TIME

ABSOLUTE VICTORY

"Yesterday, December 7, 1941—a date which will live
in infamy—the United States of America was suddenly and deliberately
attacked by naval and air forces of the empire of Japan . . .
Always we will remember the character of the onslaught against us.
No matter how long it may take us to overcome this premeditated invasion,
the American people in their righteous might will win through to absolute victory."
—Franklin D. Roosevelt

ABSOLUTE VICTORY

EDITOR	Kelly Knauer
DESIGNER	Ellen Fanning
PICTURE EDITOR	Patricia Cadley
FOREWORD	George H.W. Bush, Hugh Sidey
WRITER/RESEARCH DIRECTOR	Matthew McCann Fenton
COPY EDITOR	Bruce Christopher Carr
GRAPHICS AND MAPS	Joe Lertola
RESEARCH ASSISTANT	Rudi Papiri

ACKNOWLEDGEMENT

The following military veterans and participants in the war agreed
to be interviewed for this book. The editors thank them for their participation.

Harold Agnew, Ben Bernal, George H.W. Bush, Alfred Cassella, George Checkan, Dewey Dossett,
John Dunleavy, George Fisher, Kats Kajiyama, Armin Lehmann, George Lucht, George McGovern,
Will Souza, Gerald Thomas, George Wahlen

TIME INC. HOME ENTERTAINMENT

PUBLISHER	Richard Fraiman
EXECUTIVE DIRECTOR, MARKETING SERVICES	Carol Pittard
DIRECTOR, RETAIL & SPECIAL SALES	Tom Mifsud
MARKETING DIRECTOR, BRANDED BUSINESSES	Swati Rao
DIRECTOR, NEW PRODUCT DEVELOPMENT	Peter Harper
ASSISTANT FINANCIAL DIRECTOR	Steven Sandonato
PREPRESS MANAGER	Emily Rabin
BOOK PRODUCTION MANAGER	Jonathan Polsky
MARKETING MANAGER	Kristin Walker
ASSOCIATE PREPRESS MANAGER	Anne-Michelle Gallero
ASSISTANT MARKETING MANAGER	Candice Ogarro

SPECIAL THANKS TO:

Bozena Bannett, Alexandra Bliss, Bernadette Corbie, Suzanne Janso,
Robert Marasco, Brooke McGuire, Adriana Tierno

TIME

ABSOLUTE VICTORY

America's Greatest Generation and Their World War II Triumph

By the Editors of TIME

Contents

LIBERATION **Dutch, U.S. and British soldiers cheer as U.S. Navy vessels approach their POW camp near Yokohama. The date is Aug. 29, 1944—15 days after Japan agreed to surrender**

WINGS **Bush at the controls of an Avenger**

Growing Up in Uniform

By George H.W. Bush, as told to Hugh Sidey

Mr. Bush, the 41st President, enlisted in the U.S. Navy on his 18th birthday and flew Avenger torpedo bombers in the Pacific Theater from 1942-45, completing 58 combat missions and earning the Distinguished Flying Cross. Mr. Sidey has covered the White House for TIME and LIFE for 48 years.

BACK IN 1941 I WAS AN UNCONCERNED, CAREFREE guy, a 17-year-old senior at Andover School in Massachusetts, interested in athletics and beginning to get interested in girls, playing baseball a lot. I had little knowledge of the world around me, although I knew about the tension between America and Japan's emissaries who were then in Washington. I was offended by Hitler and what I saw in the Pathé newsreels—the marching, the *Sieg Heils*, the power of the panzer divisions and Hitler walking out of the 1936 Olympics when Jesse Owens won his races.

But I knew very little else. One Sunday morning I came out of church and was walking across the Andover campus and somebody yelled, "The Japanese have bombed Pearl Harbor!" That was the wake-up call. The news was so devastating and so clear; it was a horrible catastrophe. Now we had all these questions. How long would it take

us to recover? Could we regain control of the sea?

I enlisted in the naval aviation cadet program in Boston on my 18th birthday. My dad came to see me off at Pennsylvania Station in New York City, and it was an emotional time. Nobody knew what was ahead. We were on our way to Chapel Hill, N.C., for training. I hadn't seen much of the world: I hadn't done anything but go to school, and I didn't know a soul on that train. I was the youngest by far. I had been to Florida and South Carolina for hunting—you know, the good life—but I had not been down there for anything else. The guys on the train were from all over the States, with all different backgrounds, men I never would have met in my normal life—until then. It was fine right off. We were in this together.

The closeness was good. I found I could hold my own. I learned it all: how to do the corners on the bed, how to handle the sheets, how to stand at attention. I learned a lot of dirty words, and I learned not to judge a guy by his background but by his character. I learned how those men looked at the country.

There was always a common ground. We all wanted to fly a plane and go into combat and fight and win. Death did not really cross our minds at first. You wondered what it would be like, but not much more, not until we went into flight training, and every now and then a cadet would be killed. It really entered my thoughts after we took our carrier, the U.S.S. *San Jacinto*, from Philadelphia through the Panama Canal and were in the Pacific Theater. On the very first mission one of my cabinmates was killed.

By then the war was all around us. Officers lectured us on the brutality of the Japanese and showed us a picture of a prisoner kneeling down and a Japanese officer cutting his head off with his sword. They even showed us the prisoner's decapitated body afterward. It sure made you feel that you didn't want to be captured.

My first combat mission in my Avenger, a torpedo bomber carrying four 500-lb. bombs, was against Japanese installations on Wake Island. I was shaky in the knees, had some jitters. We had some antiaircraft fire, but it wasn't very heavy compared with the stuff we ran into later.

Once I had to land in the water. The carrier was expecting a kamikaze attack, so we had to get the planes off the deck. My fuel-pressure gauge was wobbling around, and under other conditions I probably would not have taken off. Once I was up, the plane got shaky. I did the distress maneuver, waggled my wings, flew low along the starboard side. We couldn't break radio silence. I made a pass to land, but I was waved off. So I flew up ahead of the fleet and landed in the ocean. Made a pretty good landing, pulled the life raft out, and the crew and I scrambled aboard it. Never got wet. We knew there were other ships around, and pretty soon a destroyer picked us up.

WE WERE REALLY IN THE WAR BY THEN. TERRIFYING examples of what could happen were all around us. We supported the Marine landings on Guam, and we could see the men down below on the beaches. Once, after finishing a flight, I climbed out of my plane and waited to see the fighters come in. I was standing up against the carrier's "island," its command center. All of a sudden a plane came in to land, but it stalled out, then went over on its back as it crossed the deck. Standing right in front of me was a flight-deck guy, and the propeller cut him into three pieces. His leg was over here quivering, his torso was there, and the upper part of his body was another place. I still can see the image of that leg quivering. I was totally devastated.

I knew our mission against Chichi Jima in September 1944 would be tough. We had flown through a lot of antiaircraft fire the day before. We went in and on my dive, I felt the plane jerk upward. We'd been hit! The cockpit filled with smoke. I could see a strip of flame where the wing joined the fuselage—right where the fuel tanks were—but it hadn't exploded. That was really terrifying.

I was scared. I shouted on the intercom for my crew to jump out, and I radioed the skipper I was going down. I started to jump but I had forgotten to undo my headset and I ripped that off, then dove out of the plane, and I guess I dove out far enough, but I pulled the rip cord too soon. I hit

ALL SMILES The young officer

my head on the stabilizer, and my chute hung up momentarily. Then I was falling fast and I was bleeding like hell and I looked up and saw that three panels of the chute had been ripped out. I had forgotten to hook my life raft to my "Mae West" life preserver, and the raft fell free and smashed the only water can I had.

One of the fighter pilots who had been with us dove down to show me where the raft was, and I swam over and climbed on. A bomber pilot saw I was bleeding and he dropped a big balloon filled with medicine. I was blowing toward shore and certain capture, so I began paddling like hell. I was sick to my stomach and was an awfully scared kid. I worried about my two crew members, wondering if they had gotten out. That they were both lost haunts me to this very day.

It turned out that I was also an awfully lucky kid. The submarine U.S.S. *Finback* had been alerted and picked me up, and I spent about 30 days with that crew. We were depth-charged—and how that submarine would shake! Now that was scary. Once we were pounded by a Japanese "Betty" bomber. These great submarine guys didn't seem to be concerned about it, but I was saying "What the hell is going on?" Sub service seemed much scarier than flying.

We were back in Norfolk, Va., re-forming to go back for the invasion of Japan, when V-E day came in May 1945. We had anticipated that. But we did not have an inkling about the atom bomb in August. When we heard about it, we shouted, "Hurrah, this is the greatest thing!" I felt sure the war was over. On the day the Japanese surrendered we went to church—and then we went on about our lives.

The war changed my life profoundly, and I guess that some things never leave you, because they came back when I was in the Oval Office: our determination to win, the importance of teamwork, the pride we felt in our fellow Americans and the great respect we developed for the military. My experiences of war will be with me forever. I was a scared kid floating out there in the Pacific, worrying about my crewmates, fearing that I might be captured—but knowing that all my buddies would go the extra mile to find me. You never forget that. ■

DOWN! Bush is rescued by sailors aboard the U.S.S. *Finback*

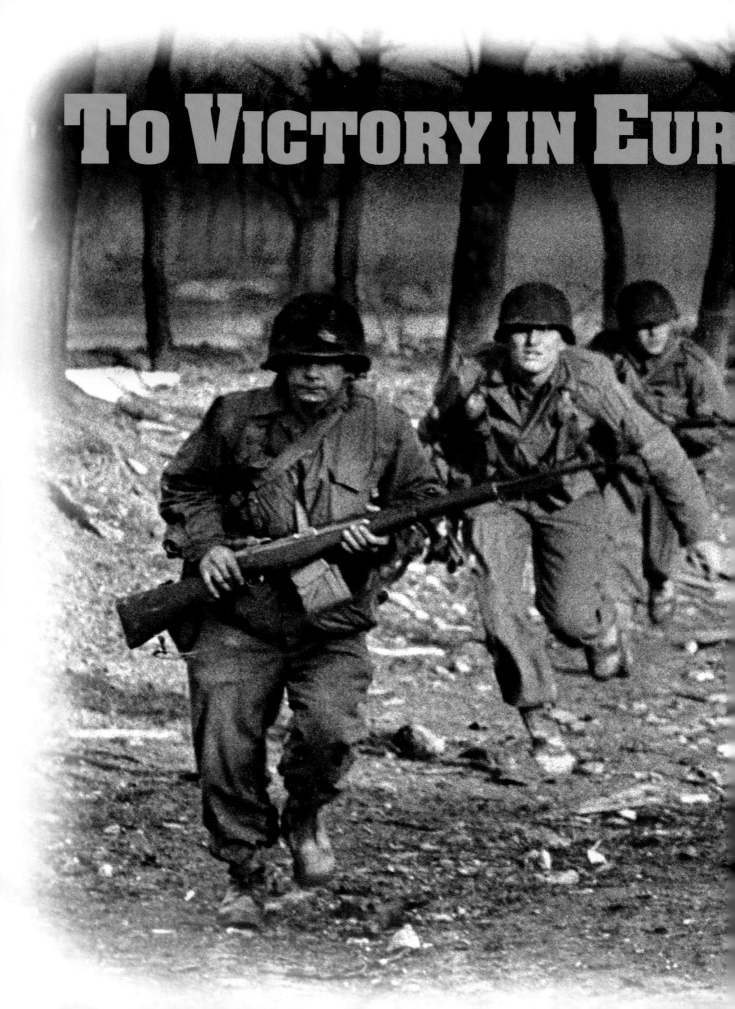

CLOSING IN U.S. Marines under fire dash for cover during fighting along the Roer River as the Western Allies continue their advance on Adolf Hitler's Germany in February 1945

MUNICH Inset: a beaming Adolf Hitler shakes hands with Neville Chamberlain in 1938. Britain's Prime Minister agreed to divide Czechoslovakia in hopes of averting war

WARSAW At left, German troops march through Poland's conquered capital in the fall of 1939

Germany Rising

Europe, 1933. The Continent whose mighty empires— Britain, France, Germany and the Netherlands—dominated the globe at the turn of the 20th century had sacrificed a generation in the mass slaughter of the Great War that ended 15 years before. The four-year conflict helped topple Russia's Czar, turned many West Europeans into pacifists—and now brought to power in defeated Germany an Austrian veteran of the conflict, Adolf Hitler, whose totalitarian National Socialist Party capitalized on the Germans' desire for revenge and sense of racial superiority.

After consolidating his control of Germany, Hitler began to terrorize his neighbors. Violating the Treaty of Versailles, he sent German troops to reoccupy the Rhineland, Germany's buffer zone with France, in 1936; France and Britain failed to respond. In April 1938 Hitler seized control of Austria. Six months later, he convinced British Prime Minister Neville Chamberlain to carve up Czechoslovakia, giving control of the Sudetenland to Germany. In London, powerless Tory backbencher Winston Churchill detailed Hitler's crimes, only to be branded a warmonger.

Success emboldened Hitler: by 1939, he was ready to unleash the military machine he had been building for years. On Aug. 23, the devout anticommunist startled the world by striking a cynical nonaggression pact with Joseph Stalin's socialist Russia. Days later, on Sept. 1, 1939, Germany's army, the Wehrmacht, and air force, the Luftwaffe, smashed their way into Poland in a surprise lightning attack, or blitzkrieg, that quickly subdued the Poles. Now, at last, Britain and France declared war on Hitler. A new conflict—a war that TIME would soon christen World War II—had begun.

BRITAIN In London, St. Paul's Cathedral weathers German bombs in 1940. In the Battle of Britain, 900 British fighter planes held off some 1,400 bombers and 1,000 fighter planes of the Luftwaffe

▢ A World at War

After Adolf Hitler's muscular military machine subdued Poland, hurling Britain, France and the Netherlands into war with Germany, the winter of 1939-40 was deceptively calm; Britons called the period the "Bore War." War for real came in May, when Hitler's armies drove around France's defensive Maginot Line. Before a startled world could catch its breath, it seemed, Hitler was the master of the Netherlands and France, while the British Expeditionary Force in Europe narrowly escaped, retreating in disarray from Dunkirk in France.

Disgraced by the policy of appeasement that had proved so frail, the government of Neville Chamberlain finally fell in Britain, and Hitler's ardent foe, Winston Churchill, was summoned to lead a coalition government. Britain now stood alone, the last surviving democracy in Europe, as Hitler contemplated Operation Sealion, a seaborne invasion of the isle. But Hitler, whose success had outrun his supply lines, lacked the boats and troops to overwhelm Britain. Instead, he decided to bomb the Britons into submission.

In the Battle of Britain, a few valiant British pilots—aided by a new technology, radar—managed to hold off Germany's Luftwaffe, while Churchill rallied his people with his unparalleled eloquence. A frustrated Hitler finally called off the bombing and, spellbound by his own success, spent the winter planning his next gambit on the world's chessboard: the double-crossing of Stalin and the conquest of his communist state.

On June 22, 1941, Hitler made the

RUSSIA German troops move into Russia in 1941. Hitler's surprise attack on Joseph Stalin's vast nation was the Führer's single greatest miscalculation

mistake that would cost the dictator his empire and his life: in Operation Barbarossa, he sent the Wehrmacht barreling into Russia, history's graveyard of empires. Propelled by surprise, the Germans rolled triumphant over the steppes, but they soon ran up against the factors that had doomed earlier invasions of Russia: the nation's vast spaces, resilient people and hostile climate.

While Europe burned, America fiddled. Hitler's racist rantings, suppression of democratic principles and rampant

expansionism were anathema to U.S. ideals, and President Franklin D. Roosevelt and many other Americans longed to enter the fray; they, however, were held back by the nation's powerful isolationists. The best F.D.R. could do was to create a program, Lend-Lease, to channel U.S. armaments to Hitler's foes.

Meanwhile, Americans were turning their eyes west, to the Pacific Ocean, where another expanding power, imperial Japan—Hitler's ally through the Axis pact of 1940—was imitating his conduct.

Resentful of European hegemony in Asia, and with a government dominated by a militarist cabal, the Japanese had invaded China in the 1930s. Now they demanded territorial and oil concessions that brought them into increasing conflict with the U.S.

The tensions exploded with Japan's surprise attack on Pearl Harbor on Dec. 7, 1941; four days after the stunning air raid, Hitler declared war on the U.S. In the great global struggle between liberal democracy and militant totalitarianism, America was no longer on the sidelines.

Battling Hitler to a Standstill

Hobbled by the isolationists who had barred attempts to prepare for war, the U.S. entered the conflict with its military readiness at a low ebb. Everything was lacking: soldiers and officers, rifles and tanks, aircraft and aircraft carriers. So—to the chagrin of America's surprising new ally of convenience, Joseph Stalin—the U.S. was a mostly silent partner in Europe in 1942. Still, at home the nation was heeding F.D.R.'s call to become "the arsenal of democracy."

Across the Atlantic, America's new allies began scratching out the first victories over Germany. Wehrmacht soldiers came within sight of Moscow in December 1941, only to be hurled back. They besieged Leningrad, but the city refused to fall. In 1942 Hitler lavished troops to win Stalingrad, but was again rebuffed: on Jan. 31, 1943, 110,000 starving Germans surrendered to the Russians. It was a resounding victory for Stalin.

South of Europe, Hitler's outsized dreams—and his alliance with his fellow Axis dictator, the Italian Fascist Benito Mussolini— led him to North Africa. Early in 1941 the panzers of General Erwin Rommel's Afrika Korps had begun rolling over the colonial lands of Britain and France. There, in late 1942, Americans finally joined the fray. In Operation Torch, U.S. troops landed in Morocco, Algeria and Tunisia; in tandem with a British army led by Field Marshal Bernard Montgomery, they finally drove the Germans from Africa in May 1943, then quickly moved closer to the Continent, invading Sicily on July 10, 1943. In the same month, the Russians beat the Germans in the Battle of Kursk, the war's greatest tank conflict.

But there was no time for gloating: F.D.R. and Churchill had promised Stalin they would open a second front against Hitler in northwestern Europe. As 1943 ended, no such front existed.

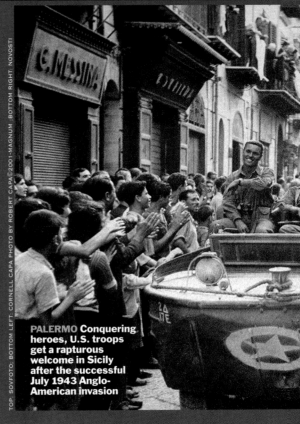

PALERMO Conquering heroes, U.S. troops get a rapturous welcome in Sicily after the successful July 1943 Anglo-American invasion

STALINGRAD The battle for the industrial city on the Volga was one of the most severe conflicts of the war. Germans attacked the city for seven months before surrendering in the depths of winter

KURSK Russian troops advance in the great 1943 tank battle, another major defeat for Hitler on the Eastern Front

NORMANDY A landing craft approaches the beach. On D-day, more than 5,000 Allied ships carried some 150,000 troops across the English Channel to attack Hitler's "Fortress Europe"

◼ Turning Point

As the year 1943 was ending, three of history's most oddly cast allies—U.S. President Franklin D. Roosevelt, British PM Winston Churchill and Soviet leader Joseph Stalin—met all together for the first time, in Tehran, the capital of Iran. Here, F.D.R. and Churchill promised Stalin, who had been holding off Hitler's armies for 30 months, that they would mount a land invasion of northwestern Europe in 1944, to draw Hitler's attention away from the Eastern Front and create an Allied pincer movement to drive on Germany from both west and east.

On June 6, 1944, the Western Allies made good on their promise in Operation Overlord, a gigantic, daring and well-executed assault on the beaches of Normandy in northern France. Although the Germans had turned the Atlantic Coast into a fortress, the British, Canadians, Poles and Americans who landed in France on D-day managed to wrest a foothold on the Continent, with the U.S. troops on the strand designated Omaha Beach fighting with notable valor.

Under the leadership of the top Allied commander, U.S. General Dwight D. Eisenhower, D-day was a success, yet for several frustrating weeks the Allied armies were unable to break out of their pocket in Normandy. Finally, in July, the Allies punched a hole in the German lines, and as more Allied men and supplies arrived in France, the Germans began retreating rapidly toward Belgium.

On Aug. 25, 1944, amid memorable scenes of exultation, Allied troops marched into Paris: France was free at last. Yet as the Allied generals eyed their maps in September of 1944, the path to invading Germany and toppling Hitler seemed far from clear.

SITUATION REPORT: SEPTEMBER 1944

200 mi.

Operation Market-Garden 9/17/44

Liberated 9/4/44

Allies invade 6/6/44

Liberated 8/25/44

Mussolini overthrown 7/25/43

Allies invade 1/22/44

Allies invade 7/10/43

Axis forces surrender 5/12/43

ATLANTIC OCEAN

NORTH SEA

BALTIC SEA

MEDITERRANEAN SEA

NORWAY
SWEDEN
FINLAND
DENMARK
ESTONIA
LATVIA
LITHUANIA
IRELAND
BRITAIN
NETHERLANDS
BELGIUM
LUXEMBOURG
GERMANY
POLAND
CZECHOSLOVAKIA
AUSTRIA
HUNGARY
SWITZERLAND
FRANCE
YUGOSLAVIA
ROMANI
BULGARIA
ALBANIA
GREECE
ITALY
PORTUGAL
SPAIN
MOROCCO
ALGERIA
TUNISIA
LIBYA
Rhine River

Oslo
Stockholm
Helsinki
Lening
Petersb
Copenhagen
Amsterdam
Berlin
Warsaw
London
Brussels
Paris
Prague
Vienna
Budapest
Belgrade
Bucharest
Sofia
Madrid
Rome
Anzio
Sicily
Athens
Algiers
Tunis
Tripoli

Legend:
- Front lines, Sept. 1944
- Axis-dominated area
- Neutral countries
- Area under Allied control
- Area formerly under Axis control

Allies with Russia 9/19/44

German siege ends 1/27/44

Moscow

U. S. S. R.

Germans surrender 1/31/43

Stalingrad

Allies with Russia 8/25/44

B L A C K   S E A

Allies with Russia 9/8/44

Ankara

T U R K E Y

SYRIA

Damascus

PALESTINE

TRANS-JORDAN

E G Y P T

Cairo

THE "BIG TWO" Canada's Governor-General, the Earl of Athlone, left, and P.M. MacKenzie King, right, join F.D.R. and Churchill at Quebec. Stalin was absent

Eyes on Victory, Fingers Crossed

When Winston Churchill arrived in Quebec on Sept. 11, 1944, for his eighth wartime conference with U.S. President Franklin D. Roosevelt, Britain's Prime Minister beamed at reporters and said, "Victory is everywhere."

Indeed it was. After years of triumph, Adolf Hitler's Germany was reeling, collapsing from the outside in, its once-vast domain visibly shrinking with each passing week.

In northern France, the Allies had brilliantly breached Hitler's Fortress Europe at Normandy in June and had broken out of the hedgerow country where they had been hemmed in for weeks. Paris had been liberated on Aug. 25, amid scenes of rejoicing that electrified the world. Although Hitler clung to a few key ports on France's northern coast, a massive Allied push had shoved his armies back toward their homeland, and the front lines had moved to the Netherlands.

In the Balkans, the Germans had lost Romania, including the rich oil fields of Ploesti, depriving their armies of their lifeblood. To the north, Joseph Stalin's advancing armies were continuing their inexorable march toward Germany's eastern borders. Farther north, Finland was moving out of the German orbit and making peace with Stalin's U.S.S.R.

Inside Germany, rumors swelled that the Nazi leaders were preparing to flee the country. Above Germany, the skies were filled day and night with Allied bombers, for the dreaded Luftwaffe was no longer dominant.

"The Nazi beast was dying," TIME said in its Sept. 11, 1944 issue, "but he was dying hard." Even as Hitler's tanks were running out of gas, Germany was terrorizing Britons with a new superweapon, the V-2 rocket, and its new jet airplanes, while few at present, were far faster than Allied craft. Stories abounded of even more deadly weapons to come. Hitler was expected to put up a mighty battle to protect his soil from invading Allied armies, then head for his retreat high in the Alps, where he might hold off the Allies for months, even years, before surrendering.

Nor was Hitler the only enemy the Allies faced. Halfway around the globe, their troops were engaged in a bloody struggle against imperial Japan. Barring a breakthrough, the war in the Pacific looked as if it might drag on for long, costly years.

Often obscured in the rush of events, another enemy loomed, albeit in the temporary guise of a friend. The third of the "Big Three" Allied leaders wasn't present at Quebec. In the Kremlin, an exultant Stalin was also consulting his maps— and watching his troops move into Romania, Bulgaria, Czechoslovakia, Hungary and Poland. In the power vacuum that would follow Hitler's fall, Churchill and F.D.R. knew they would face another struggle, with the forces of Moscow's militant communism.

The View from the Top

With Hitler's armies in desperate flight, General Dwight D. Eisenhower's chief lieutenants vied for the chance to deal Germany a knockout blow

IN THE LATE-SUMMER WEEKS OF 1944, VISIONS OF VICTORY danced in Allied heads. American and British armies had broken out from Normandy, liberated Paris and devastated the German army at Falaise. From London to Washington to the highways of France, where Allied soldiers marched seemingly unopposed toward Germany, one question dominated the chatter: Now what? Adolf Hitler's forces were reeling backward across Western Europe—in some cases so quickly that pursuing British and American troops could scarcely advance fast enough to keep up with them.

Yet even in this heady atmosphere of triumph, the end of the war in Europe was not in sight. The news was good but not good enough. The public—and even the civilian leaders to whom the generals answered—didn't understand what was taking so long. The unspoken hope was to wind up the war in Europe before a new year dawned: end the war in '44!

For Dwight D. Eisenhower, the Supreme Commander of the Allied Expeditionary Force, the impediments to this goal were as clear as they were complex: shortages of vital materials; tenuous supply lines; and, above all, the prospect of storming the Siegfried Line, a series of more than 18,000 bunkers, pillboxes and tank traps that stretched for almost 400 miles along the German border, from the Netherlands to Switzerland, guarding the western portals to the Fatherland.

Napoleon said his armies traveled on their stomach; Eisenhower's armies traveled on gas. The precious fluid was conveyed to the front lines by ships, transport planes, pipelines, fuel trucks and even dropped by parachute to the parched tanks of General George Patton's Third Army. By September 1944, the Allies were devouring more than 1 million gal. of gas per day and were using up just as much gas getting fuel to the front as they were delivering to it. Most supplies traveled to the front lines all the way from Normandy on a single highway, the "Red Ball Express," where a never-ending convoy of

9,000 trucks rolled back and forth at 40 m.p.h., day and night.

If the obstacles on the ground were daunting, so were the pressures from above. On Sept. 8, 1944, the first of the *Vergeltungswaffe* 2 rockets (Adolf Hitler's "vengeance weapon," dubbed V–2 by the Allies) began falling on London, terrorizing the British population. Meanwhile, steady, ominous grumblings from Washington and London reached Eisenhower that the élite airborne troops who had spearheaded D-day had been largely idle since June.

Eisenhower, universally known as Ike, was the very model of a modern managerial general: a self-effacing technocrat-cum-diplomat whose best battles were often fought at the head of a conference table. Now the pressure on Ike mounted for a new miracle: a swift coup de main that would match the stunning surprise and flair of D-day and bring similarly spectacular results.

In the weeks after D-day, British General Bernard Law Montgomery had been pondering the problem of a quick thrust into Berlin. Montgomery, an ascetic, eccentric military genius with an ego to match his reputation, drew inspiration from Hitler's 1940 invasion of France, which French generals had been blithely confident would be deterred (or at least delayed) by the Maginot Line, a complex of fortifications similar to the Siegfried Line. The Germans had solved this problem not by assaulting the bunkers head on but by going around them, driving their forces through the unfortified borders of Belgium and the Netherlands. Monty reasoned that a similar feint could be achieved by driving north through the Netherlands, hooking around the Siegfried Line, and then marching into the heart of Germany.

Nor was Montgomery alone in scheming for a rapid war-ending drive into Germany. His equal in strategic thinking and superior in battlefield bravado, U.S. General Patton, had also trained his sights on Berlin. The visionary tank-corps leader set his staff to work on a plan that would take his Third Army across the Rhine River and into Germany via a southern route, from the French city of Metz.

THE ODD TRIO **Eisenhower, the diplomat, confers with the gritty Omar Bradley and the gung-ho warrior George Patton in Belgium**

Eisenhower's third principal lieutenant, American General Omar Bradley, agreed with neither Patton nor Montgomery. Like Ike, the realistic Bradley, who was widely admired by the troops for his unassuming style, preferred to focus on capturing the huge Belgian port of Antwerp, through which mountains of war matériel could be funneled, cutting the overland supply route from the English Channel coast by more than half. While far less spectacular than a march into Berlin, this strategy would solve in a single stroke many of the logistical issues that were plaguing the Allied advance.

But it was Eisenhower himself who was most deeply skeptical of any grandstand play. A supremely cautious general, he was more comfortable with a "broad front" strategy that would advance slowly across a line hundreds of miles long, ensuring that supplies would be able to keep up with the advancing troops. Another advantage: the Allies' indispensable ally on

SKULL SESSION **Field Marshal Bernard Montgomery plots strategy with British Air Marshal Trafford Leigh-Mallory, right**

the Eastern Front, Joseph Stalin, was gripped by a paranoid fear that if America and Britain marched rapidly on Berlin, the capitalist democracies would control a platform from which to launch a future invasion of the U.S.S.R. Thus, Montgomery and Patton must be kept on a tight leash to avoid the risk of a rupture in the alliance.

But in the end, the opportunity to win the war in a matter of weeks was too tempting to resist. Ike decided to take a chance—and he chose Montgomery's bold northern gambit.

The Briton's plan for an air-land invasion of Holland boasted three chief virtues: it would bypass the Siegfried Line rather than attack it head on; it would make use of the paratroopers Eisenhower was being pushed to find a mission for; and it might overrun and silence the V–2 rocket bases on the Dutch coastline that were terrorizing Britain.

A subtler agenda may have been at work. Some historians now suspect that Ike had drawn two conclusions about the plan: if it succeeded, the war would soon be over; if it failed, the blame would rest squarely on the Briton's shoulders, cowing him into submission for the rest of the war. Whatever his reasoning, Ike approved the plan, dubbed Market-Garden—to the immense frustration of Patton, whose tanks ground to a halt so that fuel and supplies could be diverted to serve Monty's grand end-run. Market-Garden was on. ■

Eight Bridges To Nowhere

Operation Market-Garden, history's greatest airdrop,
was designed to end the war in '44, but a host of "snafus"
derailed Field Marshal Montgomery's grand gambit

ONCEIVED IN HASTE, EXECUTED WITH valor and sabotaged by coincidence, Operation Market-Garden was one of the Allies' most audacious and most frustrating battles of World War II. The brainchild of Britain's best warrior, Field Marshal Bernard Montgomery, the operation was born as Allied troops were barreling toward Germany, facing little opposition from Hitler's beaten armies. The war, it seemed, might end in months, perhaps even before the turn of the year, freeing Allied troops and the long-suffering British people from a sixth winter of war. The plan called for history's single largest airdrop,

and the British had the men to do the job: 10,000 paratroopers of the 1st Airborne Division—highly trained soldiers, "full of piss and vinegar," as the saying went—eager to see more action in the war; they wanted in on the so-called "party" one more time before it was over. They would deploy in tandem with 25,000 paratroopers of the U.S. 82nd and 101st Airborne Divisions, seasoned veterans of D-day.

Montgomery's strategy consisted of two principal blows. Operation Market was a massive airborne drop of more than 35,000 British, American and Polish troops along a 65-mile stretch of the Rhine River behind German

ACME—CORBIS BETTMANN

OPERATION MARKET-GARDEN

British & Polish paratroopers

Oosterbeek
Arnhem

The Ruhr

Elst
Lent
Nijmegen
Groesbeek

Waal

Rhine

U.S. 82nd Airborne
Grave
Overasselt

Reichswald

Maas

GERMANY

Uden
Veghel
St. Oedenrode
Son
Best

U.S. 101st Airborne

British Second Army

Eindhoven

Valkenswaard

HOLLAND

BELGIUM

NETHERLANDS
[Map area]
GERMANY
BELGIUM
FRANCE

100 mi.

10 mi.

lines; it would be launched in tandem with Operation Garden, a thrust by the tank forces and ground troops of Britain's XXX Corps up a single narrow road along the river.

As with D-day, the fast-moving but lightly armed paratroopers would take strategic targets (in this case, a series of eight bridges over the Rhine and nearby canals) and hold them temporarily, while the slower-moving but more heavily armed tank units would link up with the airborne units, reinforcing the positions taken by the paratroopers and digging in. This process was to take less than a week: XXX Corp was to reach the closest bridges (those in the south, nearest the Allied lines) on the first day of Market-Garden and travel the 64-mile length of the road to the northernmost bridge—in Arnhem, the farthest point inside German-held territory—in three days. Once all eight bridges were secure, a breakout by Allied infantry would cross the Rhine in force at Arnhem, execute a right hook around the northern end of the Siegfried

IMPERIAL WAR MUSEUM

HERO General Roy Urquhart led 10,005 British airborne troops into Arnhem on Sept. 17; days later, only 2,163 made it out alive

MARKET Paratroopers land in Holland on Sept. 17, far left. The airdrop was conducted in daylight and took three days to complete

GARDEN Tanks rumble past a windmill in the Garden segment of the plan, above left, as Allied motorized units rolled up Highway 69

Line, Germany's western line of defense, and march directly toward Berlin.

The plan was as brilliant as it was bold—but there were problems from the outset. Market-Garden would involve more paratroopers than D-day, yet while the Normandy invasion had been the the subject of more than a year of meticulous planning, this scheme was pulled together in eight or nine days. Its success depended on almost split-second timing, on favorable weather and, above all, on the assumption that the Germans had basically abandoned the defense of Holland, leaving only light troops on the ground to face an invasion. If any of these elements went wrong, then the entire operation would be imperiled. In fact, all of them would go wrong.

YET NONE OF THESE DOUBTS HUNG IN THE AIR AS THE FOG CLEARED OVER Britain on the Sunday morning of Sept. 17, 1944. People who lived beneath the flight path of the armada would never forget the sight of more than 1,500 transport planes and gliders as they flew the first wave of paratroopers toward their drop zones in Holland. The initial parachute landings went almost perfectly, with all units forming up at or near their intended drop zones: Eindhoven to the south, Nijmegen in the center and Arnhem at the northern end of the battle zone. Early in the day, troops from the U.S. 101st Airborne Division easily captured the bridge at Veghel, the first of the Rhine crossings called for in Montgomery's plan. A contingent from the U.S. 82nd Airborne Division took a bridge near the town of Grave. Further north, at Arnhem, British paratroopers under General Roy Urquhart were able to occupy the town and take the northern end of the bridge that was Market-Garden's most critical objective. Three bridges down, five to go.

But before the sun set on the first day of Market-Garden, things began to go wrong. In the afternoon, German troops blew up the bridge at Son, rather than allow American troops to take it. Then, units of the 82nd Airborne ran into unexpectedly stiff resistance in taking the Groesbeek Heights overlooking Nijmegen bridge—the second largest of the eight Montgomery had targeted and nearly as important as the bridge at Arnhem. The failure to take Groesbeek Heights meant that Nijmegen bridge would, at least for the time being, remain in German hands.

Meanwhile, in the south, XXX Corps ran into greater than expected German resistance and was halted in its advance up Highway 69 (the road along the Rhine that linked all the bridges), failing to reach Eindhoven, its first-day objective. To compound the growing difficulty, the British troops found that their radios had been outfitted with the wrong kind of crystal, cutting off their communications.

On the German side, matters were nearly as confused. Not grasping the plan to bypass the Siegfried Line, German commanders were baffled by what seemed to be an Allied parachute drop into an area with no strategic significance. They initially imagined that the British and American commandos were there to kidnap Field Marshal Walther Model, who had been placed in command of what seemed like a backwater after Hitler had relieved him, days earlier, as the German army's senior general for Western Europe.

Model was briefly stunned by the scale and audacity of the attack but was soon incredulous at his own good luck. A week earlier, in one of his last orders as the over-

BY PARACHUTE Most—but not all—paratroopers survived the initial drop into Holland, far left. The immense air armada that took off on Sept 17 was the largest ever assembled: 4,700 aircraft took off from Britain on the first day of the operation

BY GLIDER Operation Market called for history's largest glider drop: 478 gliders carried 18,546 troops and tons of supplies to crash landings in Holland. At center, U.S. soldiers care for the dead and wounded after one rough landing on Sept. 18

ARNHEM The battle of the surrounded and outnumbered British Airborne troops to control the Arnhem Bridge is one of the great stories of the war. At left, German troops move north as they begin to retake control of the span

BOOM! Below, British soldiers dodge an explosion outside Arnhem in late October. Fighting in the area continued in the weeks after the official conclusion of Market-Garden. Holland remained in German control until the war's end

"A great prize was nearly within our grasp." **—Winston Churchill**

"In return for so much courage and sacrifice, the Allies had won a 50-mile salient—leading nowhere."
—Official U.S. Army history of Market-Garden

all commander of the West, Model had directed two élite tank units, the 9th and 10th S.S. Panzer Divisions, to relocate to the quiet rear area he would soon be commanding, where the troops could rest while their tanks were repaired. As a result, two of Germany's best armored units, with an additional 9,000 troops, happened by coincidence to be stationed in Arnhem, beside its crucial bridge. (Montgomery had actually been informed of this fact two days before the operation was launched, but he dismissed the news, insisting that it had to be wrong or that the tanks must be inoperable.) Next, Model was told that a complete set of plans to Market-Garden had been recovered from a glider that had been shot down. Model read them and decided they were simply unbelievable; he concluded that the plans must be part of an elaborate Allied hoax. They weren't, as

Model and his men would find out the hard way.

On Sept. 18, the second day of Market-Garden, forces from the 101st Airborne were repelled as they attempted to take a bridge in the town of Best. Later, XXX Corps advancing toward Arnhem on Highway 69 reached the town of Eindhoven a day behind schedule, but they were halted at the Son bridge, blown up by the Germans the day before. More precious time was wasted as combat engineers built a new bridge.

Day Three of Market-Garden brought new trouble. Polish paratroopers arrived in the third wave of Airborne troops but were dropped into a landing zone near Arnhem that had been overrun by the Germans. British forces nearby were unable to warn them away, owing to the radio foul-up. The Polish unit was cut to pieces.

General Urquhart's British paratroopers holding the north end of the bridge at Arnhem were now surrounded and being mauled by the 9th and 10th S.S. Panzers. Although taking horrendous casualties, these troops held on, confident that they would be relieved that day by the tanks of XXX Corps—but those tanks were now two days behind schedule. As the paratroopers at Arnhem ran dangerously low on ammunition, airdrops of desperately needed supplies floated down—but landed in areas the Germans had retaken. *Danke schöen!* XXX Corps finally made it as far as Nijmegen but was halted once again. The boats they needed for an amphibious assault on the German-held bridge had to be brought forward from the rear.

Sept. 20 saw the most stunning displays of Allied gallantry. On the morning of Day Four, the boats that XXX Corps needed to assault Nijmegen Bridge finally made it to the front lines, but these craft were intended to be used under cover of darkness. Determined to relieve the besieged troops at Arnhem, a group of American and British troops volunteered to take the boats across the river in daylight. This nearly suicidal mission is now regarded as one of the bravest acts of the war. Most of the group were killed, yet enough made it to the far side of the river for the span to be attacked from both ends simultaneously. After intense fighting that lasted through the night, Nijmegen Bridge at last fell into Allied hands.

As Day Five of Market-Garden dawned, the road to Arnhem—less than an hour's drive from Nijmegen—was now open. But it was too late. The detachment of Urquhart's troops holding the north end of Arnhem bridge had completely run out of ammunition. Retreating to a group of houses on the bridge's approach road, they tried to hold out as German tanks blasted the buildings to smoking ruins. Able to do no more, the Britons (who had finally managed to coax a few of their radios to life) sent one last message—"Out of ammo, God save the King"—and surrendered.

By Sept. 22, it was clear that Market-Garden was doomed. The new goal was to minimize the disaster. South of Arnhem, British, American and Polish troops were stretched along more than 40 miles of a narrow, two-lane road now dubbed "Hell's Highway," vulnerable to attack from either side or from above (Market-Garden was the only major battle in Western Europe that the Allies undertook without overwhelming air superiority) and at risk of being trapped if the Germans cut the road and closed off their escape route. Units at the southern end of this column were ordered to retreat but did so under withering German fire, at a terrible cost in casualties. At the northern end, outside Arnhem, Allied commandos pushed across the Rhine under cover of darkness, amphibiously evacuating as many as they could. By Sept. 25, however, strong German fire put at end to this mini-Dunkirk. Every Allied soldier left alive on the German-held side of the Rhine was taken prisoner.

When Market-Garden was over, more than 10,000 Allied soldiers lay dead, half that many again were German prisoners, and very little had been gained. Yet one illusion had been firmly dispelled: the war would not be won by a single bold stroke. Now everyone knew what Eisenhower had suspected from the beginning: the Allies would beat Hitler and his armies—but victory would come one mile, one bridge and one battle at a time. ∎

THE LONGEST WALK Above left, dejected U.S. troops trudge through the streets of Nijmegen as the Market-Garden forces withdraw from the Dutch towns they had fought to win only days before; civilians clearing rubble clearly share their disappointment. In the weeks before the invasion, German troops had seemed to be rapidly withdrawing from Holland, encouraging the Dutch people to believe their liberation was at hand and fostering Allied hopes of an easy victory. But the Germans decided to halt their retreat in the days immediately preceding Operation Market-Garden

TAKING COVER Dutch civilians share a bunker with British troops in s'Hertogenbosch, outside Nijmegen. Instead of liberation, many citizens of Holland would endure what they called the "hunger winter" of 1944-45. Years after the war, Prince Bernhard of the Netherlands told chronicler Cornelius Ryan, "My country can never again afford the luxury of another Montgomery 'success'"

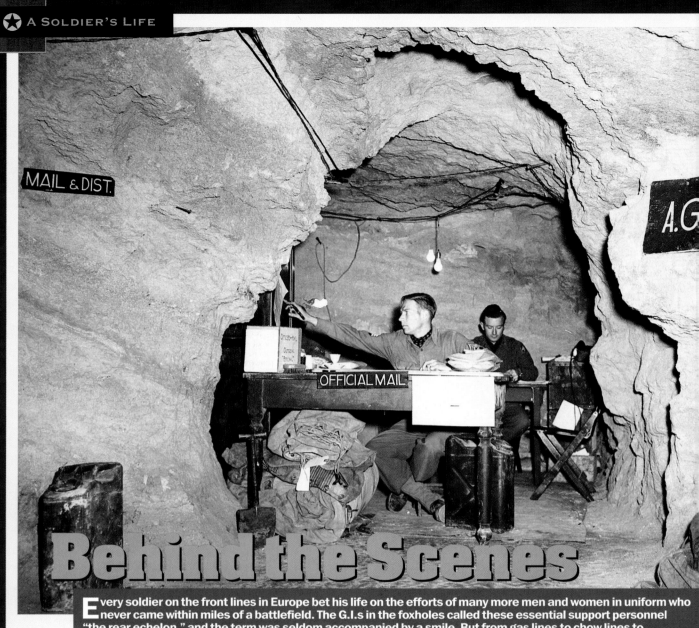

MAIL & DIST.

A.G.

OFFICIAL MAIL

Behind the Scenes

Every soldier on the front lines in Europe bet his life on the efforts of many more men and women in uniform who never came within miles of a battlefield. The G.I.s in the foxholes called these essential support personnel "the rear echelon," and the term was seldom accompanied by a smile. But from gas lines to chow lines to reconnaissance and communications, the support troops played crucial roles in winning the battles in Europe

■ **MAIL HANDLERS** With 2.7 million Americans serving in uniform in Europe in 1944-45, the military put a premium on delivering the mail. Neither rain nor snow nor glaciers nor Germans could stop Army couriers from their appointed rounds. Above, a cave becomes a mail room in Italy

■ **BY AIR** Traveling on skis, Sergeant Wallace Hansen of the Greenland Base Ice Cap Detachment collects airmail dropped via parachute to the communications and weather station. The skis visible in the foreground probably belong to the photographer

■ **BY HOOF** Mail reaches an antiaircraft crew stationed along the Saar River valley via "pony express." While we think of World War II as a great mechanized struggle, in reality both the German and U.S. armies used horse power to haul equipment and carry the mail

■ **ELECTRICIAN** A member of Britain's WAAF—the Women's Auxiliary Air Force—adapts a Canadian-made Mosquito fighter for eventual use on the Pacific front. Some 190,000 women served in the WAAF in the war

■ **WEATHERMAN** An R.A.F. meteorologist tinkers with a new invention, the radiosonde. Attached to a balloon, the device will collect readings in the upper atmosphere, then transmit them via radio back to ground stations in Britain

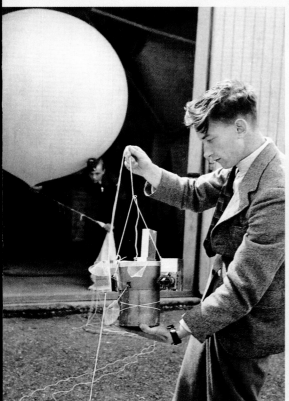

■ **AIR CONTROL** Personnel at a Royal Observer Corps Center at an undisclosed location in Britain plot the position of every airplane, friendly and hostile, currently in the air over Europe; the information will be sent to the Fighter Command unit

■ **NURSE** An Army nurse tends a patient at a field hospital in France; he will be evacuated by air to Britain. The innovative use of forward field hospitals near the front lines and fast evacuation of the wounded saved thousands of lives in the war

■ PROPAGANDISTS Soldiers load pro-Ally leaflets, written in German, into empty smoke-bomb shells on the Italian front: they will be shot across enemy lines to reach German troops

■ RADAR OPERATOR A member of the Women's Auxiliary Air Force (WAAF) tracks aircraft on a radar screen. This photo was embargoed and not released until after the war's end

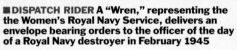

■ DISPATCH RIDER A "Wren," representing the the Women's Royal Navy Service, delivers an envelope bearing orders to the officer of the day of a Royal Navy destroyer in February 1945

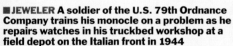

■ JEWELER A soldier of the U.S. 79th Ordnance Company trains his monocle on a problem as he repairs watches in his truckbed workshop at a field depot on the Italian front in 1944

■ TECHNICIANS Workers assemble war matériel beneath the Houses of Parliament, in a vaulted basement corridor of Britain's Palace of Westminster that was formerly a ventilation shaft. The original captions for such pictures often strain for effect: the text on this photo declares the assembly station "grew overnight, like some giant mechanical mushroom"

■**HAULER** Though trained as an evacuation nurse, Oklahoma-born Lieut. Irena Steffens pitches in to help unload precious gasoline from a C-47 in Rheims, France; it will then travel on land to George Patton's tanks

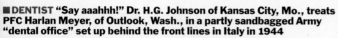

■**DENTIST** "Say aaahhh!" Dr. H.G. Johnson of Kansas City, Mo., treats PFC Harlan Meyer, of Outlook, Wash., in a partly sandbagged Army "dental office" set up behind the front lines in Italy in 1944

■**CENSOR** Holed up in a bunker in Italy, Lieut. Warren W. Pingleton uses his knee as a desk as he reviews his company's outgoing mail while an officer makes a phone call and a sergeant brews coffee

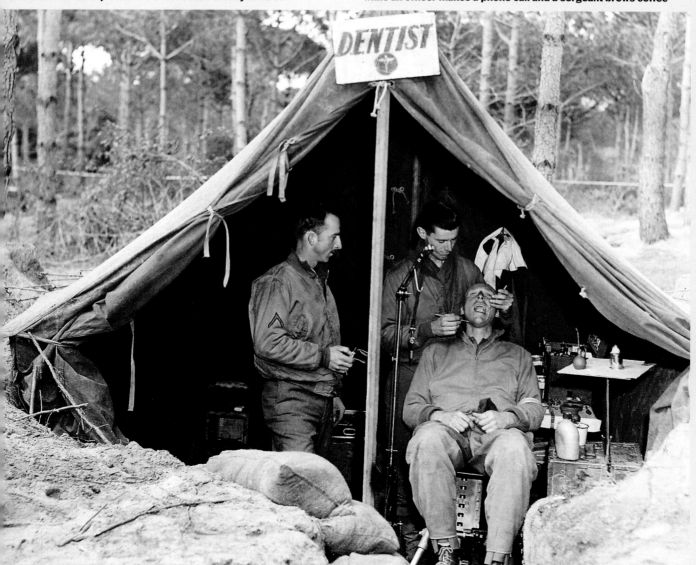

Twilight of the Reich

Cosseted by Hitler, seduced by Nazi propaganda and supported by slave laborers, ordinary Germans escaped war's misery—for a while

"We'll never capitulate. Never. We can go down. But we'll bring a world with us." —Adolf Hitler

JUNKED Bronze statues, church bells and other metal pieces from Germany and its occupied countries lie in a Hamburg smelting yard, where they will soon be melted down and turned into weapons. It is an apt memorial for Adolf Hitler's bizarre career: the man who had risen to power by exalting his vision of Germany's history and culture ended up trashing it

N THE BEGINNING, IT HADN'T SEEMED LIKE A WAR. IN THE early years of the conflict their Führer began, ordinary Germans were largely untouched and untroubled: casualties were light, the skies over Germany were unclouded by Allied bombers, and life went on much as it had before. Nazi-controlled media concealed the occasional bad news and whipped up giddy euphoria with each new victory.

But by the autumn of 1944, the war had moved in, a constant, nagging presence in German lives. For more than a year, the American and British air forces had been taking turns bombing German cities into rubble, day and night. For months now, the big bombers had operated without apparent opposition from the Luftwaffe. German civilians watched, aghast, as their homes and streets were bombed and members of their families died in the flames.

Slightly more than a year earlier, the Germany economy had finally shifted to a war footing, ushering in rationing and shortages. At Hitler's insistence, Germany had not converted to full wartime production until this preposterously late date, a factor that would hasten its defeat. For the first time, German parents now saw hunger in their children's eyes.

Nor were there victories to report: Hitler's "thousand-year Reich" had reached its greatest geographical extent for less than 12 months. By the early autumn of 1944, the tempo of Germany's collapse was speeding up: the Fatherland was ceding hundreds of square miles of territory in a typical day.

Secret reports on German public opinion compiled for the Nazi leadership by the security police show that by late 1944, the majority of Germans no longer believed that the war could be won. Indeed, many civilians put their odds of personal survival at little better than fifty-fifty. For most, the only question that remained was whether their country would be ruled by the Russians or the British and Americans. Other reports indicated that many Germans now feared that Hitler had lost his mind, with some asking about rumors that he had convulsions during which he would chew on the carpet in his Berlin chancellery. Germans had lost their mystical faith in the Führer. The sorcerer who had delivered Munich and the Anschluss, whose blitzkrieg had overrun Poland and Western Europe, then brought German troops to the gates of Moscow, could not be expected to deliver another miracle.

For many Germans, the turning point seems to have come in the hours after the failed attempt on Hitler's life on July 20, 1944, when the dictator delivered a nationwide radio address in which he said, "Now I finally have the swine who had been sabotaging my work for years." To many Germans, Hitler seemed to be admitting finally (if only tacitly) that Germany had been losing the war for a long time. Coming after years of insistence by the Nazi leadership that victory was drawing ever closer, this was a bitter disappointment.

In place of the love and loyalty that had once guaranteed Hitler's hold on the German people, fear would now have to do. Fear of the retribution that the Russians would take if they over-

The War Comes Home

In one of the war's great ironies, the German people—who cheered as their leaders spread misery, exile, starvation and death across broad swaths of Europe—managed to avoid privation through the first four years of the war. Not until 1943 did the Germans begin to experience rationing. Meanwhile, their economy was subsidized by the unpaid toil of some eight million slave laborers from conquered nations. But by the fall of 1944, the sting of war reached deep into the Fatherland

Necessities Were in Short Supply . . .

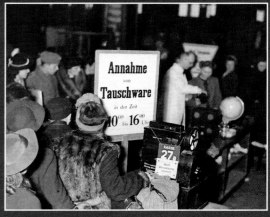

TRADING Civilians swarm a swap center in Berlin in 1944. The government established such markets in major cities to encourage noncash commerce

WATER LINE As Allied bombers hammered Berlin—U.S. planes by day, British planes by night—water mains were destroyed, forcing citizens to rely on public faucets

FILL-INS By early 1944 the government was routinely issuing papier-mâché replacements for shattered windows after each devastating Allied bombing run

. . . and Civilians Were Pressed into Uniform

WOMEN As Allied armies closed in on Germany in 1945, the Wehrmacht began training civilian women in military skills

TEENS As Hitler's élite troops were chewed up in combat, German boys ages 12 to 16 were trained for war and even sent to the front

SENIORS Wearing the armband that identifies him as a member of the *Volkssturm*, Hitler's army of old men and young boys, a geezer checks his rifle

ran the country. Fear of Hitler's secret police, who could arrest and execute anyone even suspected of defeatism. Fear of the Morgenthau Plan, an abortive scheme by Franklin Roosevelt's Treasury Secretary, Henry Morgenthau, to reduce postwar Germany to an agricultural vassal state.

The outward signs of this shift were usually subtle. Among civilians, the greeting *"Heil Hitler,"* which had been enthusiastically adopted in the late 1930s, increasingly gave way to a simple *"Guten tag."* In other cases, Nazi Party members stopped wearing party emblems on their clothing, no longer sure they would bring deference and sometimes fearing they would bring something far worse than disrespect.

But some indications of the public's disaffection were unmistakably stark. In a few cities that had been extensively bombed, young boys and deserting soldiers organized themselves into bands of ersatz resistance fighters, who came to be called "Edelweiss Pirates." Before being hunted down and wiped out by the Gestapo, these groups would attack small police detachments and lightly armed military units, stealing their weapons and using them to stage larger raids. In some cases they even attempted to assassinate local officials.

At the top of the regime, the Third Reich's death rattle was more pronounced. Apart from the hundreds of senior officers who were arrested and executed for their involvement (real or imagined) in the 1944 plot against Hitler's life, the list of German generals who were dismissed, demoted or otherwise disgraced by Hitler after reversals on the battlefield runs to more than 100. (In many cases, the officers were reappointed to command weeks or months later.) In several instances, Hitler sent messages to generals whose command posts were about to be overrun, urging them to commit suicide.

As for the man who had brought his nation to such a desperate impasse, by the close of 1944, Adolf Hitler had begun to admit to his closest associates—at least in unguarded moments—that hope was fading and that something other than victory might be his goal. When his last gamble in the West, the winter offensive in the Ardennes, was stymied, he said to his Luftwaffe aide, Nicolaus von Below, "We'll never capitulate. Never. We can go down. But we'll bring a world with us." ■

The Plot to Assassinate Hitler

A NEAR MISS Hermann Göring, in white, Martin Bormann, left, and other high-ranking Nazis view the wrecked conference room shortly after the bomb blast

In the first weeks of September 1944, the Germany army was reeling from a series of devastating blows from which it would never fully recover—defeats inflicted not by artillery and air power but by piano wire and meat hook, in the basement interrogation rooms of Hitler's secret police, the Gestapo. After the failed attempt on Adolf Hitler's life on July 20, 1944, the Gestapo arrested and executed as many as 5,000 Germans, including many high-ranking officers.

Displaying what biographer Ian Kershaw would later call "the luck of the devil," Hitler had dodged a series of assassination attempts for more than a decade, but this was his closest call. The bomb plot, led by Colonel Claus von Stauffenberg, took shape in the weeks after D-day. It wounded the Führer and killed many of the people who had been standing near him in a conference room at his field headquarters in East Prussia. This latest "miracle" stoked Hitler's most paranoid fantasies: his recent defeats in Africa, Italy, Russia and now

France had not been his fault but sprang from the treachery of his generals. And his survival was clear evidence to Hitler that he was destined not only to survive but also to win the war.

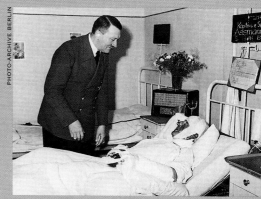

ESCAPE Hitler comforts a survivor of the bomb attack that almost killed him

But first, vengeance must be taken. Hundreds of senior officers as well as opposition figures who had nothing to do with the July plot were arrested and tortured to death. A few, such as Field Marshal Erwin Rommel, once a favorite of Hitler's, were afforded the more generous end of taking their own life. For most of the others, the last act was a show trial before a "People's Court," followed by a grisly death, with all of the defendants haunted by the certain knowledge that their wives and children would share a similar fate.

SUICIDE The Nazis claimed—and TIME and the Allies initially believed—that Erwin Rommel died of wounds suffered while serving in Normandy

Knocking on Hitler's Door

U.S. troops first strike at Germany's heartland in the battle of Aachen—and the price is high

INTO THE WOODS **These U.S. infantrymen marching through the forest toward Aachen on Sept. 10 were among the first Allied troops to enter the German homeland**

MID-SEPTEMBER 1944: AS MARKET-GARDEN REACHED ITS TRAGIC, BLOODY dénouement in the north, a new flash point was beginning to take shape 50 miles to the south, along Germany's border with Belgium, where fast-moving U.S. troops were poised to enter German territory. If the lesson of Montgomery's misbegotten air-land operation in Holland was that Germany would have to be strangled slowly rather than stabbed in a single decisive thrust, then the ancient city of Aachen would be where Hitler first felt the hands of the Allies closing around his throat.

Aachen was a stark contrast to Market-Garden. The British took the lead in the airborne invasion of Holland, emphasizing speed and surprise. But the siege of Aachen was an exclusively American operation, emphasizing massive firepower on the ground and overwhelming air superiority. Still taught at military schools, it became a case study in the gritty, grinding nature of urban warfare.

All of which is ironic, for Aachen was a battle that neither side courted. U.S. commanders deemed the city of little military value and originally intended to push forward in columns to its north and south, bypassing Aachen rather than taking it. The Germans hoped to preserve the historic site, known to the French as Aix-la-Chapelle, where Charlemagne had been born and later crowned Holy Roman Emperor. German commander Gerhard von Schwerin evacuated most of Aachen's 160,000 civilians and sent a courier to the U.S. lines on Sept. 13 with a message offering to surrender the city in order to spare it from Allied bombs.

But Adolf Hitler wasn't made for surrender. He had Von Schwerin arrested and quickly transferred several battle-hardened units from the Eastern front, along with 5,000 *Volkssturm* troops (young boys and old men) to reinforce the city. He ordered them to make Aachen for the Americans what Stalingrad had been for the

31

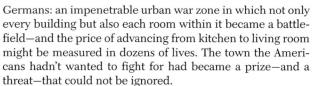

Germans: an impenetrable urban war zone in which not only every building but also each room within it became a battlefield—and the price of advancing from kitchen to living room might be measured in dozens of lives. The town the Americans hadn't wanted to fight for had became a prize—and a threat—that could not be ignored.

"Aachen was doomed," TIME reported in mid-October, after U.S. troops began entering the city; the fighting ran the gamut "from dive-bombing of German headquarters buildings, through tank skirmishes, to the rooting out of individual Germans from cellars." American units poured as many as 5,000 artillery shells per day into the city, followed by hundreds of tons of bombs. "The enemy fought as if the city were the cornerstone of the whole front," TIME said. The tragedy was that Aachen possessed no such significance. But Hitler, true to form, "chose certain destruction of the city rather than surrender a point that had become tactically valueless."

The countryside around Aachen was significant, however: it was there that the Americans under General Courtney Hodges applied the other lesson they took from Market-Garden: that they must punch straight through Hitler's Siegfried Line, instead of trying to maneuver around it. The line, Germany's main defense against invasion from the west, ran for almost 400 miles along the border of Belgium and France; it bristled with the X-shaped antitank "hedgehogs" and reinforced concrete bunkers connected by underground tunnels familiar to the Allies from Normandy. But the men of the U.S. 1st Infantry Division (the "Big Red One") now besieging Aachen had land-

MANSELL COLLECTION—TIME LIFE PICTURES (2)

ed on Omaha Beach in June and had learned much from the Germans' "impenetrable" Atlantic Wall. If artillery and air power could cut off German bunkers from supply and reinforcement, then it mattered little how bravely or well the soldiers inside them fought: it was only a matter of time before they would be killed or forced to surrender. And troops in the pillboxes would almost always surrender as soon as U.S. troops were in position to attack the fortifications from the rear.

Despite these new tactics, the Siegfried Line proved more formidable than Hitler's Atlantic Wall: the soldiers here were defending their homeland rather than occupied foreign territory. Yet though the barrier held somewhat longer than the fortifications at Normandy, it finally collapsed in the face of relentless U.S. firepower.

After weeks of battle, both Aachen and the segments of the Siegfried Line around it were subdued. The price was high: more than 2,000 U.S. soldiers and 5,000 German troops were dead; 5,600 Germans were prisoners, and Charlemagne's ancient city was a smoking ruin. All that remained was the capitulation that Von Schwerin had first offered five weeks earlier—and that Hitler had forbidden the city's new commander, Colonel Gerhard Wilck, to sign, on pain of death. On Oct. 21, Wilck signed an unconditional surrender: for the first time, a major German city had fallen into Allied hands. The path to the Rhine, and beyond it to Germany's heartland, now lay open. After signing the surrender and saying a few words to his troops, Colonel Wilck, TIME reported, "went off to the prisoners' cage and sobbed." ■

"I was refused by the Americans the authority to give the Sieg Heil and Heil Hitler. But we can still do it with our minds."

—Colonel Gerhard Wilck, to his soldiers, in surrendering

Winged Victory

Former U.S. Senator George McGovern shares the view from the
cockpit as gutsy Allied bombing crews strangle Hitler's war machine

ALBERT SPEER, ADOLF HITLER'S ARCHITECT AND, BY 1944, his Armaments Minister, knew once and for all that the war was lost when he visited the Italian front in the closing weeks of the year. His conclusion came not from battlefield reversals or from a loss of faith in Hitler but from the sight of a column of German trucks headed toward the front. The 150 vehicles, which were in perfect working order and were packed with desperately needed troops and supplies, were crawling along a road at about 3 m.p.h.—because that was as fast as the team of oxen pulling each truck could go. The vehicles had no fuel.

All over the shrinking territory that Germany still controlled, the same was true for tanks and half-tracks, airplanes and armored personnel carriers: the Nazi war machine was dying of thirst. By the fall of '44, the war in the skies had begun to matter as much as (sometimes more than) the fighting on the ground. For all the heroism on the beaches, D-day had succeeded largely owing to Dwight Eisenhower's Transportation Plan, which used Allied air superiority to prevent German reinforcements and supplies from reaching the front lines. Two days after D-day, General Carl Spaatz, the commander of the U.S. Strategic Air Forces in Europe, formalized a new strategy for the air war, ordering that "the primary strategic aim of the U.S. Strategic Air Forces is now to deny oil to enemy armed forces." From that day forward, all the concentrated might of the U.S. Eighth, Ninth, Twelfth and Fifteenth Army Air Forces would focus on oil.

"From the time I arrived in Europe, in September 1944," recalls George McGovern, then a 22-year-old bomber pilot from South Dakota, later a U.S. Senator and presidential candidate, and now a proud veteran of 83, "oil was the top priority. We hit refineries wherever we could find them—in Roma-

nia, Austria, Czechoslovakia, Germany and everyplace else the Nazis processed oil. Our second priority was railroads, but the difference was that you could wreck a rail terminal and the Germans would have it back in full operation, or nearly so, in a few days. But if you clobbered an oil refinery, it would be out of commission for weeks, maybe months."

After the first massive raids against German oil facilities, Speer reported to Hitler that "the enemy has struck at one of our weakest points. If they persist at it this time, we will soon no longer have any fuel production worth mentioning. Our one hope is that the other side has an Air Force General Staff as scatterbrained as ours."

Speer's hope was almost realized: the planners guiding the U.S. and British bombing campaigns altered strategies several times throughout the war, as the Allies searched for the one pillar that, if removed from service, would cause the German war effort to collapse. Intensive raids on ball-bearing factories, railroad facilities, munitions plants and dams caused serious difficulties for the Germans, but none turned out to be the body blow that air-raid planners had hoped for. Oil was.

"When I began flying combat missions," says McGovern, who was stationed in Italy with the Fifteenth Army Air Force, "there was still opposition from German fighters. But by the end of 1944, we almost never saw enemy planes in the air. Our intelligence people told us that the Germans still had plenty of fighters—but no fuel to fly them with."

For bomb crews, though, the grounding of the Luftwaffe didn't mean the end of danger. "The Germans were pulling their antiaircraft guns back with them as they retreated," McGovern explains. "So as many guns as they had used to protect all of Western Europe and North Africa and half of Russia were now concentrated into a much smaller area—maybe

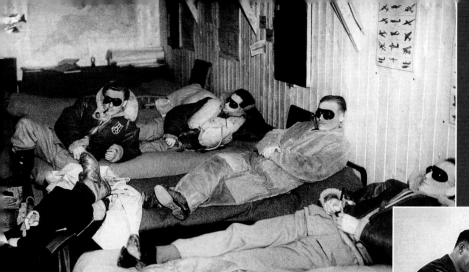

one-third of that size. That meant that the antiaircraft fire was much thicker and heavier with each mission and our job became progressively harder in the last months of the war."

For U.S. bomber pilots, the day would typically begin several hours before sunrise. "They would wake us up around 4 a.m.," McGovern says, "and after a light breakfast, we would gather in the briefing room to hear about the target we were supposed to hit that day." A "milk run" was an easy target that presented little danger. But in other cases, "when you heard the name of the place you were going," McGovern says, "you knew that not all of the planes would be coming back. Even aircraft that made it back would be carrying people who had been badly shot up. You knew that somebody in that room was probably going to die."

Although aviators were often envied by ground troops—because they came back to a warm bed, hot meal and a shower each night (assuming they did come back)—flying combat missions was actually considerably more dangerous than fighting from a foxhole. Only about one-third of all the crews that flew bombing missions over Europe survived the standard rotation of 25 missions (later raised to 35) without at least one member being wounded or killed. In the Army Air Force in Europe, almost 10,000 bombers (each carrying a crew of 10 men) were shot down during the war.

THE PLANES THEMSELVES WERE THE STUFF OF LEGEND, four-engine behemoths that hauled tons of ordnance across the breadth of Europe on missions that routinely lasted eight or nine hours. The workhorses of the U.S. fleet were the B-17, which carried 6,000 lbs. of bombs, and the B-24, which carried 8,000 lbs. Both planes had a top speed of around 300 m.p.h. U.S. factories turned out more than 12,000 B-17s during the war and more than 18,000 B-24s.

Six decades after the war, George McGovern remains partial to the plane he flew, the B-24 "Liberator." He maintains that it "could fly farther and faster with a heavier bomb load than any other plane. It was also amazingly durable. We came back from one mission with more than 100 holes in the fuselage from flak. The hydraulics were shot up, so we had to

crank the landing gear down by hand. And because the flaps were gone, the only way we could slow up was to tie parachutes to the ribs of the plane and toss them out the gunners' windows in the back as we touched down. But the plane got us home, which seemed like a miracle."

After the morning briefing, pilots and crews would head to their planes and, as dawn broke, begin taking off, one bomber every 30 seconds. "The liftoff was enough to put a few gray hairs in your head," McGovern says. "You used every foot of that runway. Even after you were in the air, you had to fly forward and level for quite a distance before you could gain much altitude. And if you tried to pull up too quickly, the plane would stall on you."

Once airborne, American bombers would remain above their airfields, waiting for other aircraft to join the formation. "Because there were usually more than 100 planes on a mission—sometimes more than 1,000—we would spend most of the first hour forming up in the air. You'd climb to about 21,000 ft. and begin circling while other planes that had taken off after you flew alongside." Most bombers were not pressurized, so the crew had to don oxygen masks once a plane climbed above 10,000 ft.; electrical wiring ran through their jackets, pants and gloves to keep them from freezing.

The Army Air Force trained bomber pilots to fly close together ("near enough that you could recognize the faces of guys you knew in other planes," McGovern says) because this made the entire group a smaller target for ground-based gun-

"We did not recognize our street anymore. Fire, only fire, wherever we looked."

—Lothar Metzger, Dresden bombing survivor, 1999

WOE A medieval angel regards the ruins of Dresden, where on the night of Feb. 13-14, 1945, 773 British planes unleashed incendiary bombs designed to create firestorms. Estimates of civilian deaths range from 30,000 to more than 200,000

ners and enemy fighters (while also focusing the return fire that the 50-cal. machine guns on each plane could direct at German fighters). The downside: if one bomber was hit, it might take down one or more of the planes close to it.

Bombers flew straight and slow, often at low altitude, on their final approach to the objective. "This was the time when we were most vulnerable to flak fire," McGovern says, "but it was necessary if we were going to hit targets with any accuracy. Ideally, we wouldn't be over the target for any more than 10 or 12 minutes. After unloading the bombs, we'd turn and head home—almost always taking a different route than the flight path in, to make it harder for enemy planes or guns to intercept us."

The trip back was easier—"the B-24 handled better with a lighter load," McGovern says—but there was always the possibility of more flak. "I never really relaxed until we were back on the ground," he recalls. "We were always met by Red Cross people, who gave us each a shot of bourbon."

While American flyers drew the tough duty of precision bombing by daylight, British bomber command usually opted for the less precise (and less dangerous) task of bombing German cities under cover of darkness. That reflected not a failure of nerve but a competing theory of how to wage the air war: British planners believed that setting entire cities aflame would psychologically devastate the German population. Yet studies conducted after the war would show that, just as German bombs and rockets failed to break British morale, the carpet bombing of German cities not only failed to smash the resolve of German civilians but also actually increased it. The Allied fire-bombing of major German cities like Dresden was sharply criticized by many Britons and Americans during the war and remains a notable, controversial exception to the generally humane Allied war strategies.

As the air raids against German oil refineries (especially at Ploesti, in Romania, which produced more than half of the Third Reich's fuel supply) effectively choked off the supply of gasoline, the engine that had driven the conquest of Europe, North Africa and much of Russia all but sputtered to a halt.

But like a caged animal, Hitler remained dangerous to the last. Allied bombers continued to suffer heavy losses; dozens of planes were shot down even in the last month of the war in Europe. George McGovern flew his final mission on April 25, 1945, against the Austrian city of Linz—Hitler's hometown. "For me, it was the worst mission of the entire war," he now says. The terrifying ordeal involved almost continual enemy fire all the way into Austria and nearly the entire journey back, during which McGovern's plane sustained heavy damage. (This turned out to be the last bombing run for the Fifteenth Army Air Force and one of the last flown by American bombers in Europe.)

Reflecting on that last mission, and others like it, McGovern now says, "What sustained me was the rightness of what we were doing. I didn't think that America had any honorable course other than to go after Hitler and the Nazis with everything we had. When you're looking at the possibility of dying, that can make a big difference. I was still afraid, yes, but I was able to do the job in spite of the fear, because I believed that what we were doing was vitally important." ■

Secret Weapons Of the Third Reich

RUINS Emergency personnel work amid a market in Faringdon Street, London, after it was hit by a V-2 in 1944

Adolf Hitler's secret weapons programs might have altered the course of the war—if only they could have been kept secret from Hitler. Early in the war, Germany's program to develop an atom bomb was scuttled, in part, because Hitler dismissed theories about nuclear fission as "Jewish physics."

By mid-1944, groundbreaking research into missile technology conducted by rocket pioneer Wernher von Braun and his team fed hopes that Germany could take back control of its skies, which in turn might have revived fuel production, helping reverse the nation's military losses. A small, inexpensive missile designed by Von Braun, code-named Waterfall, proved able to hit targets at altitudes of 50,000 ft.—more than twice as high as the operational ceiling of any Allied bomber—with great accuracy, in skies that were dark or light, cloudy or clear.

But Hitler demanded that these rockets be enlarged to carry hundreds of pounds of explosives (rather than the small charges need to knock an airplane out of the sky) over a range of many hundreds of miles. The dictator was

FLIGHT As V-2 rockets menaced London in the fall of 1944, some 55,000 British children were evacuated from the city on trains dubbed "the Doodlebug Express"

DEADLY German technicians work on a V-2 rocket at the Peenemünde base on an island in the Baltic Sea. The V-2 stood 46 ft. tall and carried a 2,000-lb. payload for 200 miles

achieved by German engineers in the last year of the war: jet aircraft. The Me-262 fighter flew higher and faster than any plane in the Allied arsenal. Used properly, it could have cut to shreds the vast herds of Allied bombers that were pouring destruction onto German cities day and night. But Hitler demanded that the Me-262 be reconfigured to serve as a bomber—a task for which it was manifestly ill-suited—again for the unstrategic task of carrying out bombing raids against Allied cities. His plan drove Luftwaffe designers to distraction, because bombers are primarily offensive weapons, whereas fighters play a largely defensive role. At a moment when the Third Reich was fighting for its life, Germany had little need for the former and a desperate need for the latter.

Perhaps the primary role played by Hitler's star-crossed search for new weapons was to deceive the German people. All through 1944 and 1945, when there were no more victories to report, the Nazi propaganda apparatus prattled endlessly about the wonder weapons that would shortly be unleashed upon Germany's enemies.

Ordinary Germans weren't the only ones deceived by such fantasies: Armaments Minister Albert Speer would later recall being told by Nazi Labor Front leader Robert Ley in Hitler's bunker—in April 1945, as Russian troops massed only miles away— that "death rays have

deaf to protests that the added expense would allow only a few hundred large missiles to be produced each month, rather than thousands of the smaller rockets. And he didn't care that Waterfall's pinpoint accuracy would be diminished to the point where no target smaller than a major city could be hit.

For Hitler wasn't interested in achieving tactical control of the skies over Germany; he was interested in revenge. His fury at Allied air raids on German cities led him to order rockets big enough to batter London, Paris and Antwerp. Von Braun's team reluctantly followed Hitler's orders. The result was the V-2 rocket. By

war's end, the Germans had launched 1,358 of them at London, killing 2,700 civilians—to no strategic gain.

As Germany collapsed in May 1945, both Russian and U.S. occupation officials frantically searched for any scientists who had worked on missile technology, for it was clear that rockets would play a key role in future wars. This race was mostly won by the Americans, who spirited a willing Von Braun and many of his colleagues back to the U.S., where they worked on long-range missiles and eventually in NASA's space program.

The story was much the same with the other major technical breakthrough

PLANT This German jet-plane factory, manned by 2,400 slave laborers, was discovered in a salt mine near Schonebeck

been invented!" This giddy declaration was followed by a squabble among Hitler's paladins over who would be honored with the chance to serve as "Commissioner for Death Rays."

In the end, Hitler was probably incapable of using any technology that surpassed his understanding. As Speer wrote in his memoirs, "Amateurishness was one of Hitler's dominant traits ... The tendency to wild decision had long been his forte; now it speeded his decline."

IN PROGRESS: A U.S. soldier examines a nascent V-2 at an underground assembly plant in Nordhausen, Germany, that fell to the Allies in April 1945

War in the Mountains

The Allies' advances in Italy are hard-won, yet this front is a sideshow
after D-day—and that knowledge makes every soldier's burden heavier

DISPLAYING HIS CELEBRATED GIFT FOR THE TELLING phrase, Winston Churchill dubbed Italy "the soft underbelly of Europe" when arguing for a 1943 invasion designed to liberate the Italian peninsula in a few short months and open a southern front against Germany. But in this case, reality defied the phrasemaker: for Allied soldiers, Italy turned out to be a hard spine rather than a bloated gut. The troops met determined German resistance from the mo-

ment they landed in Sicily in July 1943, and the fighting grew tougher as they advanced northward. More than a year after the initial punch to this supposed Axis soft spot, the battle for Italy was still undecided, and some of the bloodiest fighting that U.S. and British troops would see at any time during the war had flared up at Anzio and Monte Cassino in central Italy. Churchill, quotable even in dejection, would grouse after the Allies' January 1944 landing at Anzio that "I had hoped we

were hurling a wildcat onto the shore, but all we got was a stranded whale."

By September 1944, though, much had been accomplished. Rome had been in Allied hands for three months; it was captured on June 5, the day before D-day. Hitler's feckless Italian ally, the strutting Benito Mussolini, was safely bottled up. Deposed and briefly imprisoned in 1943, the erstwhile dictator had been freed in September of that year, when German commandos staged a daring glider and parachute raid on his mountaintop prison in the Abruzzi region. Hitler then installed Mussolini as the head of the new Repubblica di Salo in northern Italy. This puppet state was run entirely by the Nazis, a fact underscored when one of Mussolini's first official acts in his diminished new role was to cede Trieste, Istria and South Tyrol to Germany, while promising to hand over Venice in the near future.

On the battlefield, where German divisions had largely replaced Mussolini's disorganized and dispirited Italian troops, Wehrmacht soldiers had retreated into the Apennine Mountains and the site of what would be their last stand on the Italian peninsula: the Gothic Line. This series of fortified passes and mountaintop strongholds north of the Arno River stretched from the Ligurian Sea, on Italy's west coast, through the cities of Pisa, Florence and the strategic crossroads of Bologna (a major rail and road hub) to the Adriatic, on Italy's eastern shore. Here the Germans dug in, building more than 2,300 machine-gun nests with interlocking fields of fire and hundreds of heavy-gun emplacements.

Faced with this formidable obstacle, American and British commanders found themselves stalemated—not by the Germans but by each other. The last phase of the Italian campaign illustrates, perhaps better than any other chapter of World War II, the difficulties of coalition warfare. Churchill was growing alarmed at the gathering speed of Stalin's advance across the Russian Front, believing that it posed a postwar threat to British and American interests in Eastern Europe and the Medi-

> **"I had hoped we were hurling a wildcat onto the shore, but all we got was a stranded whale." —Winston Churchill**

terranean. For this reason, he argued for a quick thrust through what remained of Italy, followed by a push into Austria, Hungary and the Balkan states.

The Allies' top commander on the Continent, Dwight Eisenhower, didn't agree: he was more interested in winning the war than in trying to influence what the map of Europe would look like after it. Flush with the success of D-day, Eisenhower wanted to assign top priority to northwestern Europe and the drive across France, Belgium and the Netherlands to the German border. What's more, Ike believed that Churchill and British generals vastly underestimated the number of troops and the amount of supplies that would be required to break the Gothic Line.

In some ways, the argument over Italy was a reprise of the debate about a "broad front" strategy (which the Americans favored) as opposed to a quick drive on Berlin (the preferred British strategy), which resulted in the ill-fated Operation Market-Garden. Even if storming the Gothic Line would be costly, Churchill reasoned, the prize behind it was tempting. Beyond the Apennines lay the broad flat plains of the Po Valley, which offered no natural defensive line, making it nearly impossible for the Germans to rally there and make a stand. A German retreat across this terrain would almost certainly devolve into a slaughter. But this time, with the expensive lesson of Market-Garden fresh in his memory, Eisenhower refused to take the bait. He declined to send more Allied troops to Italy, and even siphoned off some units, transferring them

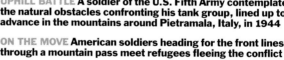

UPHILL BATTLE A soldier of the U.S. Fifth Army contemplates the natural obstacles confronting his tank group, lined up to advance in the mountains around Pietramala, Italy, in 1944

ON THE MOVE American soldiers heading for the front lines through a mountain pass meet refugees fleeing the conflict

BRUNI FOTOGRAFICO

THE END A few U.S. troops mingle with the crowd of taunting Milanese as the bodies of Mussolini, far right, his mistress and two fellow Fascists are displayed in public on April 28, 1945

to the Western Front. The role that he envisioned for the British and American troops left facing the Apennines was to keep German troops pinned down there, preventing Hitler from transferring them either to the Eastern or Western front.

To placate Churchill, however, Eisenhower reluctantly agreed that British Field Marshal Sir Harold Alexander, the overall commander of Allied troops in Italy, could use the remaining troops of the British Eighth Army (under General Oliver Leese) and the American Fifth Army (led by General Mark Clark) to attack the Gothic Line if they saw an opportunity. In October, Alexander saw just such an opening—or so he believed. Egged on by the hard-charging duo of Leese and Clark—both of whom were frustrated at being relegated to a

"Blood alone moves the wheels of history." —Benito Mussolini

theater of war that was increasingly treated as a sideshow—the somewhat ineffectual Alexander approved Operation Olive, in which British forces would launch a feint from the Adriatic, while U.S. forces would try to punch through to Bologna. Deprived of a vital transportation center and pushed back from the coast, German resistance would disintegrate.

"Now we begin the last lap," Leese predicted confidently before the start of Operation Olive. "Victory in coming battles means the beginning of the end for the German armies in Italy." But the British Eighth Army met stiffer resistance than

expected, getting bogged down in bloody, prolonged and intense combat in Adriatic coastal towns like Rimini and Gemmano. While the Eighth didn't lose any of these battles, neither did it win them. Through October and November, towns with little strategic value evolved into costly quagmires. In the center, Clark's Fifth Army advanced on Bologna, only to be repeatedly pushed back by the entrenched Germans. The mountainous territory favored the defenders, and Clark's troops paid dearly for every yard of territory they gained.

With the onset of winter, it was no longer practical for Alexander to contemplate a major offensive in the mountains. The Gothic Line had held, and the German army would remain in Italy until the spring. In the wake of Operation Olive, Leese complained that "this campaign is a hard row to hoe. It is the most difficult country in Europe, and yet we always get troops and equipment taken away from us for elsewhere."

With warm weather came renewed offensives. Bologna finally fell on April 21, 1945, followed by Verona four days later. German resistance on the Italian peninsula was effectively over. As German troops retreated across the Alps, they tried to smuggle their ally, Mussolini, out of the country with them. But on April 28, one day before Germany's formal surrender in Italy, Italian partisans on patrol near the Swiss border stopped the convoy in which the deposed dictator was hiding, disguised as a German soldier, and arrested him. As they prepared to execute Mussolini, his mistress Clara Petacci insisted on joining him in front of the firing squad. A moment later, they were machine-gunned together, followed by a dozen of Mussolini's Cabinet and close associates. Afterward, their bodies were brought to Milan and hung upside down in a public square, where crowds that had once roared their approval of Il Duce threw stones at his corpse. ∎

In the Balkans, Webs of Alliance and Betrayal

Southeastern Europe, cradle of WWI and a crazy quilt of warring allegiances even in peacetime, saw ferocious combat in 1944 and '45, as partisan irregulars battled German and Soviet divisions for power

Bulgaria

Alone among Hitler's Balkan allies, Bulgaria did not send troops into Russia in 1941. Even so, on Sept. 5, 1944, Russia declared war on Bulgaria. Three days later, as Russian troops surged across its borders, Bulgaria switched sides and declared war on Germany, which used the nation as a transit hub and avenue to Greece. Hitler's ally, King Boris, died in 1943, leaving his son Simeon, only 6, to rule as regent. He was pushed aside by the Soviets, who took control after the war. Below, cheering partisans enter Sofia in 1944.

Yugoslavia

The factious nation was originally a German ally, but Hitler ordered an invasion after the Fascist Prince-Regent Paul was toppled from power in 1941. This triggered a years-long partisan campaign in which two warring groups of Yugoslav nationalists waged guerrilla war against German troops. Allied support (weapons and supplies dropped by parachute) originally went to the Chetniks, who supported a restoration of the monarchy. But when this group began working with the Germans, the Allies switched their aid to the communist-leaning Josip Tito. By November 1943, Tito was running a rump government in the countryside; a year later he entered Belgrade in triumph. After the war he carved out a uniquely independent path for Yugoslavia within the Soviet sphere. Above, as many as one-third of Yugoslavia's partisans were women.

Greece

In October 1944, 30 months after German troops arrived in Greece to relieve Italian forces in their failed invasion, they were stranded: British ships were approaching from the south, while retreat was cut off in the north by Bulgaria's recent entente with the Allies. These troops were saved when, for once, Hitler agreed to deal with his enemies. German forces were permitted to evacuate Greece without being attacked by British naval units. In return, Hitler ordered German troops to hold Salonika against advancing Russian troops and surrender it instead to the British. Said the Führer: "This is the only time we have consented to anything like that." Below, British soldiers visit the ruins of the Acropolis in Athens in 1944.

Romania

Romanian strongman Marshal Ion Antonescu became Hitler's ally in 1941; he even sent troops to fight alongside the Germans in their invasion of Russia. But in August 1944, Antonescu was toppled from power and troops loyal to his successor, King Michael, reached the Danube one day before German troops, who were retreating at top speed before advancing Soviet tanks, above. Michael switched sides and declared war on Germany, while his troops barricaded the Danube bridges, cutting off the German retreat and exposing 16 German divisions to Soviet slaughter. The Romanians then joined the Russians in their battle against Germany. But that didn't save the country from occupation—this time by Russian troops after the war—followed by decades of Soviet domination.

The Bare Necessities

You'll never get rich by diggin' a ditch … or by taking an outdoor shower, bedding down with a few close friends or "liberating" a string of German sausages. But for weary, hungry Allied soldiers in Western Europe, everyday acts taken for granted at home—a bath, a bunk, a break, a butt—now became treasured moments of luxury amid war's brutal privations

■ **DO NOT DISTURB** Above, after weeks of sleeping in the open, men of a combat patrol of the U.S. First Army, 69th Division, bed down in a German town in March 1945

■ **CLEANUP** An outdoor shower, hand-fed by a watering can and decorated with a pinup girl, draws a smile from Eugene Morell of Rochester, N.Y., in March 1945. His turn is noted on the chalkboard at left

■ **GLORIOUS FOURTH** Perhaps eyeing a patriotic cookout, U.S. soldiers smile as they return to their camp in Cherbourg, France, with captured German sausages on July 3, 1944

■ **SIGN OF SPRING** Corporal Carmen Padelino of Belleville, N.J., enjoys a scrub in a metal tub his company found in a German pillbox. The date is March 15, 1945; the war in Europe will be over in six weeks

■ **SPOILS OF WAR** Five U.S. infantrymen take a break from duty on the front lines in the Neuf Brisach area of France, above. At night, their full squad is in position on the front; during the day the men retire to this captured German dugout in two teams to rest and recuperate

■ **SCRUBDOWN** A bombed-out building in Lanfroicourt, France, serves as a field kitchen for these soldiers from a U.S. artillery division in October 1944; they are washing their mess kits in hot water before being served their grub

■ **SACK TIME** British rifleman H. Stanborough of London grabs some sleep amid relics of Italian grandeur as Allied troops close in on Rome in 1944

■ ROOST Unfazed by his grand surroundings, left, an infantryman of the U.S. Third Army enjoys a snooze on Hermann Göring's bed in the Luftwaffe boss's residence in Neuhaus, Germany, in May 1945

■ CLOSE SHAVE Enjoying a rare interlude of downtime during the six weeks of the wintertime Battle of the Bulge in the Ardennes, an American soldier grabs the chance to clean up amid the snow

■ LAUNDRY DETAIL Two Canadian soldiers in Normandy crank the handles of a homemade washing machine engineered from a wine barrel, as a third inserts clothes; washed-up duds will hang out to dry on the clothesline at rear

■ SPECIAL HOLIDAY DELIVERY Above, PFC Edmund Dill of Cumberland, Md., on left, opens a Christmas packet he received from his wife and shares the booty. The three soldiers are members of the U.S. Army 30th Infantry Division

■ THE LINEUP An Italian priest and his donkey, left, seem to be enjoying the spectacle as American soldiers perform their morning ablutions in the portico of a 15th century monastery

■TAKE FIVE Two U.S. soldiers grab a few moments of rest al fresco on Sept. 23, 1944, during the first days of the battle for the German town of Aachen. The U.S. Army laid siege to the town after Adolf Hitler refused to allow surrounded Germans inside to surrender

■NOT LIKE THE ONES HE USED TO KNOW Perhaps dreaming of a white Christmas, a British soldier lines his foxhole in Holland with Christmas cards as he enjoys his holiday "feast" on Dec. 25, 1944

■RUB-A-DUB-DUB . . . Five men, five tubs, as troops from Britain's Dorsetshire County Regiment enjoy a hot bath in France in 1944

ALLIES In Greece, local partisans aid a British airman who has bailed out and landed in their area

Secret Sharers

Across an occupied empire, local heroes conspire to aid the Allies and undermine German rule

FROM CAPTURED ENEMY ORDERS AND PAPERS," A November 1944 German military intelligence report on civilian sabotage in Czechoslovakia reads, "it has been learned that the enemy intelligence service has tried to infiltrate single agents and teams to build up resistance groups in the rear of the present German front." The report could have applied to all of Nazi-occupied Europe. Across the Continent, citizens united to counter Nazi aggression and brutality. Motivated by patriotism, ideology, religion and moral outrage, such groups employed tactics that ranged from the prankish (slipping laxatives into German food supplies) to the serious (bombing train tracks) to the deadly (ambushing and slaughtering isolated units of German troops).

While many of these groups were independent, some took direction from London, Moscow or Bern, the Swiss city where the U.S. spy organization, the Office of Strategic Services, was headquartered. When all the gears meshed, the resistance could make a real difference in the war effort. Eisenhower later estimated that the Maquis, France's paramilitary rebels, had been worth the equivalent of two divisions during the Battle of France. In Normandy, a French civilian bicyclist carefully mapped the German fortifications guarding the beaches and smuggled them to the Allies before D-day. In Denmark, a heroic resistance effort managed to deliver almost the entire Jewish population of the country—thousands of innocent people who would otherwise have been bound for the gas chambers—to neutral Sweden. Everywhere, ongoing acts of civil disobedience helped tie down entire German divisions, keeping them away from the front. In Russia, Poland and Yugoslavia, even territory that was hundreds of miles behind the front lines was never fully under the German's control, thanks to partisan campaigns.

To battle the occupiers was to risk your life—and those of your friends. Rebels who fell into German hands faced not only the certainty of torture and death but also the policy of *Sippenhaft* ("kin reprisal"): their families were also punished. In more than a few cases, when German anger was not slaked by the murder of a small number of relatives of resistance members, civic leaders or the populations of entire towns were machine-gunned to death.

Nazi retaliation could take more ghoulish proportions. When members of the Dutch resistance emerged from hiding and began fighting on the side of U.S. and British troops during Operation Market-Garden in September 1944, the Germans took their revenge the following winter by halting food shipments to the parts of Holland still in their grip. More than 20,000 Dutch civilians died of starvation.

The tales of the resistance are not always heroic. The anti-Nazi factions in Greece were so fragmented and beset by bickering that they accomplished almost nothing. In Yugoslavia, communist and anticommunist resistance units ended up fighting one another. British, U.S. and Russian intelligence services often operated at cross purposes.

But for the Allies, the value of having people on the ground who were prepared to gather information and risk their lives in confronting the Germans was incalculable. Several thousand American and British pilots who had been shot down by German gunners were saved from capture, hidden (sometimes for months) and then returned to friendly territory through an elaborate "pipeline" system that stretched across the breadth of Europe. In other cases, bombing missions were guided to their targets at night with signal fires set by the resistance.

While the rebels could not, by themselves, throw off the yoke of German oppression, they played a significant role in the outcome of the war—and paid a significant price. Across Europe, historians now estimate, more than 2 million resistance fighters were killed by the Germans during the war. ∎

Tales of the Resistance

Tracing the history of resistance movements is difficult: secrecy, after all, was their lifeblood. Most such organizations were networks of civilian informers, some highly organized and many in direct touch with Allied personnel. Not all resistance fighters were civilians; several of the movements were quasi-military outfits, including the Home Rule group in Poland and France's famed Maquis. Women, excluded from the front lines except in the Balkans, played major roles in several resistance movements

INGE ASCHER-SCHOLL

The White Rose

By 1942, resistance to Hitler's Nazi regime within Germany was almost nonexistent: indoctrinated young people were among the regime's most enthusiastic supporters. The most notable exception was a small group of students based in Munich who called themselves the White Rose. The leaders included, from left above, Hans Scholl, his sister Sophie Scholl and their friend Christoph Probst, as well as two other students, Willi Graf and Alexander Schmorell. The core of a group that later numbered as many as 80 young people, they blasted Germany's leaders in a series of pamphlets that began appearing in Munich in June 1942. The first of them accused the Nazis of killing 300,000 Jews—one of the earliest references to Hitler's genocide.

Emboldened by a positive response to their broadsides, White Rose members also wrote anti-Hitler graffiti on Munich walls on three nights in February 1943. A few days later, the two Scholls were detained and arrested after a pro-regime janitor at the University of Munich saw them drop White Rose pamphlets from a third-story atrium into a school courtyard. On Feb. 22, 1943, the Scholls and Probst were beheaded by a guillotine.

O.F.I.C.

The Marr Family

In its Dec. 11, 1944 issue, TIME ran a full page of photographs of the ongoing resistance in France, noting that a few rogue German units were still active near the mouth of the Garonne River. TIME reported that Madame Marr and her son and grandson, above, had sheltered 17 U.S. and Canadian soldiers in their home in the town of Laguepie, allowing them to escape detection by German search parties.

Hannie Schaft

Remembered by the Dutch as the legendary "Red-Headed Girl," Hannie Schaft , a law student specializing in civil rights at the University of Amsterdam, was only 20 when the Germans occupied Holland in May 1940. Her first acts of civil disobedience were directed at the Germans' harsh anti-Jewish restrictions. She dropped her studies in 1943, after the Germans ordered that all Dutch students spend a year in Germany. Back in her hometown of Haarlem, she began distributing anti-German news-papers, sheltering Jews and collecting information on German activities. Dying her telltale hair black, she stepped up her activities, becoming a saboteur and assassin.

DUTCH WAR ARCHIVES

In June 1944, the Germans arrested Schaft's parents and confined them in a concentration camp, hoping to persuade her to come forward, but she remained in hiding. On March 21, 1945, Schaft was stopped by German soldiers as she was delivering resistance dispatches; she was identified, interrogated, probably tortured, shot to death and buried in a shallow grave. Three weeks later, the Netherlands was liberated.

Marie-Madeleine Fourcade

Known by her code name "Hedgehog," Fourcade was a divorced Parisian who in 1941 assumed control of Alliance, a network of some 3,000 agents who collected information for the British. The only woman to head a major French resistance group, Fourcade was arrested by the Gestapo in 1944 in the act of sending secret coded messages to London. Imprisoned by the Germans and awaiting torture and probable execution, Fourcade stripped off her clothes and squeezed through the bars of the cell window; she was not captured again.

COURTESY MARIE-MADELEINE FOURCADE

"I learned that good judgment comes from experience, and that experience grows out of mistakes." —Omar Bradley

Destroy the Enemy

Three weeks before the Germans launched their last great assault in the west, TIME profiled the man universally revered as "the G.I.s' general"

LIEUT. GENERAL OMAR N. BRADLEY, commander of the Twelfth Army Group, can get the weather forecast at any time from his meteorological staff, but he likes to see things for himself. So he keeps three barometers in his headquarters office, jots down the readings twice a day in his notebook.

Most of last week the barometers told kindly, soft-spoken Omar Bradley (whose oldest friends call him "Omar the Tentmaker") that the weather would not be good. He was out a lot himself in the rain and snow, wiping the steam from his glasses, getting plenty of mud on the paratroop boots into which he tucks his G.I. pants. He knew what the cold, dirty, wet and often hungry doughboys were going through. He wanted to get them out of there, and out of the war, as soon as possible. He looked forward to fishing, back in the U.S. "I know," he said recently, "a lot of nice river banks."

Bradley is already acknowledged as one of the finest ground commanders of this war. If he beats the Germans to their knees in front of the Rhine, his name will go down the centuries as one of the great captains of history. Less than two years ago, when this quiet son of a Missouri schoolteacher was sent to Tunisia to serve under George Patton, he had never seen any actual fighting. But he had an exhaustive knowledge of infantry tactics, and of infantrymen as human beings, and he knew training. He had made a resounding success as Commandant of the Infantry School at Fort Benning. In Africa and Sicily, Bradley so distinguished himself that Dwight D. Eisenhower picked him to head U.S. forces in the assault on Hitler's Atlantic Wall on D-day.

Bradley and his staff were responsible for all joint planning and coordination of Army, Navy and Air for the two U.S. landings on the Normandy beaches. But the General never for a moment forgot the doughboys. An officer of the 4th Infantry Division later recalled a meeting at which Bradley addressed the division officers a week or so before D-day:

"He said that in his experience—and he had had plenty—

OLD SOLDIER After the war Bradley was named a five-star general; he served as the first Chairman of the Joint Chiefs of Staff and as chair of NATO's first board of military advisers

our training was absolutely sound. He said that if we remembered the simple things we had been taught, the division would make a name for itself ... It was good, because it took away the idea that this war was any different than what we had been trained for. You can't kid the infantry; they know they've got to go in and do the fighting; and Bradley was an ex-infantryman. It inspired confidence."

As a tactician, Omar Bradley is blessed with powers of accurate observation and shrewd analysis, a natural affinity for maps and a prodigious memory which endears him to countless juniors whose names he recalls. He will accept bold risks if his basic horse sense, of which he has plenty, tells him they are sound. After D-day, Bradley was the line smasher as well as quarterback for the Allied operations (as he is now). He did not fumble, and he invariably capitalized on the errors of the enemy.

It was Bradley who designed the breakthrough to the west side of the Normandy peninsula, cutting off Cherbourg, and the breakthrough at Saint-Lô which began the battle of France. Bradley also designed the Argentan-Falaise pincers, and the scythelike sweeps to the Seine which ruined the German Seventh Army. His rush to the German border was a bid to knock out German resistance once & for all, before his supply lines snapped. He was philosophical about not winning that one; nobody can win them all.

Bradley is not the kind of man to worry about his place in history, and he is too busy for that now, anyway. He pops awake every morning at 7, breakfasts an hour later, has a briefing on the previous day's operations at 9:15. The rest of his day is spent in conference or in driving or flying along the front. After dinner Bradley usually sees a movie (e.g., *Janie, Heavenly Body, Bride by Mistake, Dragon Seed*) screened by his aides in his quarters, pecks out a letter to his wife on his portable typewriter, goes to bed early.

Most G.I.s seldom discuss officers except for the juniors with whom they come in contact. Bradley is an exception. They sometimes speak of him as Robert E. Lee's men spoke of their general around the campfires of the Civil War. Bradley's men know that he never forgets them, that he wants to send as many of them home alive and whole as he can. ■

Showdown in the Snow

Outmanned, outgunned and out of gas, Adolf Hitler risks all on a final gamble, but after early success he is beaten in the Battle of the Bulge

DEC. 16, 1944. ALL ALONG THE FRONT LINES IN FRANCE and Belgium, Allied troops were shoring up their positions—not against the Germans but against the elements. "We were dug in and ready to settle down for the winter," recalls George Checkan, then a 20-year-old infantryman in the First Army's 9th Division, serving under General Omar Bradley, and now, at 82, a retired Washington

Post employee in Maryland. "Everybody told us that the Germans didn't have the equipment for a new offensive, that they couldn't get ready before the spring." A U.S. Army intelligence report issued that day declared, "The enemy is at present fighting a defensive campaign on all fronts; his situation is such that he cannot stage major offensive operations."

An hour before dawn on that bitterly cold morning, Check-

an recalls, heavy German shelling began hitting his unit's position near Aachen. "Before then, we would occasionally take some fire," he remembers, "but this was different. They fired shell after shell, blanketing the woods around us. The .88s were a terrible weapon, just incredibly destructive. So we took whatever shelter we could find and hung on."

That morning, Checkan was a pawn on a mighty chessboard: the final major battle on the Western Front had begun.

For months now, at opposite ends of Western Europe, the two men who held his future in their hands had pondered their next moves. At the Supreme Headquarters of the Allied Expeditionary Force in Verdun, France, General Dwight D. Eisenhower fantasized about getting his hands on a major harbor. One trophy city after another—including Rome, Paris and Brussels—had fallen to advancing British and American troops in 1944. Yet by the beginning of September, the Allies

"A single breakthrough on the Western Front! You'll see! It will lead to collapse and panic among the Americans."
—Adolf Hitler, to his generals

ON THE OFFENSIVE: Driving deep into territory held by the Allies, German troops pass burning U.S. vehicles on a road in Belgium after their successful surprise attack. This film was taken from captured German soldiers

still held only one natural port of any consequence: Cherbourg, which the Germans had sabotaged so completely as to render it nearly useless. Ike's supply lines now stretched almost 400 grueling miles from Normandy to the front lines.

In Berlin, Adolf Hitler was also dreaming. On his right flank, a ferocious Russian onslaught was continuing; there, the dictator saw no possibility of a change in his fortunes. But the West might be different. For Hitler knew what Ike did: that the Allies had advanced farther and faster than they had originally believed possible. Their supply lines were pulled taut. Meanwhile, along the broad 1,100-mile front lines to Germany's west, U.S. and British troop concentrations were thin.

Hitler's considerations were political as well as military. He knew that the U.S. and Britain were deeply suspicious of Joseph Stalin's postwar ambitions. If he could split his Western foes' alliance of convenience with Stalin by battling them to an accommodation, then the Third Reich could devote its full strength to the fight against the Russians. It is emblematic of the convoluted workings of Hitler's mind that he decided to attack the people he didn't want to fight anymore.

On Sept. 4, 1944, Eisenhower finally got his wish—or at least half of it. The Belgian port of Antwerp fell to the Allied advance, with its harbor facilities intact. But the Germans continued to control the Schedlt estuary, the 100-mile stretch leading from Antwerp to the North Sea. It would take another 12 weeks, until Nov. 27, before the estuary was secure and the Allies could exploit Antwerp's full potential.

During those 12 weeks, Hitler reeled between despair and new determination. After the fall of Antwerp, he lost 16 lbs. and was confined to bed for days. During that time, he conceived a plan reminiscent of his brilliant stroke of 1940, when he bypassed France's Maginot Line by attacking through the Ardennes Forest on the German border with Belgium and Luxembourg. A new thrust in the Ardennes would take the Allies by surprise, revisit the scene of an earlier triumph and again prove the Führer a war strategist superior to his generals.

By mid-September 1944, Hitler had rallied from his initial shock at the loss of Antwerp. The Allied advance toward the German border had slowed, as Nazi troops formerly in full retreat turned and began to fight. Eisenhower's forces were tak-

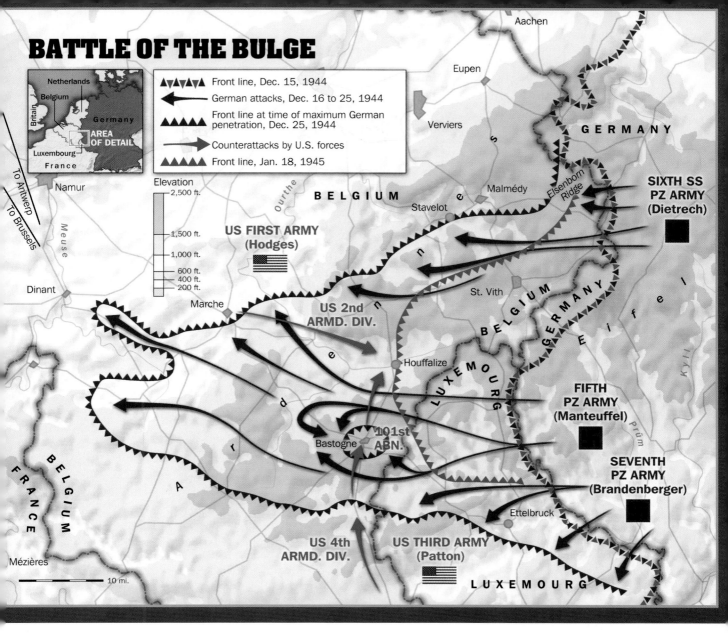

BATTLE OF THE BULGE

Netherlands
Belgium
Britain
Germany
AREA OF DETAIL
Luxembourg
France

To Antwerp
To Brussels

Namur
Meuse
Dinant
Mézières
Marche
Houffalize
Bastogne
Ettelbruck

BELGIUM
FRANCE
LUXEMOURG
GERMANY

Aachen
Eupen
Verviers
Malmédy
Stavelot
St. Vith
Elsenborn Ridge

Ourthe
Our
Eifel
Kyll
Prüm

US FIRST ARMY (Hodges)
US 2nd ARMD. DIV.
101st ABN.
US 4th ARMD. DIV.
US THIRD ARMY (Patton)

SIXTH SS PZ ARMY (Dietrech)
FIFTH PZ ARMY (Manteuffel)
SEVENTH PZ ARMY (Brandenberger)

---

ing heavy casualties in their siege of Aachen and along the Siegfried Line. The U.S. and British advance in Italy had also stalled, as German troops dug into fortified positions along the Gothic Line in the Apennine Mountains. Later in the month, as Hitler began planning in earnest for the new offensive in the Ardennes, the Allies faltered once more—this time in Holland, with the ill-fated Operation Market-Garden. Every indication seemed to confirm Hitler's hunch: he must strike—and strike soon—on the Western Front.

T HE RAPIDLY EVOLVING PLAN, CODE-NAMED "WATCH ON the Rhine," called for audacity and aggression, swiftness and surprise. The Germans would time their attack to coincide with bad weather, negating Allied air superiority. Charging down from the high ground of Germany's Eifel region, armored and motorized units would explode out of the Ardennes forest in a reprise of the blitzkrieg tactics that had succeeded so spectacularly in 1940.

The tip of the spear would be two armies of German tanks: the Fifth Panzers, which would push toward Brussels, and the Sixth Panzers, driving toward Antwerp. Behind them would come an additional 14 German divisions, supported by 10,000 heavy artillery pieces and hundreds of V-1 and V-2 rockets. The initial thrust would be directed at a sparsely manned section of the Allied lines, near the Belgian town of Bastogne, where the onslaught of German troops would quickly overwhelm the five understrength, unsuspecting American divisions bivouacked nearby.

Hitler's goal was to split the U.S. forces in the south from the British troops in the north. As the Sixth Panzers captured Antwerp, the British would be encircled and either slaughtered or captured. In the south, the advance of the Fifth Panzers would drive the Americans backward in a headlong rout.

Russia and the East remained uppermost in Hitler's mind: the new offensive had to begin before the Russians launched their inevitable winter offensive, expected for December or January. Hitler settled on Nov. 27 for the start of the Ardennes campaign but was delayed by the need to move large numbers of troops close to the Allied lines in secrecy. Most units moved gradually, usually at night. They brilliantly achieved

their objective, successfully arriving at the front without the Allies' knowledge.

A larger problem was the question of supplies: Hitler's armies were literally running out of gas. To provide the 17,500 tons of fuel needed for "Watch on the Rhine" to begin, Albert Speer, Hitler's Armaments Minister and supply czar, had to begin siphoning supplies away from other fronts a month earlier.

Germany's generals were skeptical. Sepp Dietrich, a personal favorite of Hitler's, who would command the Sixth Panzers, remarked upon learning of the plan, "All Hitler wants me to do is to cross a river, capture Brussels and then go on and take Antwerp. And all this in the worst time of the year, when the snow is waist deep." Indeed, Hitler's plan required every possible variable—from the weather to the element of surprise to the prospect of stumbling over treasure troves of fuel—to break in favor of the Germans. And as the Allies had learned in Operation Market-Garden, expecting a dozen flips of the coin to come up heads 12 times in a row is not a prudent way to plan battles.

After repeated delays, the final date for the launch of Hitler's Ardennes offensive was set for Dec. 16. Six days before, Hitler moved his field headquarters to a series of specially built bunkers in the forest code-named Alderhorst, "the Eagle's Nest," where he had cheered on the successful 1940 blitz. On Dec. 15, the first of the coin flips that would determine the fate of the dictator's high-stakes gambit came up heads: the weather turned to clouds, snow and rain. Allied fighters and bombers were grounded.

■ **December 16** AS DAWN BROKE OUTSIDE AACHEN, ABSTRACT strategy took the form of hot metal for George Checkan and his fellow soldiers. "Right after the sun came up," Checkan recalls, "the small-arms fire started. There was so much of it that we knew immediately that the Germans were closer— and in much greater numbers—than we had thought possible. But we didn't know anything more than that."

In Eisenhower's headquarters, at Verdun, nobody knew much more than that either. The day began with good news:

Ike received word that he had been given a fifth star and promoted to the rank of General of the Army. As a relaxed Eisenhower met with General Omar Bradley for a game of bridge, initial reports showed that the Germans were beginning to engage troops along a sparsely manned 50-mile section of the front. Some U.S. units near the front lines had already been overrun or surrounded. But intelligence officers initially believed that this was a tactical action by the Germans, trying to assume more defensible positions. Bradley told Eisenhower that he believed the attacks were insignificant.

At the Eagle's Nest, Hitler was jubilant: his forces were advancing almost unopposed, and there was little evidence that the Allies grasped the scale and significance of what was afoot. At the end of the first day, the motorized units of the Fifth and Sixth Panzers had advanced as far as 30 miles into the U.S. lines. This didn't quite meet Hitler's audacious goal of pushing 50 miles through the lines—all the way to the Meuse River—on Day One, but it was still a huge gain. Germany had battered the Americans, and it now held the initiative.

Part of what kept German forces from reaching farther into Allied territory on that first day was a level of courage under fire that Hitler had not reckoned on. Small U.S. units, some composed mostly of young replacement troops who had not yet seen combat, rallied in the face of the advance and hung on even after being surrounded, holding off much larger German units until they were completely out of ammunition.

On the northern flank of the German attack, outside the town of Elsenborn, young Americans of the 99th Infantry Division, an untested outfit, stopped Sepp Dietrich's advancing tanks cold, preserving Allied control of the vital Elsenborn Ridge, which dominated two vital roadways. Meanwhile, just to the south, U.S. troops of the 106th Infantry Division managed to stave off the initial German attack at St. Vith, then were reinforced by fast-moving troops of the 7th Armored Division, moving south from Aachen. Ultimately, the Americans' stand at St. Vith would frustrate the German advance for days; it would be a critical factor in the eventual Allied victory.

In many cases, U.S. units that were forced to fall back would rally each time they came to a crossroads and fight a delaying action. This was vital, because it hindered the Germans' north-south mobility behind U.S. lines, avoiding an encirclement of the Americans and a push toward Antwerp. Every intersection whose roads were strong enough to support tanks became vital real estate.

At Verdun as Dec. 16 drew to a close, only one voice dissented from the view that the German breakout was a minor irritant. Eisenhower saw early on that if German troops reached two nearby objectives, the Meuse River and the crossroads town of Bastogne, they would be ready to drive on Antwerp.

■ **December 17** BLITZKRIEG! FLUSH WITH victory, Hitler's armored units pressed farther into Allied territory. But now, as Allied troops that had been billeted in rear areas were rushed forward, resistance stiffened. For the second day, Hitler's troops failed to take any of the vital crossroads. But, also for the second day, the bad weather held, and the numerical superiority enjoyed by the German troops meant that the Allies were still fighting a losing battle. Many U.S. soldiers displayed extreme courage, yet their valour couldn't compensate for their utter confusion.

Much of that confusion had its roots in a November meeting between Hitler and his commando chief, Otto Skorzeny, who had led the spectacular glider-borne rescue of Benito Mussolini from a mountaintop prison in 1943. Hitler charged Skorzeny with creating chaos behind U.S. lines; the commando chief's response was "Operation Seize." He recruited hundreds of German soldiers who spoke fluent English. Dressed in captured U.S. uniforms, wearing dog tags stripped from POWs and dead Americans, they were to roam freely behind Allied lines, spreading misinformation, cutting down signposts and doing all they could to encourage panic.

In the initial days of the attack, these "Trojan horse" troops were very effective, even managing to rattle the unflappable George Patton. He told Eisenhower that Germans "speaking perfect English [are] raising hell, cutting wires, turning road signs around, spooking whole divisions and shoving a bulge into our defenses." (This may have been the earliest use of the word by which history knows the campaign.) But Americans began to notice the slightly guttural inflection of some of these troops

In Bastogne, a Discouraging Word

BETTMANN CORBIS

AFTER THE ONSLAUGHT On Jan. 8, after the relief of Bastogne, a U.S. soldier examines a blasted truck; behind him are hedgehogs thrown up as roadblocks

On Dec. 22, all eyes focused on the small Belgian town of Bastogne, now the Alamo of the Ardennes. Constant bombardment from German units ringing Bastogne was wearing down the some 15,000 U.S. troops within, who had reached it only hours before German units arrived and surrounded them. To the south, the tanks of General George Patton's Third Army were racing to Bastogne's relief, in a grim duel against time and the elements.

About 10 a.m. the German firing stopped, and a squad of officers approached the American lines waving a white flag. They carried a two-page letter for General Anthony McAuliffe, the senior U.S. officer in Bastogne. It read, in part:

From the German commander to the USA Commander of the encircled town of Bastogne:

The fortune of war is changing ... There is only one possibility to save the encircled troops from total annihilation: that is the honorable surrender of the encircled town.

After McAuliffe read the message, he is said to have uttered an offhand remark that would soon become immortal: "Aw, nuts!" But when the leader of the besieged Americans turned to the more serious business of drafting a written reply, he found himself at a loss for words. One of his staff officers suggested, "That first crack you made would be hard to beat,

TERSE General Anthony McAuliffe entered the ranks of the great phrase-makers with a single four-letter word

General." So a clerk typed up the following letter:

To the German Commander:
Nuts!
The American Commander

A U.S. colonel helpfully explained McAuliffe's vernacular to the Germans who had delivered the ultimatum: "If you don't know what 'Nuts' means, in plain English it is the same as 'Go to Hell.' And I'll tell you something else, if you continue to attack we will kill every goddam German that tries to break into this city." Meanwhile, McAuliffe's single defiant syllable galvanized the man who was driving his tank units to the Americans' relief. "A man so eloquent must not be allowed to perish!" George Patton is said to have exclaimed.

U.S. ARMY

CASUALTIES: The bodies of dead German soldiers litter the fields outside besieged Bastogne. These troops had followed in the wake of a group of tanks that were also knocked out by U.S. soldiers of the 101st Airborne Division. The date: Christmas Day, 1944

almost immediately, and word went out on the second day of the battle to question anyone who seemed suspicious. Within five days, however, almost all of the impostors who hadn't been arrested and shot had fled behind German lines.

The second day of the battle also marked a high point of savagery in the campaign. When a U.S. field artillery observation battalion was overrun near the village of Malmédy on Dec. 17, SS troops marched more than 100 American soldiers into a field and mowed them down with machine guns. A few managed to escape by running into nearby woods, but most were killed. One U.S. officer who survived later recalled: "when they ceased firing after approximately five minutes, they came into the group to those men who were still alive—and of course writhing in agony—and they shot them in the head."

■ **December 18** ON DAY THREE, HITLER'S PREDICTIONS ABOUT a windfall of captured gasoline almost came true. As a tank column headed by SS Colonel Jochen Peiper headed into the Belgian town of Stavelot, it overran a small fuel depot, containing about 50,000 gal. of gasoline. Captured Americans were forced to fuel up the tanks and then were shot. As Peiper's column moved forward, it came to the edge of a much larger depot. In fact, this was the biggest Allied gasoline storage facility in Europe. The 2.5 million gal. of fuel held there (guarded by only a few dozen troops) was enough to fuel all the German armored units in the Ardennes offensive for the coming 10 days. But Peiper had no idea how much fuel was in front of him or how lightly defended it was. He turned his tanks northward and bypassed the Stavelot depot.

"By rushing out from his fixed defenses, the enemy may have given us the chance to turn his greatest gamble into his worst defeat."
—Dwight D. Eisenhower

Near Elsenborn, not far from Peiper's wrong turn, a frustrated Sepp Dietrich tried to outflank the Elsenborn Ridge but ran smack into the battle-hardened troops of the U.S. 1st Infantry Division, the "Big Red One," which had just arrived from Aachen. Dietrich wasn't getting any closer to Antwerp. Hitler's coin toss was beginning to come up tails.

By the end of three days of battle, Eisenhower had drawn two important conclusions. First, he realized that Bastogne would be the linchpin of the Ardennes offensive. In this small town, several major roads converged, vital to supporting the rapid movement of tanks, artillery and significant numbers of troops. Ike ordered the 101st Airborne Division and troops from the 10th Armored Division to reinforce Bastogne. Because the weather wouldn't permit the U.S. paratroopers to

reach the town by parachute or glider, they would instead race toward Bastogne in trucks. Every nearby supply convoy in the "Red Ball Express" was told to dump its loads and instead ferry men into Bastogne. If they got there before the German advance, it might be possible to hold the town.

Second, Ike concluded that he had two options: either limit the depth of the German salient but not its width, or keep it narrow while allowing the Germans to stab as deeply into Allied territory as the flow of the battle would carry them. He chose the latter, knowing that if the Germans pushed large numbers of troops through a small opening in the Allied lines, these troops could be surrounded and defeated once the Americans succeeded in closing the gap. A repeat of the debacle at Falaise would all but finish the Germans in the West.

■December 19 BEFORE THE SUN ROSE, EISENHOWER MET WITH his senior commanders at a bunker in Verdun. Alone among the generals, Ike thought that the Bulge might present an opportunity. Ike argued that, in spite of initial reversals, the Allies now at last had the Germans out in the open. As Ike would say to his troops in an Order of the Day 48 hours later, "By rushing out from his fixed defenses, the enemy may give us the chance to turn his great gamble into his worst defeat."

Encouraging words—but before the Allies could seize the offensive, Bastogne must be held. The 10th and 101st divisions had beaten the Germans to the town by only a few hours, but that had been time enough to take up defensive positions. As Ike was meeting with his generals, they were fighting bravely, but ever larger numbers of German troops were surrounding Bastogne, preparing to destroy it.

Eisenhower went around the table, asking who among his generals was prepared to relieve the defenders of Bastogne. One by one, they begged off, explaining that their own units were under siege and on the run. But when Eisenhower came to Patton, whose units were then 125 miles south of Bastogne, the tank commander said he could be ready to attack with three divisions as fast as he could get to the town—which would be less than 72 hours. The other generals rolled their eyes, initially dismissing this boast as more of Patton's trademark swagger. But unknown to anyone at the table (including Eisenhower), Patton had begun readying his tank units for a push north toward the center of the battle days earlier, the moment he had heard about the German breakout in the Ardennes. Eisenhower ordered Patton to relieve Bastogne.

John Dunleavy, then a 21-year-old tank commander in the 737th Tank Battalion of Patton's Third Army and now a retired FBI agent living in Virginia, doesn't mince words when he recalls his former leader 60 years later: "We hated that s.o.b.," he says of Patton. "He wanted you fighting all the time. He didn't care about being exhausted, wounded or out of supplies. He just wanted you to keep going. We admired his ability as a soldier, but we didn't love the way he constantly exposed us to enemy fire."

PALLBEARERS Supervised by an American, German POWs carry the body of a fallen U.S. soldier. Tens of thousands of prisoners were taken by both sides during the winter conflict, the largest Allied battle of the war

When Dunleavy's unit, which had been stationed outside of Metz, received its orders, they turned northward and began pushing toward Bastogne. "Patton drove us even harder than usual," he says. "We'd generally fight during the day, then spend most of the night taking on supplies. After that was finished, we might get two or three hours of sleep before the sun came up and then start all over again. But on the way to Bastogne, we didn't stop to sleep."

Spurred on by George Patton's furious command—"There are brave men dying up there!"—the Third Army covered more than half the 125 miles to Bastogne in one day. The next morning, as they passed U.S. infantry units, they picked up word of the massacre of the U.S. prisoners at Malmedy. This, if anything, inspired them to push harder and move faster. "Once we knew that the SS were killing Americans," Dunleavy says, "we were looking for a chance to kill the SS. After you're in the war for a while, you become a little crazy. You're exhausted most of the time and heavy combat makes you unstable, mentally, emotionally and physically. In order to survive, you have to hate the enemy—you cannot continue unless you hate the person who is trying to kill you all the time."

"The road to Bastogne," Dunleavy recalls, "was jammed with thousands of vehicles—tanks, trucks, ambulances, you name it. There were two lanes of traffic moving in the same direction, 24 hours a day. We were driving through a snowstorm, and we had to have all the hatches open to be ready to fire. I was riding in the top hatch and the tank was like a wind tunnel. It was so cold that my clothes literally froze solid. On the second day, when we stopped to take on fuel, the only way I could get down from the turret was to slide down the side."

■ December 22 ALMOST FOUR DAYS OF ROUND-THE-CLOCK fighting, heavy casualties, dwindling stocks of ammunition, and fears that the Germans were about to overrun their positions had taken a heavy toll on the soldiers within Bastogne. That morning, the lead elements of Patton's Third Army reached the outskirts of Bastogne. Nearly frozen and pushed beyond the point of exhaustion, the troops "had about three hours to get ourselves into position," Dunleavy recalls, "while we took on fuel and ammunition. Then, of course, Patton orders us to attack immediately."

While the 4th Armored Division began trying to punch through the German lines, into the heart of Bastogne, Dunleavy's unit assaulted German units to the north and the east of the town, engaging in a ferocious, prolonged firefight. By dusk, the 737th had charged three miles into the German lines, but the advance had come at steep price. "We had 27 tanks left, out of a total complement of 68," Dunleavy recalls. "We had a good day against the German infantry, but then we ran out of gas and ammunition and had to stop for the night."

The hours between dusk and the dawn of Dec. 23 were anything but restful. "If anything, this place was colder than it had been on the road in." Dunleavy remembers. "And we were now inside the German lines and vulnerable to counterattack. We were also surrounded by our own supply trucks, which had come up from behind and were loaded with gasoline and ammunition. Meanwhile, German shells were landing all around us."

Within Bastogne, the freezing, encircled members of the 10th and 101st divisions were heartened to learn that the 4th Division was close by and fighting its way toward them: one message from within the town advised the relieving troops, "only one more shopping day till Christmas."

But the morale-boosting arrival of the first trickle of Patton's advance units did little to change the trapped men's immediate situation. It would still take the 4th Division several days to open a corridor to the defenders trapped within Bastogne. And without new supplies, especially of ammunition, the men of the 10h and 101st divisions weren't sure they could withstand the German attacks for even another 24 hours. The next day, they feared, might go down in history like the Alamo—a heroic last stand that ended in utter defeat.

U.S. ARMY

A Winter's Tale

Even today," George Fisher says, "when it gets cold, or it snows, it has an effect on me. The same with fog—it brings back some very bad memories." In December 1944, Fisher was a 19-year-old PFC in the 26th Infantry. His unit, part of George Patton's Third Army, was operating near Metz, 100 miles south of the Ardennes. "It was warm there," he recalls, "so we were all wearing light field jackets, like cotton overcoats."

On Dec. 16, he says, "We got an urgent order: 'Pack up and be ready to ship out in one hour.' We had no idea where we were going, but they loaded us into trucks and we started driving north. Along the way, we drove into a snowstorm—one that didn't let up for the next three weeks."

Still clad in light uniforms, Fisher and his unit were headed not only into the Battle of the Bulge but also into the 20th century's coldest winter to date in central Europe. "When it didn't snow," Fisher says, "it rained or you were covered with fog. The ground was frozen so hard that we couldn't dig foxholes. A lot of guys died because they couldn't take cover belowground. Our rations were always ice cold, and we started to dehydrate, because the water in the canteens froze."

The troops couldn't even build a fire. "That was a guaranteed way to get killed," Fisher says. "At night, the

MUSH! A long way from a parachute, troopers of the 82nd Airborne Division march toward Herresbach in Belgium during the frigid battle

glow from a fire would attract sniper or artillery. During the day, they would site on the smoke. We'd take our guns apart at night, in the pitch dark, and then reassemble them, just so frost wouldn't accumulate. You'd wake up every hour or so and throw the bolt on your rifle, to be sure it hadn't solidified." One novel strategy for thawing frozen weapons: gathering in a circle and urinating on them.

"On Christmas Day," he remembers, "we finally found a barn that was outside the range of German shells. We camped out inside, built ourselves a small fire, and it was like the finest hotel in Europe. But a buddy of mine who had grown up on a Kentucky farm decided there had to be a chicken somewhere nearby. He was going to make us all chicken soup. I told him it was a bad idea, but he went out to find one. A few minutes later, we heard sniper fire. He never came back."

George Fisher did. Wounded by shrapnel in his thigh on Jan. 3, he was evacuated and hospitalized for nine months but recovered the use of his leg. He felt lucky. "For me," he says, "the fighting, the cold and the whole war were over." Fisher, 80, now lives in Florida—for obvious reasons.

■**December 23** "AND THEN," AS ALBERT SPEER WOULD LATER RE-call, "the skies opened up." Every gain made by the Germans in the previous seven days had been dependent on bad weather preventing Allied fighters, bombers and supply planes from leaving their bases. Hitler himself had admitted before the offensive began that, "we must have bad weather. Otherwise the operation cannot succeed." But as Dec. 23 dawned clear and cold, the words "visibility unlimited" were broadcast from control towers on air fields stretching from south England to Belgium. Within hours, every Allied plane that could fly—more than 5,000 aircraft—roared into the sky. German tank and infantry columns, which had spent a week using the open roads without risk, were now slaughtered by dive bombers. German supply convoys, coming up from the rear, were now flattened by massive armadas of bombers.

Hitler, anticipating that the weather would not hold indef-initely, had massed the last stocks of German fighter planes within striking distance of the Ardennes breakout. But, be-cause of the Germans' worsening fuel shortage, fewer than half of these planes could fly on any given day. And the ones that did were outnumbered and outgunned by the combined, concentrated might of Allied airpower. More than 250 German planes would be shot from the skies in the following days.

In Bastogne, the early hours of Dec. 23 found the besieged men of the 10th and 101st divisions lifting hopeful eyes to the sky. They didn't have long to wait: by 9 a.m., the first of more than 240 cargo planes had begun dropping tons of ammuni-tion, food, medicine and other matériel by parachute. These were followed by gliders bringing in doctors, nurses and chap-lains. P-47 fighter escorts lingered over Bastogne to rain fire and steel down on the German positions ringing the town. That same day, the final U.S. troops withdrew from St. Vith, where their brilliant stand against overwhelming odds had foiled the German strategy from the first day of the attack.

■**December 24** ONCE AGAIN, THE LEADING EDGE OF THE GER-man salient charged toward the Meuse River, and was once again repelled. This marked the end of the German advance. On the same day, General Hasso von Manteuffel, the com-mander of the Fifth Panzers, requested Hitler's permission to withdraw to behind the Siegfried Line. Hitler refused and or-dered him to continue pushing forward.

On Christmas Day, a return of heavy weather brought a brief lull in the fighting. "We had been scheduled to lead an attack in battalion strength against a nearby town called Consdorf," recalls Dunleavy, "but it was called off. So we dug in and opened our rations. Then an infantry supply wagon came up, and they had hot turkey and ham, mashed potatoes and pie, plus whiskey. Since we were in a different unit, they weren't supposed to feed us. But an infantry mess sergeant called us over and invited us to join them. That was the first hot meal we had eaten in …" Recalling these experiences in 2005, Dunleavy paused at this point, and his voice cracked at the memory of a few minutes of peace more than six decades earlier. "That was a pretty good Christmas," he says quietly. "We had a hot meal, and I was still alive. Plenty of guys in my outfit didn't get either one of those things."

The next day, Dec. 26, the lead elements of the 4th Ar-mored Division finally broke through the German ring and into Bastogne. The quotable General McAuliffe greeted his rescuers with a terse, "Gee, I'm mighty glad to see you."

Whatever lingering hope the Germans may have harbored for the success of the Ardennes offensive was gone. Ten days after the battle started, neither of the indispensable objec-tives the Germans had planned on taking in the first 48 hours—Bastogne and the Meuse River—were in Hitler's hands. Allied air superiority was now decimating German ranks, Nazi armored units were out of fuel, and all the German forces were running out of ammunition.

Now it was Eisenhower's turn to contemplate a strategic thrust to cripple his enemy. At the Dec. 19 conference in Ver-dun, Eisenhower had put British Field Marshal Bernard Montgomery in command of U.S. and British troops north of the German breakout and ordered him to push south. Monty took his time, as always, but on Jan. 3 these forces finally went on the offensive, chasing German units whose commanders had enough sense to retreat and cutting to pieces those that obeyed Hitler's order to give up no ground.

SURRENDER An American soldier captures a German in the fields surrounding Bastogne. The picture was taken some time in the days between Dec. 23 and Dec. 26—photographer Robert Capa could not recall the exact date

On the same day, Hitler at last faced reality, issuing an order to halt the advance. By Jan. 10, German forces had to abandon even their defensive positions and retreat behind the Siegfried Line. Three days later, Patton's and Monty's troops linked up at the Belgian town of Houffalize, cutting off escape for tens of thousands of German troops trapped inside the resulting pocket. On Jan. 14, the German general staff issued an order to its field units, advising that "the initiative in the area of the offensive has passed to the enemy."

The costs on both sides had been enormous. The Americans had suffered more than 20,000 casualties. But the German side had lost more than 100,000 soldiers. In addition, more than 800 of Hitler's tanks and the last of the Third Reich's fighter aircraft were gone. But the numbers don't tell the full story. The starkest, simplest difference between the two sides is that the Americans and British could afford to take the losses that had been inflicted on them, but the Germans could not.

As Albert Speer wrote in his memoirs, "The failure of the Ardennes offensive meant that the war was over. What followed was only the occupation of Germany, delayed somewhat by a confused and impotent resistance."

The next day, Jan. 15, Hitler abandoned the Eagle's Nest and retreated to Berlin, where he took up full-time residence in his underground bunker. He would never leave the city again. Nor could he deny the magnitude of the defeat. As the dictator remarked bitterly to one of his staff shortly after arriving in the shattered capital, "I know the war is lost. The superior power is too great … I'd like most of all to put a bullet through my head." His apocalyptic tone sprang not only from the loss he had just endured, but also from one that was soon to come. The Russian winter offensive, which Hitler's Ardennes gamble had been designed to avert, had begun three days earlier. The Third Reich, which Hitler had boasted would last for 1,000 years, had slightly more than 100 days left to live. ■

"The failure of the Ardennes offensive meant that the war was over."
—Albert Speer, Hitler's Armaments Minister

At Ease

Every soldier knows the drill: "Hurry up—and wait." Yet while you were waiting, there just might be time to play a game of cards or cheer up a local kid or, for a lucky few, take in a USO show. Meanwhile, for Europeans starved for simple pleasures after five years of war, shortages and Occupation, the sight of liberating American and British troops—some bearing candy bars, all wearing smiles—was an occasion that would long be cherished

■ DRAW! Above, five soldiers from an Army ordnance unit put their slack time to use in Normandy on July 22, 1944, six weeks after D-day. This gaggle of American poker players includes two men from Brooklyn, a Michigander, a Texan and an Oklahoman

■ RESPITE With Aachen, Germany, safely in Allied hands after a weeks-long siege, U.S. soldiers gather round a swastika-bedecked piano on Oct. 25, 1944. Captain Gilbert Fuller of Ludlow, Vt. (third from left, standing) assured the photographer that he was the "Mayor of Aachen"

■ JOY RIDE With most of France cleansed of Germans, three U.S. soldiers enjoy a ride in a bicycle taxi in Nice, where the Army established an R.-and-R. area. The Allies' amphibious landing along France's Mediterranean coast on Aug. 15, 1944, was almost unopposed by sparse German troops

■ **TROUBADOUR** The stars at night are big and bright … deep in the heart of Belgium, where P.F.C. Laurence Hoffman, a Montana ranch hand, plucks a tune on Oct. 14, 1944

■ **FROSTY** As the Battle of the Bulge ends, two U.S. soldiers take time out to create "Agnes," an anatomically correct snowwoman; they're plying her with Camels and a Coke

■ **TIME FOR A STITCH** Two women of the Free French ambulance corps take time out for knitting while awaiting their next call somewhere on the Italian front in 1944

■ **REFLECTION** A British paratrooper assigned to guard duty at the Acropolis Museum in Athens enjoys a letter from home, his pose echoing that of the ancient statue behind him

■ **SHOWTIME** On Aug. 8, 1944, Allied troops have finally broken out of the confines of the "hedgerow country" of Normandy and are moving to liberate Paris. Somewhere behind the front lines, singer Dinah Shore dazzles a crowd of soldiers at a large USO show in France

NIGHT LIFE Violinist Vlastri Krikava was hired by the U.S. Army to entertain troops enjoying R. and R. on the Riviera in April 1945. The young woman at right is Betty McGabe, a USO entertainer whose troupe was performing in Nice

PLAY ON! Amid the rubble of a bombed-out home, Russian troops enjoy a tune. As with many photographs from the Eastern Front, documentation of time and place is scanty; this impromptu concert took place sometime in 1945

DECK THE TENT Dec. 18, 1944: WACs Dorothy Dittwald and Dorothy Charpenter trim a tree (with .75-mm shell casings) while a sergeant hangs a wreath in Italy's Apennine Mountains

THE BATHERS They're not exactly Wagner's Rhine maidens, but these young German women swimming at a local pool in August 1945 have drawn an appreciative audience of G.I.s

ALL SMILES Fraternizing with the (former) enemy, U.S. troops are invited to an al fresco meal in Germany in 1945

■ **A PINCH MORE, S'IL VOUS PLAIT?** An American soldier offers advice to a Frenchwoman pouring a celebratory glass of wine for U.S. troops who have just liberated her hometown, Brignoles, from German occupiers in August 1944

■ **HELPING HAND** P.F.C. Walter Trohan of Caplan, Louisiana stoops to conquer … the heart of a French orphan

■ **WHEE!** At left, Sergeants Harman Barber of Kansas and John Aylor of Tennessee have time for a bit of sledding in Belgium on Jan. 12, 1945, as the Battle of the Bulge ends

■ **PARADE** Below, G.I.s escort a a group of Dutch children, dressed up for a concert of folk songs, on the grounds of Hoensbroek Castle in Holland in February 1945. The tykes lived in the castle, cared for by Roman Catholic nuns

"The Germans are losing the war in Russia, which means they are losing World War II." —TIME, Dec. 14, 1942

Endgame in the East

After U.S. and British troops hold off Hitler's surprise attack in the Ardennes, Soviet armies continue their deadly march into Germany

WE ONLY HAVE TO KICK IN THE FRONT DOOR AND THE whole rotten structure will come tumbling down," Adolf Hitler had boasted to his nervous generals in the weeks before his betrayal and surprise invasion of Soviet Russia in 1941. Three years later, by the first weeks of autumn 1944, no one in Hitler's inner circle dared remind him of these words. The 1941 German advance, Operation Barbarossa, had verged on miraculous for the first six months but had been stalemated at the gates of Moscow during the Russian winter. The following year had brought the lost siege of Stalingrad, which cost Hitler more than a quarter of the 2 million men he had sent into Russia.

In the summer of 1943, the German offensive at Kursk, the largest tank battle in military history, had devolved into a bloody rout. The following summer a new Soviet offensive, Operation Bagration, had resulted in the single most devastating German defeat of the entire war: more soldiers were killed, wounded and captured than had been at Stalingrad, and Soviet troops finally recaptured all the territory the Germans had taken from Russia since the war began.

Yet even in the face of such disaster, Hitler might have won a reprieve. In the first week of September 1944, Japan's ambassador to Germany passed the word that Moscow (which still had diplomatic relations with Tokyo) had indicated a willingness to enter peace talks with Berlin. Stalin knew that he would soon be competing with his allies of convenience, the U.S. and Britain, to shape Europe after the war; with Germany as an ally, he might dictate the future of the Continent. As if to signal his receptiveness, Stalin ordered his armies, then advancing through Poland, to halt at the gates of Warsaw.

The gambit failed, for Hitler was less rational—and more filled with hatred—than Stalin. The German dictator's loathing for communism, and for the Russian people, was exceeded only by his hatred for Jews. Hitler brushed off Stalin's peace feelers, assuring his inner circle that new secret weapons would soon turn the tide on the Eastern Front.

For the rest of the war, the quickening tide would flow in only one direction, carrying Soviet troops toward Berlin. A week after Hitler dismissed Stalin's overture, Finland, formerly Germany's ally, signed an armistice with Russia. Within a month, other Axis allies began to defect; Yugoslavia, Hungary, Romania and Bulgaria all began moving out of Hitler's orbit. As Hitler's armies retreated and Stalin's advanced, national leaders across Eastern Europe began tossing German phrase books into the fire and stocking up on vodka.

In October, the Soviets overran Hungary and entered Czechoslovakia, then slowed in preparation for a new winter offensive. Meanwhile, the ongoing Soviet pause outside War-

CLOSING IN As Soviet armies tighten the noose around Hitler's remaining armies, Germans in Breslau seem stunned to find that Russian troops have brought the battle to their streets

Across Hitler's East and Stalin's West, the Longest Front

On the Western Front, German officers learned they could keep troops in line by threatening to send them to the Eastern Front. Here, for four long years and amid scenes of horrendous carnage, Russian, German and East European armies fought the largest, costliest battles in military history. A final estimate of the dead: 40 million

From the Steppes ...

TIME compared the Soviets' long, horse-drawn columns with the armies of Napoleon's day

... to the Mountains

Russian troops (here in the Carpathians) were expert at conducting operations in the winter

... to the Farms ...

Fighting was particularly fierce in Belorussia, where the Germans put up a last-ditch stand

... to the Cities

Soviet troops battle Germans in the heart of Budapest, Hungary, in February 1945

THE EASTERN FRONT 1944-45

FINLAND
Helsinki
SWEDEN
Stockholm
Tallin
ESTONIA
BALTIC SEA
LATVIA
Riga
Copenhagen
LITHUANIA
Vilnius
East Prussia (Germany)
Minsk
U.S.S.R.
Berlin
Warsaw
GERMANY
POLAND
Kiev
Rhine
Prague
CZECHOSLOVAKIA
Vienna
Bratislava
aduz
Budapest
AUSTRIA
HUNGARY
Chisinau
Ljubljana
ITALY
Zagreb
YUGOSLAVIA
ROMANIA
150 miles
Belgrade
Bucharest

- - - Front line, June 1944
- · - Front line, Aug. 1944
——— Front line, Jan. 1945

Sarajevo
BULGARIA

FALL OF THE REICH

Stralsund
Hamburg
British 2nd Army
Army group Vistula
Szczecin
2nd Belorussian Front (Rokossovsky)
Elbe
Aller
U.S. 9th Army
Oder
Berlin
1st Belorussian Front (Zhukov)
Magdeburg
Frankfurt
50 miles
Dessau
April 25 U.S. and Russian forces meet
1st Ukrainian Front (Konev)
U.S. 1st Army
Army group Center
Dresden

——— Front line, April 16, 1945
····· Front line, April 18, 1945
– – – Front line, May 8, 1945
+ + × Berlin defense line
○ Surrounded German pockets

saw yielded a dividend for Stalin: his propagandists urged the Poles to rise up against the Germans, promising Russian aid. It never arrived. The hapless insurgency decimated the ranks of the Polish resistance, thus easing the way for the Kremlin's planned conquest—as opposed to liberation—of Poland.

The start of the new Soviet offensive was delayed by a few weeks as the ever cautious Stalin awaited the outcome of the Battle of the Bulge. As soon as the Germans had clearly failed, the new Russian onslaught began. In the hours before dawn on Jan. 12, Soviet armies under the command of Marshals Georgy Zhukov and Ivan Konev broke through the German lines in Poland, pushing south toward Silesia and the Oder River, the last natural barrier in the east before Berlin.

As TIME reported in its Jan. 29 issue, "The Russians swept forward with an impetus which no losses, no barriers, had been able to break. By this week, it seemed that its momentum could not be slowed short of the banks of the Oder ... Joseph Stalin had decided, probably months before it started, that the goal of his winter offensive was Berlin." Further south, Russian troops overcame the last pockets of resistance in the Baltic states. Across this lengthy front, more than 2 million Russian troops gathered for the kill, enjoying a 10-to-1 numerical advantage over the remaining German soldiers.

O N JAN. 30, HITLER ADDRESSED THE GERMAN NATION FOR the last time. After railing about "Jewish Asiatic Bolshevism," he concluded, "however grave the crisis may be at the moment, it will, despite everything, finally be mastered by our unalterable will, by our readiness for sacrifice and by our abilities. We shall overcome this calamity, too, and this fight, too, will [be won by] our Greater German Reich ..." By now, few of his listeners believed him.

A flailing Führer next resorted to desperate measures. He appointed secret police chief Heinrich Himmler, who had

even less military experience than Hitler himself, to command a new force, Army Group Vistula. Himmler tried to raise troops from Russian POWs. Several thousand volunteered, but most defected back to the Russian side as soon as they reached the front lines. It did them little good: after the war, Stalin's secret police treated every Russian who fell into German hands as a traitor, but they reserved especially ghoulish tortures for those who had volunteered to fight for the Nazis.

Himmler displayed the ruthless resolve that Hitler believed his generals lacked, yet he quickly found that well-armed Russian troops were far tougher opponents than the defenseless civilians and prisoners he had been murdering methodically in concentration camps for the previous 10 years. Himmler's fanatic SS troops succeeded only in slightly delaying the Russian advance, now swallowing up some 25 miles a day, at a cost of tens of thousands of their own lives.

"Minefields, German armor, and heavy snows so thick that correspondents said they felt, rather than saw, the movement of endless hordes of Russian men could check, but could not permanently halt the hate-filled Russian juggernaut," TIME observed in its Feb. 12 issue. As the Russian advance quickened, Hitler cashiered Himmler, only 10 weeks after appointing him. In February, the Russians captured the border regions of East Prussia and Pomerania and crossed into Germany itself, reaching the outskirts of Frankfurt by the end of the month. In every German town, Soviet troops exacted bloody vengeance for the crimes Germany had committed in the East. An estimated 2 million German women were raped by Soviet troops, and tens of thousands of civilians were killed.

In March, the Red Army entered Austria; by April, it had crossed into Germany from the south. On the northern flank, Russian troops advanced as far as the outskirts of Berlin by the last week in April. They had only to kick in Hitler's door, and his whole rotten structure would come tumbling down. ∎

FALSE DAWN **Victorious Czech resistance fighters join Russian soldiers atop a Soviet tank barreling through the streets of Prague in May 1945**

"He has a hard face, which can break into a wonderful smile.
He's a man of the earth: short, pudgy fingers and a lot of brains."
—U.S. General James Gavin

A Dragoon's Journey

Ten years after World War II ended, in the depths of the cold war, TIME reviewed the remarkable life of the general who drove Hitler from Russia

I N THE 10TH REGIMENT OF THE NOVO-grod Dragoons, few were younger and none was braver than Georgy Zhukov, the kid from Kaluga province. The 10th dashed in behind the German lines and with saber and carbine cut down the enemy gunners. This was World War I, and twice young Georgy received the coveted St. George Cross, awarded for valor in battle; he was a doughty figure in the Czarist Army.

[*Zhukov joined the Red Army after World War I, studied at Russia's top military academy in Moscow, then went to Germany for further training. In the 1930s he excelled as a young tank commander, and he survived Stalin's purge of the Soviet Army, in which some 30,000 officers were killed.* —ED.]

The first effect of a weakened Red Army was a Japanese penetration deep into Outer Mongolia in 1939. Stalin sent Zhukov there. By bringing tanks from a railhead 150 miles away and using them with air support, Zhukov achieved complete tactical surprise, annihilated the Japanese Sixth Army and drove the Japanese back into Manchuria.

Then, in June 1941, Germany sent the whole weight of the powerful, victorious Wehrmacht charging into Russia. Zhukov fought a battle outside Smolensk, which drove the invaders back 20 miles. It was one of the few successful delaying actions. Within four months the Wehrmacht was at the gates of Moscow and Leningrad, and 4 million Russian army men were prisoners. Stalin was forced to yield all military decisions to the best professional soldier in Russia: Georgy Zhukov.

Zhukov brought the Siberian army across the trans-Siberian railroad and deployed them in five columns around Moscow. The fresh, well-officered Siberians pushed the Germans back out of artillery range of the capital. Then the Russian winter, the severest in 50 years, halted all but patrol activity. In the six months of snow and thaw, Zhukov created and equipped vast new armies. One of his first field commands after Moscow was near Kaluga, not far from Strelkovka, his home village. As the Germans were driven from Strelkovka, they prepared to destroy it. They rounded up the Zhukov family, locked them in a cottage and set fire to it. The story goes that Zhukov's men dashed into Strelkovka just in time to rescue their commander's family.

UPS AND DOWNS **Zhukov fell from Stalin's favor shortly after the war, but he returned to power in the mid-1950s. He died in 1974**

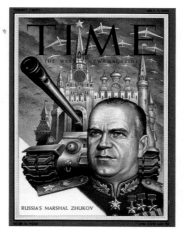

RUSSIA'S MARSHAL ZHUKOV

The turning point was the tough, bitter, bloody battle of Stalingrad. Zhukov masterminded the battle but was not there to take the German surrender, because he had to fly to besieged Leningrad. "Our next step in the war," says Zhukov, "was to prevent Hitler maneuvering." This he did in a series of masterly battles, the sweep and magnitude of which have never been equaled.

Over a front that stretched from far inside the Arctic Circle down to subtropical Sukhumi, Zhukov manipulated some 300 divisions. His strategy and tactics were orthodox: there was no time for trickery. He would hit a 20-mile sector of the German line with successive waves of infantry, each wave 20 to 30 divisions strong. Sometimes the German gunners would run out of ammunition. When he had punched a hole in the line, Red Army tanks with infantry riding on their backs would drive through, sweep around and encircle the enemy flanks. Sometimes Zhukov trapped as many as 10 German divisions this way. He would then stand off and pound them to pieces with his artillery.

Dwight Eisenhower once asked Zhukov how his men negotiated minefields. Zhukov's answer chilled Ike: "When we come to a minefield, our infantry attacks as if it were not there. The losses we get from personnel mines we consider equal to those we would have gotten from machine guns and artillery if the Germans had chosen to defend that particular area." Mass attack was Zhukov's master weapon, massive casualties his expectation. Driving through birch woods, through forests of fir, bridging huge rivers, filtrating through the great marshlands, fighting, always fighting, in winter blizzard or in blistering summer heat, the Red Army recaptured half a million square miles of territory in two years.

The last great push to Berlin cost the Red Army 1 million casualties. Zhukov arrived, tough and imperturbable, fully conscious of his great feat but also plainly glad that the war was over. Eisenhower and Zhukov became friends; at a football game at Moscow's Dynamo Stadium, Ike put his arm around his ally's shoulder as they took the wild cheers of 100,000 Russians. The two used to argue the relative merits of capitalism and Communism, and Ike never heard from Zhukov a despairing word about Communism. But of course they usually talked through a Russian interpreter. ∎

UNEASY ALLIES: The Big Three at Yalta. Thirteen months later, Winston Churchill would declare, "From Stettin in the Baltic to Trieste in the Adriatic, an iron curtain has descended upon the Continent"

In War, Visions of Peace

Meeting in Yalta, the Big Three Allied partners make their plans for a world after Hitler, igniting lasting controversy and a new kind of war

MARK TWAIN MUST HAVE BEEN LOOKING INTO HIS crystal ball when he visited Yalta in the Crimea in the grand tour described in his 1869 travelogue, *The Innocents Abroad*. "O geeminy, what a stir there is!" Twain exclaimed of the resort town on the Black Sea coast. "What a calling of meetings! What an appointing of committees! What a furbishing-up of swallow-tail coats!"

Seventy-six years later, it was in this unlikely setting that three larger-than-life heads of state called a meeting—with their armies on the cusp of victory over a common enemy—to put in place a new world order. Their goals: to ensure that Germany would not only be dismantled but also stopped from re-arming; to create an international system that would foil the rise of any future Hitlers; and to help shape the destiny of the lands recently liberated from the dictator's grasp.

The three men had wildly varying hands to play. Winston Churchill represented the past. Britain had commanded the greatest empire of the 19th century, but it had been bled dry in its two victorious battles against Germany. Franklin D. Roosevelt and Joseph Stalin represented the future. Each led a nation of vast natural resources, enormous populations and grand ambitions. With Britain in decline, these two allies— natural enemies united only by their fear of Hitler—would soon find the radically different systems they represented butting up against each other from Italy to Indochina to India.

So Yalta was not simply the last major conference of the war; it was the first major event of the war taking shape. As TIME noted in its Feb. 4, 1945, issue, which showed Stalin on its cover, "The line of Russia's 800-mile military front practically bisected Europe. How much farther west was it going to move? And what went on behind that line, where the Western Allies had no effective power and little real information?"

The editors were more cheerful weeks later, as the conference concluded. "If words mean anything," TIME declared, "the Big Three did more for their nations and their world at Yalta than they did at Tehran [where they had met in December 1943] ... they not only proclaimed agreement on every point taken up in their announcement, but on the most difficult points broke down the agreement into hard specifics."

Among those agreements was the founding of a new international body, the United Nations, to guarantee world security. Its first meeting was set to be called at San Francisco on April 25; China and France would join the Big Three as founding partners. As for the enemy: "Nazi Germany is doomed," the official announcement declared. It would be split up into four zones, occupied and administered by Britain, France, the U.S. and the Soviet Union. Although the capital city, Berlin, was within the Soviet occupation zone, it would be jointly administered by the four Allied powers. The Nazi Party would be outlawed, the nation would be disarmed, and its current leaders would be tried as war criminals.

As for the nations now being released from Germany's grasp, the document established new boundaries for Poland and promised other newly freed nations that the Big Three Allies would join "in assisting the peoples liberated from the domination of Nazi Germany, and the peoples of the former Axis satellite states of Europe, to solve by democratic means their pressing political and economic problems."

Fine-sounding words ... if words mean anything; and such words meant little to Stalin, who was already putting in place his plans for the political takeover of Eastern Europe, now conveniently occupied by huge Soviet armies. As TIME noted, "The Big Three's words presumably applied to Russia's sphere (Bulgaria, Romania, etc.)." Bulgarians and many others would soon learn that Joseph Stalin presumed no such presumptions.

In addition to the documents made public, the Big Three reached secret agreements on the Pacific region. Russia would join the war against Japan within three months of the surrender of Germany and would receive territorial concessions in return, including the Kurile Islands and an occupation zone in Korea. These agreements were not announced at Yalta, leading to later charges that a number of secret protocols were agreed to at the conference, though this was the only such case.

THE CONFERENCE AT YALTA, IN FACT, GENERATED CONtroversy almost as soon as it concluded and still breeds criticism and conspiracy theories. Some critics insist that Franklin Roosevelt betrayed the peoples of Eastern Europe at Yalta, condemning them to decades of life under Soviet hegemony. Others argue that Stalin simply outmaneuvered Roosevelt and Churchill. Indeed, Roosevelt was a visibly ailing man at Yalta. Though he was only 63 years old, he seemed years if not a full decade older. He would die within two months.

Did Roosevelt undermine U.S. interests and ideals at Yalta? Such large questions are far beyond the purview of this book, but most historians agree that both Roosevelt and Churchill held weak hands at the conference. Britain was exhausted, and the U.S. was fighting Japan island to island across the Pacific even as the conferees met. Stalin, meanwhile, had millions of troops on the ground in Eastern Europe; the proximity of the U.S.S.R. to these nations guaranteed that Soviet influence in the region could only be overthrown by a massive, long-term military commitment that would have severely strained America's resources and might have started World War III. What Yalta did start, without question, was a new, nerve-grinding kind of conflict that came to be called the cold war. ∎

DAWN OF THE COLD WAR

Areas agreed to be transferred under treaties

19XX Year entered Soviet orbit

HIS LAST BOW On March 1, Roosevelt reported to Congress on the conference at Yalta. As TIME noted weeks later, "The well-fleshed strong face had begun to look wasted and faintly wistful, and sometimes the firm jaw quivered unaccountably … the ringing radio voice seemed now & then to drag with weariness"

An Untimely Departure

With Allied armies poised to ring down the curtain on Adolf Hitler's toppling Reich, President Franklin D. Roosevelt leaves the world stage

ANYONE WHO LOOKED CLOSELY AT PHOTOGRAPHS OF the "Big Three" conference at Yalta could not fail to see that President Franklin D. Roosevelt, at 63, was a frail, ailing man. Yet for many Americans, the man universally known as F.D.R. seemed immortal. Children born in 1933, when Roosevelt was sworn into office for his first term, were now 12 years old and had known no other President. F.D.R. had shattered a tradition established by George Washington when he ran for a third term, in 1940, and had been sworn in for his fourth term on January 20, 1945. So when the news broke on the afternoon of April 12 that the President had died of a cerebral hemorrhage at his vacation retreat in Warm Springs, Ga., Americans were stunned. Their grief was magnified by the knowledge that "the Old Man" had died even as his hard-won goal, the destruction of Adolf Hitler's Germany, was

in clear sight. For many, Roosevelt's premature death brought to mind an earlier April: 80 years before, President Abraham Lincoln had been assassinated on April 15, 1865, with the end of the Civil War only weeks away.

"At home," TIME reported in its April 23, 1945, issue, "the news came to people in the hot soft light of the afternoon, in taxicabs, along the streets, in offices and bars and factories. In a Cleveland barbershop, 60-year-old Sam Katz was giving a customer a shave when the radio stabbed out the news. Sam Katz walked over to the water cooler, took a long, slow drink, sat down and stared into space for nearly ten minutes. Finally he got up and painted a sign on his window: ROOSEVELT IS DEAD. Then he finished the shave. In an Omaha poolhall, men racked up their cues without finishing their games, walked out. In a Manhattan taxicab, a fare told the driver, who pulled

over to the curb, sat with his head bowed, and after two minutes resumed his driving. Everywhere, to almost everyone, the news came with the force of a personal shock. A woman in Detroit said, 'It doesn't seem possible. It seems to me that he will be back on the radio tomorrow, reassuring us all that it was just a mistake.'"

Roosevelt did not return. Vice President Harry S Truman was sworn into office at 7:08 p.m. in the Cabinet Room of the White House on the evening of F.D.R.'s death. Truman, a World War I veteran and formerly a Senator from Missouri, had been chosen as a compromise candidate on the 1944 Democratic ticket; he had risen to prominence as the head of a Senate committee that investigated government and military waste during the war. The plain-talking Midwesterner was the antithesis of the courtly, urbane Roosevelt; TIME told its readers, "Harry Truman is a man of distinct limitations." Moreover, declared TIME, "with almost complete unanimity, Harry Truman's friends—in Washington and across the land—agreed last week that he 'would not be a great President.'"

History would prove TIME a poor prognosticator. History would also reveal that Roosevelt and his close-knit inner circle of advisers, despite their awareness that the President's health was failing, had utterly failed to prepare Truman to take

F.D.R.'s place. When sworn in, Truman had not been briefed on the highly significant talks in Yalta and did not know that the Manhattan Project scientists were close to testing the first atom bomb. Fortunately, the war in Europe was so close to its conclusion that Truman's ignorance of the situation on the battlefields did not alter the outcome of the conflict.

No one was more affected by Roosevelt's death than his great friend and ally Winston Churchill. Yet as Churchill would tell Truman in 1952, "I must confess, sir, [when you became President] I held you in very low regard. I loathed your taking the place of Franklin Roosevelt. Since that time, you, more than any other man, have saved Western civilization." ∎

The Home Front

Millions of young Americans dreamed of home while serving abroad, but they might not have recognized the land they were longing for, even if they could have returned to it. Back in the States, the war was a constant intruder, touching and changing everything, from the first taste of coffee-with-chicory in the morning to the search for cigarettes or gas to nighttime curfews. Some Moms didn't have a curfew—they were working the night shift

■ **HOE, HOE, HOE** The government encouraged the creation of "victory gardens," especially in cities and towns, so farm produce could be sent to the millions of Americans serving abroad. Above, in March 1945, people of all ages pitch in to till the soil so planting can begin

■ **WAITING** As the war progressed, shortages and rationing introduced a new, unwelcome element into American life—long queues for products that once were widely available. At left, Atlantans line up for cigarettes outside a drug store in November 1944; a sign reveals that they will ante up 16¢ for a pack of Lucky Strikes or Camels

■ **CHOMP** At right, the 7-month-old Bachant triplets—Janet Lee, Nancy Sue and Karen Ann—do their part to sell war bonds, joining a host of celebrities who supported federal bond issues to fund the conflict. This happy picture has a sad postscript: the triplets were chosen because their father, a soldier, had been killed in Europe

■ **ALL CLEAR** At top, night-shift workers at a Douglas Aircraft factory in Long Beach, Calif., polish the nose cones of A-20 bombers. The influx of millions of women into the work force was one of the war's significant alterations of U.S. society

■ **PRAISE THE LARD ...** And pass the ammo. Above, urged on by a federal sign, a woman turns over a can of bacon grease to her local butcher; it will be shipped to the Army for reuse

■ **WIN WITH TIN!** In New York City, three women help collect and recycle cans in the cafeteria of a Western Union building

SAVE WASTE FATS FOR EXPLOSIVES!

■BIG SQUEEZE As raw materials were diverted to the war effort, every smidgen of household material was recycled. Above, soldier's wives in Newark, N.J., sort through leftover toothpaste tubes

■SIGNS OF CHANGE Right, a man collects paper for recycling. Posters promoting various war efforts were unavoidable, as the federal government took a more prominent role in people's daily lives

■PARTY POOPER In an era of rationing, even festivities were kept on a short leash. Below, a "curfew man" rings in the midnight hour, halting festivities at Cafe Zanzibar in New York City on Feb. 28, 1945

Across the Roer River

With Hitler's last desperate push repelled in the epic Battle of the Bulge, natural barriers become the enemy as the Allies close in on Germany

IT WAS THE HEAVIEST BARRAGE I HEARD DURING THE WHOLE war," George Lucht recalls. "Hundreds of guns—they had 105-mm howitzers and 155s, plus mortars and hundreds of tanks." Then a 22-year-old infantry sergeant in K Company, 3rd Battalion (333rd Regiment, 84th Division), Lucht was dug into a foxhole overlooking the Roer River, the last natural obstacle between U.S. forces and the Rhine River—the path to the center of Germany. Fortunately, on this early morning in late February 1945, the hundreds of heavy guns were American; they were aimed over Lucht's head to the east bank of the river, "but all that noise and fire still made the ground shake and gave you the jitters," he says.

Lucht, now 82 years old and a retired professor at Kent State University, had no way of knowing it at the time, but this barrage was the opening salvo of Operation Grenade, in which American, British and Canadian troops were to cross the Roer River in force and then march on the Rhine. The original plan had called for Grenade to begin in December, but it had been much delayed—first by Hitler's surprise Ardennes offensive and then by German troops who blew up dams along the Roer, causing it to flood. "We were originally told it was essentially a large stream," Lucht recalls, "but when we got there, it turned out to be almost a quarter of a mile wide, with fast-moving currents and deep water.

"We had hit the Siegfried Line in November," Lucht says, "and then fought in the Bulge. Finally, at the end of January,

we were pulled back to rest and regroup. They stationed us in a small Belgian town near the border, and for the first time in months we were beyond the reach of German artillery and sleeping indoors." But K Company's respite didn't last long. "We had been there for a little more than a week," Lucht says, "when a Belgian woman told us we were going back to Germany that night. This was the first we had heard about it, but somehow the local civilians always knew what our orders were going to be about 12 hours before we did.

"So we shipped out that night, and a few days later, we were at the Roer," Lucht recalls. For the next three weeks, his unit, along with hundreds of others, dug into positions overlooking the river along a 20-mile front. "On Feb. 22, we were told that D-day was scheduled for 24 hours later. Our orders were to wait for combat engineers to put bridges in place before sunrise, then cross at first light and begin fighting." In the early-morning hours of Feb. 23, the artillery barrage began—it was intended to explode the minefields the Germans had laid on the far bank and drive back any German units positioned there—and Lucht remembers that "another battalion came up from behind, and passed through our positions carrying boats."

The mission of these combat engineers was to row, under German fire, to the far side of the river while trailing steel cables. Once the cables were anchored on the east bank of the Roer, the metal segments of a footbridge could be threaded along them, and the infantry would be able to cross. "I recall thinking that I didn't love sitting in that foxhole," Lucht now says, "but I was thankful not to be in one of those boats."

In the swift current, some of the plywood assault boats overturned, while others spun out of control, sliding downstream and colliding with other boatloads of engineers. In several cases, when capsized or wayward boats were dragged into one of the steel cables that had been successfully pulled across the river, their combined weight would part the line, and the bridge—along with anybody on it—would be swept away in the current.

With these mishaps, the process of erecting bridges went slower than planned. So small numbers of infantry began crossing the river in the assault boats supplied by the combat engineers. As Glen Lytle, of the 413th Infantry Regiment, would later recall for *Timberwolf Howls*, an oral history compiled by veterans of the 104th Infantry Division, "Our short trip across the Roer seemed like a lifetime due to the German machine-

DOWN! Right, dodging intense mortar and machine-gun fire that has already claimed one of their comrades, two infantrymen race across a pontoon bridge spanning the Roer. On left, fellow soldiers from the U.S. Ninth Army cross the river in boats

GEORGE SILK—TIME LIFE PICTURES

"The Germans fought for the Roer River as if it were the Meuse, the Marne and the Somme of the last war all rolled into one."
—TIME, DEC. 11, 1944

HARD SLOG You'll never get rich by bridging a ditch, but that's the job these G.I.s were assigned, as Allied engineers struggle to put a Bailey portable bridge into position across the Roer

gun fire and the mortar shells coming in. We managed to steer a fairly direct route to the east bank, and made only one '360' on the way. As we landed on the opposite bank, I immediately searched in the dark for a hole to jump into for protection. Unfortunately I found one already occupied by a dazed German. But he was ready to end his part in the war and was waiting for an appropriate time to surrender, and he had just reached that moment."

By dawn, several footbridges had been successfully connected to the far side of the river, and it was time for the infantry to cross them in large numbers. "We were supposed to have smoke cover," George Lucht recalls, "but for some reason there wasn't any. But at a moment like that, you're too damn scared to think about anything except pushing forward. So when we got the order, we ran from our foxholes down to the edge of the river, and began running across.

"The bridge was just wide enough for a line of soldiers to cross in single file," Lucht remembers, and it had a single steel cable at waist level that a soldier could hold with one hand. "It was already bucking up and down from the speed of the current," he continues. "And then German artillery started landing in the water on either side of the bridge." Some of Lucht's companions fell into the water. "I never found out if they made it," he says "but it's hard to imagine that anybody could survive long in that water wearing a 40-lb. pack.

"I tried to keep my head down and watch where I was walking," he says. "I was less interested in seeing what was on the far side of the river than I was in getting there, so I kept looking down to watch my footing on that bridge."

But as the Americans approached the east bank of the Roer, enemy artillery was joined by small-arms fire from German foxholes and pillboxes. "We got across pretty well," Lucht says philosophically. "We took a few casualties, but most of my unit got to the far side." Once across the river, Lucht found a burned-out German tank and took momentary shelter behind it while his 12-man squad regrouped. "We realized pretty quickly that the artillery had done a good job the night before," he recalls. "Nobody in my squad got hit by a mine."

By sundown on Feb. 23, several footbridges were in place, and more than 1,000 American infantrymen were consolidating their positions on the east bank of the Roer. By the afternoon of Feb. 24, the first of the larger treadway bridges, which would allow tanks, trucks and artillery to cross the river, were in place. Lucht's unit, and all the others assigned to the six divisions that were now crossing the Roer, moved inland over the gently rolling hills that separate the Roer from the Rhine.

"Part of the frustration of combat," says Lucht, "is that you never have the big picture. The only information that a foot soldier has is literally what's in front of him, so it's usually impossible to know whether you're winning or losing the battle." One man who could see the big picture was Adolf Hitler, but that didn't stop him from making an elementary mistake in this last week of February 1945.

Field Marshall Gerd von Rundstedt, Hitler's chief commander in the West, pleaded with the dictator for permission to move his troops, now retreating from the east bank of the Roer, into position behind the natural defensive line of the Rhine River. But true to form, Hitler refused to give up even an inch of ground without a fight. As a result, the men trapped between the Roer and the Rhine were cut to pieces by the Allied advance—and another 250,000 soldiers Hitler couldn't afford to lose were killed, wounded or captured. Only 35 miles now stood between the Allies and the Rhine. ■

RUINS Once inside heavily shelled German territory, Allied troops found a wasteland; here, U.S. soldiers trudge through the ruins of Jülich, near the Roer River, in February 1945

■ **ENOUGH!** A German boy, pressed into service by Hitler, surrenders in Lemgo. Moving through a region where some German units were still active, Vandivert feared his jeep would be "easy meat" for their guns

William Vandivert

TIME-LIFE photographer William Vandivert accompanied U.S. troops on the first incursions into Germany in the fateful spring of 1945. Traveling through a ruined land, he found conditions more akin to anarchy than civilization. As thousands of starving slave laborers from around the Continent were finally liberated, they found themselves far from their homes with no food, no money and no family. The captions on these pages quote from Vandivert's original reports—typed in haste on the scene, recording his reflections on what he saw through his lens. They are preserved in the TIME archives

■ **FREED** These Hungarian Jewesses, coats marked with a yellow cross, worked in a factory in Lippstadt, packing war materials. "They didn't work fast enough, and soldiers were beating them as the first American tanks rolled down the road," Vandivert reported

■ **BOOTY** Germans join liberated workers from Russia, Poland and France in looting a liquor warehouse. Said Vandivert: "I have every sympathy for the slave labor, but these Germans sickened me …"

■ **SLAVES** At right, Greek civilians freed from forced labor show U.S. soldiers the sores on their feet, telling tales of constant beatings and starvation. One American said, "Now I'm beginning to get mad"

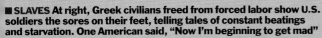

■ **SQUATTERS** Outside one town, Vandivert found liberated Italian laborers had set up a camp in a lumberyard; they were eating food they had looted from local stores. One day, when Vandivert's jeep driver stopped to inquire about directions, "a young Russian boy began yelling: 'Oh, *prima! … prima! …*' and beat his chest. 'Me Russki, you Americanski … Oh, *prima!*'" Vandivert's report concluded, "The day has been *prima* ever since"

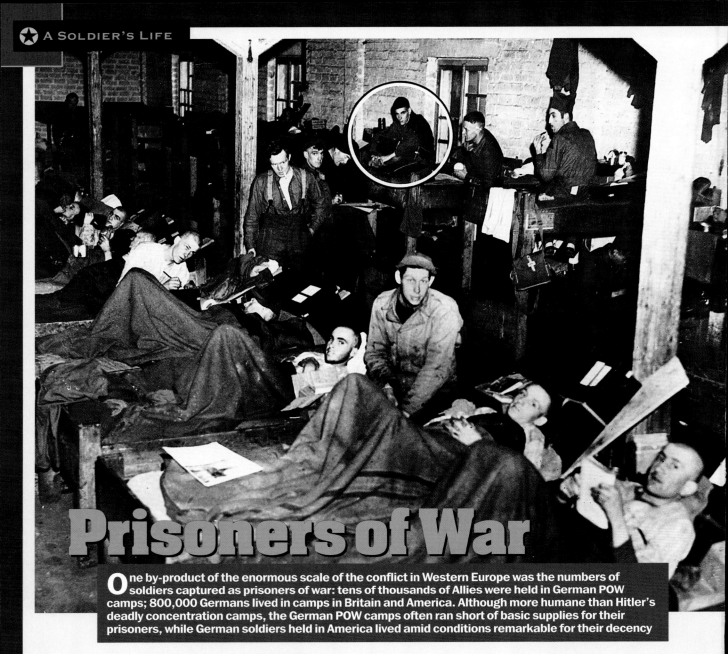

Prisoners of War

One by-product of the enormous scale of the conflict in Western Europe was the numbers of soldiers captured as prisoners of war: tens of thousands of Allies were held in German POW camps; 800,000 Germans lived in camps in Britain and America. Although more humane than Hitler's deadly concentration camps, the German POW camps often ran short of basic supplies for their prisoners, while German soldiers held in America lived amid conditions remarkable for their decency

■AILING Above, U.S. POWs are held in a hospital at Stalag Luft XIIA outside Limburg, Germany. The soldier whose face is circled (due to confusion over his identity in 1945) is Leslie H. Woolf. Once some men from this camp were being moved on a German train that came under fire from Allied aircraft; they fled the halted train and spelled out POW with their bodies in a nearby field, saving their lives

■TAPS An American POW is buried with proper honors at Stalag Luft III in February 1945. The POW camps of both sides generally abided by rules of the 1929 Geneva Convention. The Stalags were operated by the Luftwaffe, and while food and heat became increasingly scarce in the final months of the war, Allied prisoners at these camps were usually treated with some respect

■STARVED Four liberated American POWs are interviewed while recuperating at an Allied field hospital in April 1945. They are demonstrating how they used to eat from helmets with wooden spoons

■PLOTTING? At left, captured R.A.F. officers at Stalag Luft III. On March 24-25, 1944, 76 POWs managed to flee the camp through an underground tunnel, a feat celebrated in a 1951 book and a popular 1963 film, *The Great Escape.* Only three escapees reached home

■CRAMPED: At one time, this tent in a German Stalag Luft housed 450 British prisoners. Stalag Luft III, scene of the "great escape," held 10,000 Allied POWs at its peak in 1944-45. Stalag Luft is a contraction of the German term *Stamlagger Luft,* or Permanent Camps

American Camps

Seldom remembered today, POW camps in America held some 400,000 German prisoners at their peak—in conditions that were notably humane

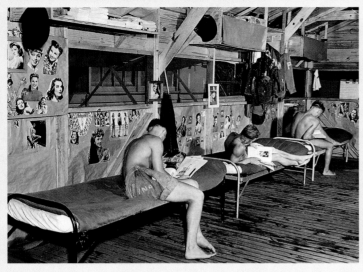

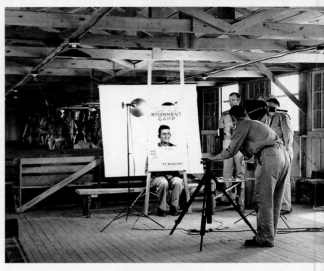

■ DREAMING Languages and customs may vary, but soldiers and pinup girls appear to be a universal constant. Favorites of the German POWs at Camp Blanding in Florida were Claudette Colbert and Hedy Lamarr

■ FRAMED A German POW, T.E. Burleigh, holds a cardboard cutout as his ID picture is taken in July 1943, upon his admission to the compound at Camp Polk, one of five POW camps in Louisiana

■ FAR FROM THE FRONT Life seems sweet for these POWs drinking beer in the canteen at Fort Custer in Michigan, where some 5,000 Germans were held

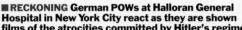

■ RECKONING German POWs at Halloran General Hospital in New York City react as they are shown films of the atrocities committed by Hitler's regime

■ LAST RITES "Only in America could this picture be made," reads the Army-approved caption for this 1944 photo, which shows a German officer giving a stiff-armed Nazi salute as a comrade is buried with honors at the POW camp at Fort Sheridan, Illinois

■ COURT DATE Two German POWs grip and grin after a game of tennis in 1944 on a court built by prisoners at Camp Breckenridge, Kentucky. German POWs being transported in the South were allowed to use segregated areas denied to local blacks

FREEDOM! In a frenzy of elation, British POWs race toward their liberators at a Stalag Luft in Germany, in April 1945. While most of the prisoners are still wearing their uniforms, a few of the men at right have apparently been forced to turn blankets into clothing

GOING HOME Allied airmen salute their liberators on March 29, 1945, as they are freed from a camp outside Wetzlar, Germany. The signpost behind them shows the distances to some longed-for cities

■ **BUSTING IN** A U.S. tank rolls over a camp's fences in an undated photo. Camps in Germany often held political prisoners, while the extermination camps were generally in occupied countries to the east

Lifeline on the Rhine

Seizing an unexpected opportunity,
U.S. troops capture a bridge across
the Rhine, changing the war's course

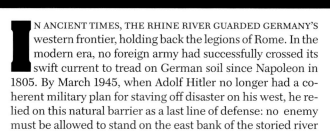

I N ANCIENT TIMES, THE RHINE RIVER GUARDED GERMANY'S western frontier, holding back the legions of Rome. In the modern era, no foreign army had successfully crossed its swift current to tread on German soil since Napoleon in 1805. By March 1945, when Adolf Hitler no longer had a co-herent military plan for staving off disaster on his west, he re-lied on this natural barrier as a last line of defense: no enemy must be allowed to stand on the east bank of the storied river

that for centuries had coursed like a unifying thread through Germany's landscape, history and national memory.

Hitler's plan called for destroying the numerous bridges that spanned the Rhine before advancing Allied troops could use them. After the Battle of the Bulge, the Germans had done so a dozen times. Allied troops had largely given up hope of capturing a bridge across the Rhine intact and had resigned themselves to the long, bloody process of erecting their own

Allied commanders knew nothing of this, of course, so they could scarcely believe the initial bulletins that came in from the field on the morning of March 7, when advanced units of the U.S. First Army's 9th Armored Division came to the outskirts of the town of Remagen, on the west bank of the Rhine, midway between Cologne and Coblenz. On a promontory overlooking the river, scouts had reported seeing what was supposed to have been impossible: Ludendorff Bridge, a railway span crossing the Rhine, was still intact.

Built in 1916, the Ludendorff Bridge had been constructed for only one purpose: to wage war. Designed to speed troops into combat against the French, it included chambers at key points built to accommodate explosives, so it could be destroyed quickly if necessary. But when the French took control of the bridge for several years after the First World War, they had filled those chambers with concrete, and the Germans later found that this act of reverse sabotage could not be undone without completely rebuilding the structure.

By the time General William Hoge, one of the commanders of the 9th Division, reached the heights overlooking

"I'll see you on the other side, and we'll all have chicken dinner."

—U.S. Major Murray Deevers, to fellow U.S. soldiers crossing the bridge

CAPTURED! Four days after the bridge was taken intact, U.S. troops in the railway tunnel on the eastern side of the Rhine look back across the span. TIME's March 19, 1945, issue compared the twin towers at both ends of the Ludendorff to "massive beer mugs"

Remagen on March 7, a few minutes past noon, the morning's planned attack on the town was already under way. Three platoons under the command of Lieutenant Karl Timmermann raced through Remagen, encountering light resistance. Less than an hour later, the town was almost entirely subdued and the American troops stood facing the bridge.

From the heights above, Hoge watched large numbers of German troops and vehicles retreat across the Ludendorff and waited for the Germans to destroy it, as they had every other Rhine crossing before it. As minutes ticked by and the bridge was not engulfed in flame and smoke, Hoge began to consider the possibility of taking it. Beneath him, Timmermann's men could see German engineers feverishly stringing charges and electrical lines along the length of the trestle; German infantry and mortar units, along with several tanks, massed on the eastern end of the bridge, prepared to rake its deck with fire should the Americans appear on its surface.

The Americans assumed that the Germans were waiting for them to venture out onto the bridge before blowing it to pieces. Clearly, any attempt to rush across would be met with a rain of fire. But as he looked down on Timmermann's position, Hoge made a decision: he would risk whatever was necessary to win the prize of an intact bridge over the Rhine, which would allow Allied penetration into Germany's center much sooner and faster than expected.

On the eastern end of the bridge, German activity was even more frantic than the Americans realized. It was dawning on the German combat engineers that there was something wrong with the network of charges they had laid along the length of the bridge. In fact, they had been issued less dynamite than the high command had promised, and when the explosives arrived, they were of poor quality.

On the west bank of the Rhine, Timmermann and his men were so sure that they would remain in defensive positions facing the bridge that they began to relax and joke about how

pontoon bridges under German fire and fighting their way across them, as they had done on the Roer River.

By now, blowing bridges had become a dangerous business in Hitler's Germany. In February, demolition charges on a bridge near Cologne were set off by a U.S. bombing raid, destroying the bridge long before the Germans intended, trapping entire divisions. Furious, Hitler established an elaborate new protocol for the destruction of river crossings.

much they would enjoy sleeping indoors and eating hot meals while they waited in Remagen for a Montgomery or a Patton to begin the next offensive. Then Hoge's order came down: Attack the bridge—now! Suddenly, they *were* the next offensive.

An appalled Timmermann asked Hoge's messenger what to do if "the bridge blows up in my face." The emissary repeated the order, then turned and walked away. Before he had taken 10 steps, a large batch of German explosives planted in the nearby ramp to the bridge exploded, gouging a large crater into the road. That seemed like an obvious sign that the bridge was about to be destroyed, and the men hesitated. But within minutes, the order came down again: Attack now!

from Hoge's command post overlooking Remagen: Get every American who can move across the bridge immediately.

Certain that they were about to die, Timmermann and his three squads began a headlong dash across the span. They were momentarily aided by the shock of the Germans, who were even more surprised than the Americans to see that the bridge was intact. In less than a minute, the first U.S. platoon had reached the foot of the twin stone towers that stood at the western end of the bridge. Germans inside began raining machine-gun fire on the Americans advancing beneath them. That was the cue for tanks, heavy machine guns and mortar units still in Remagen—and blocked from advancing behind Timmer-

> "We were across the Rhine, on a permanent bridge; the traditional defensive barrier to the heart of Germany had been pierced." —**Dwight D. Eisenhower**

As Timmermann's three platoons began to advance toward the bridge, they could see Germans on the far side frantically compressing the plungers used to detonate explosives. Seconds passed and nothing happed. Then a huge flash and roar erupted from the deck of the span, about two-thirds of the way to the eastern end. The engineers had succeeded in detonating part, but not all, of their charges. Timmermann's men watched, dumbstruck, as the steel arch that supported the Ludendorff's deck appeared to lift several feet from its footings and levitate momentarily before disappearing into an enormous cloud of smoke and dust.

When the cloud lifted, the Americans were amazed: the bridge was still standing. And once more the order came down

mann's squad by the crater the Germans had blown into the western approach ramp—to join the fight. They blasted the two towers, silencing the guns inside.

As Timmermann's unit advanced to the middle of the bridge, they quickly overwhelmed the handful of German engineers who were still there, desperately trying to rewire the explosive charges suspended from the underside of the deck. The larger, better-armed group of Germans on the eastern end of the Ludendorff kept up its fire at the rapidly advancing Americans, but it was engaged from the west bank of the Rhine by U.S. artillery and tanks.

Within 15 minutes, Timmermann and his men had advanced two-thirds of the way across the bridge, pausing every few steps to take momentary cover behind a girder and return German fire, then sprinting forward once again. Behind them, U.S. combat engineers fanned out across the western half of the bridge, cutting wires and dropping the German demolition charges into the water below.

Moving east, the Americans in the vanguard were once again pinned down by German fire, this time from the two towers on the eastern end of the bridge. They were now beyond the help of U.S. gunners on the west bank, who could not target the embattlements without the risk of hitting the Americans beneath them. In the heaviest fighting yet, Timmermann's men rushed into the fortifications and dashed up their circular staircases, shooting as they went. Within 15 minutes, the towers had been cleared.

By 4:00 in the afternoon, the bridge was in U.S. hands, along with a small foothold on the east bank of the Rhine. Sergeant Alex Drabik, one of the three platoon leaders, was the first American to set foot there, followed closely by Timmermann. Within an hour, more than 100 American infan-

BY BARGE At left, Allied armor crossed the Rhine on rafts and barges, in addition to the pontoon bridges built by engineers

BANG! At right, Winston Churchill, who was never happier than when playing soldier at the front lines, mans a gun in late March while crossing the Rhine. He landed on the river's eastern shore but was persuaded to "retreat" when a German shell exploded only 50 yds. from where he was standing

BY BRIDGE Below, as the Allied foothold across the Rhine expanded, putting German troops on the defensive, pontoon bridges were built in several locations. This crossing south of Remagen is being used on March 27 by the U.S. 87th Infantry Division, a unit of George Patton's Third Army

trymen were digging in on the far side of the river that Hitler had expected to be Germany's impassable western moat.

By nightfall, not just infantry but also tanks, half-tracks, supply trucks and armored personnel carriers were streaming across the Ludendorff Bridge, and four additional divisions were rushing toward Remagen. For the next few days, German units put up a bitter fight to retake the bridge, and Luftwaffe planes repeatedly tried to bomb it, but the Allies hung tough, gradually expanding their foothold in central Germany.

Years later, writing his memoirs, Dwight D. Eisenhower could still barely contain his delight. "This was completely unforeseen," he would recall. "We were across the Rhine, on a permanent bridge; the traditional defensive barrier to the heart of Germany was pierced." Meanwhile, Adolf Hitler could not contain his anger: he ordered courts-martial for a dozen of those responsible for the fiasco and had four officers executed for good measure. But the damage was done.

By the morning of March 8, a sign was erected on the west bank of the river: CROSS THE RHINE WITH DRY FEET. COURTESY OF THE 9TH ARM'D DIV. And for the next 10 days, that's exactly what more than 25,000 Americans would do, beginning the vast encirclement of the industrial Ruhr region that would effectively mark the end of German resistance on the Western Front. To the north, an Allied airborne drop later in March successfully put thousands more troops across the Rhine.

On March 17 the Ludendorff Bridge—taxed to the limits of its endurance by repeated shelling from both sides—plunged into the Rhine River, taking 28 American servicemen with it. By that point, its destruction mattered little. U.S. engineers had already erected two pontoon bridges parallel to it and were streaming even more men and matériel across them than the original structure could handle. The capture of the bridge, in Eisenhower's estimate, shortened the war by as much as six months. Ike later wrote, "The final defeat of the enemy, which we long had calculated would be accomplished in the spring and summer campaigning of 1945, was suddenly now, in our minds, just around the corner."

As for the bridge, it was never rebuilt. Today its four stone towers stand watch over the Rhine across an invisible span, bullet-pocked monuments to the men who fought there. ∎

Robert Capa

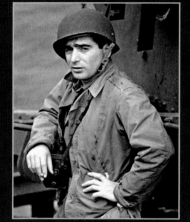

Publisher Henry Luce got two-for-one coverage from legendary photo-journalist Robert Capa: his powerful images often appeared on the oversized pages of LIFE magazine, while his first-person accounts detailing his exploits in shooting the pictures would run in TIME. In March of 1945, Capa joined U.S. paratroopers of the 17th Airborne Division in an enormous airdrop across the Rhine. Capa, who always maintained a pose of utter sangfroid in the face of danger, told TIME readers, "We dropped at 10:25, four miles north of the Rhine. Our plane was a hell of a lot hit before we got out of it ... I jumped with three cameras and a canteen of Scotch and I pointed out to myself that the canteen was very important ... [once on the ground] I started getting out of my harness. Then somebody started shooting at me and I started a beautiful long Hungarian swear. The guy next to me said, 'Don't start those Jewish prayers now. They won't do you any good.'"

■REGROUPING Outside the town of Wesel, paratroopers advance through a wooded area. Capa said, "There were some paratroopers hanging in the trees and they were murdered by the Germans. They were shot twenty times. It is fine in practice if you land in a tree, but if there is a guy with a gun shooting at you you are a dead duck." Despite such losses, the war's last big drop was highly successful

■REFUGEES With their town a battlefield, citizens abandon their burning homes and farms outside Wesel. "[The Germans] knew we were coming," Capa reported, "but they had no defenses"

■SCALPED In a show of esprit de corps, some U.S. paratroopers gave themselves Mohawk haircuts before the big drop. Capa told TIME that on this day the phrase the men yelled as they jumped from 600 ft. was not the traditional "Geronimo!" but "Umbragio!"

■MARCH! German soldiers are rounded up outside Wesel. Capa said, "Much as I hate to make primitive statements, the Germans are the meanest bastards. They are the meanest during an operation and afterwards they all have cousins in Philadelphia. That is what I like about the French: they do not have cousins in Philadelphia"

"I don't give a damn what color you are, so long as you get out there and kill those sons of bitches in the green suits."
—George Patton, to black U.S. soldiers

The Star Halfback

With Germany nearing final defeat, TIME profiled America's single most charismatic—and confounding—commander, General George S. Patton

LAST WEEK EUROPEAN CORRESPON-dents were telling another war story about unpredictable Lieut. General George S. Patton Jr. An Allied officer had asked Supreme Commander Dwight D. Eisenhower where in Germany General Patton might be. Ike's reply: "Hell, I don't know. I haven't heard from him for three hours."

George Patton was sitting in his head-quarters van, his high-polished cavalry boots cocked on the glass top of his desk. He listened now & then over his command radio to battle reports. They were good. His tankmen were rampaging around, deep in Germany, on the loose and on the prowl, raiding and rolling on. Patton could turn off the radio and turn on one of his favorite topics: the Civil War battle of Fredericksburg. Willie, the General's white bull terrier, snuffed sleepily on the rug.

Where General Patton might be in the next three hours he himself did not know. If Patton got a hunch—and Ike Eisenhower gave him the green light—he might peel off with a tank column for Berlin, or Leipzig or Berchtesgaden, at a moment's notice. If Patton's wildest dream came true, he would find Adolf Hitler in a German tank and slug it out with him. Bur for the moment, dreams aside, Patton had reason for calm and happy reflection. He was having the time of his action-choked, 40-year Army career.

His armor-heavy Third Army was performing brilliantly all the tricks he had worked hard to teach it. Patton's tankmen were carrying out his prime rule of battle: fire and movement. If they were stopped they did not dig in. They moved around the obstacle and kept firing. Patton was playing his favorite role. He was the swift, slashing halfback of Coach Eisenhower's team. His quarterback, General Omar N. Bradley, had set up a climax play and had called Patton's signal. Halfback Patton had had superb blocking from Lieut. General Courtney Hodges' First Army. Now the star open-field runner was ripping into the secondary defense.

Basically it was the play on which Patton had sped to a

TIME
THE WEEKLY NEWSMAGAZINE

THIRD ARMY'S PATTON

touchdown in the Battle of France, after the First Army had opened up a hole for him in the Saint-Lô breakthrough. There, as at the Rhine, it had been Quarterback Bradley's precise timing and teamwork that had shaken Patton loose to do his spectacular stuff. Now, as he had after Saint-Lô, it was Halfback Patton who captured the headlines. He is fast becoming a legend. The U.S. public, always more interested in the ballcarrier than in the blockers who open a hole for him, liked Patton's flourishes, his flamboyance, his victories.

Long forgotten is that emotional storm of 19 months ago in which Patton literally gave the back of his hand to a soldier sitting on a hospital cot. The U.S. has not forgotten the episode—but it has begun to misremember it, to transmute it into the Patton legend. The U.S. newspaper with the largest circulation—the tabloid New York *Daily News*—a few weeks ago editorially referred to him as "Patton, who ... slapped a soldier ... for going in the wrong direction from the front."

In slim, big-chested Patton, hero-worshipping Americans had a candidate to fit the mass idea of what a Hero General should be—the colorful swashbuckler, the wild-riding charger, the hell-for-leather Man of Action, above all the Winner. A favorite story with his officers is how the General stopped the rain in the Battle of the Bulge last December. The German offensive was blessed by soupy days at its start. No planes flew. Tankmen could not find the enemy in the endless drizzle. Patton, who can be reverent and blasphemous in the same breath, called one of the Third's chaplains. The conversation:

Patton: I want a prayer to stop this rain. If we got a couple of clear days, we could get in there and kill a couple of hundred thousand of these ... krauts.

Chaplain: Well, sir, it's not exactly in the realm of theology to pray for something that would help to kill fellow men.

Patton: What the hell are you—a theologian or an officer of the U.S. Third Army? I want that prayer!

The General got his prayer; it was printed on thousands of small cards with Patton's Christmas greeting on the reverse side. On the fifth day of rain, it was distributed to the troops. On the sixth day the sun shone, and the Third proceeded to its warlike harvest. ■

DRESSED TO IMPRESS Patton's military model was Colonel John S. Mosby, the Confederate cavalryman who rode into battle in a scarlet-lined cape, a brilliant plume in his campaign hat. Mosby lived until 1916; Patton's father was a friend

"There was a sense of finality, of nearing climax: this grand offensive might be the last big battle in the west." —TIME, April 2, 1945

MAN DOWN After a series of deadly street battles, troops of the U.S. Third Army advance into Coblenz; one comrade's war is over

Tightening the Noose

Stabbing deep into Germany's industrial heartland and linking up with the Russians at the Elbe, U.S. and British troops take charge in Germany

"GERMANY HAS TWO HEARTS," DWIGHT D. EISENHOWER was fond of telling his staff. "One, the political heart, is in Berlin. But the other, the industrial and economic heart, is in the Ruhr." And now, in March 1945, with American and British troops pouring across the Rhine by the tens of thousands, Eisenhower had to decide which of Germany's hearts to cut out.

The obvious answer was Berlin. After the failed Ardennes offensive, Hitler had fled to the German capital to await his personal Götterdämmerung. Berlin was also the objective that America's allies, the British, most wanted to take. And Berlin was the trophy the average American and Briton craved, after long years of war and new revelations of Hitler's dark deeds. But the obvious answer troubled Eisenhower. After U.S. troops crossed the Rhine at Remagen Bridge on March 7, he asked his staff for estimates of what it would cost to overrun Berlin, and the answers had been sobering: an estimated 100,000 American and British troops would probably die in the street-to-street fighting that SHAEF planners anticipated.

Eisenhower also knew that Roosevelt, Churchill and Stalin had already agreed, at the Yalta conference in February, upon the occupation zones that their forces would control in postwar Germany. And Berlin was deep within the Soviet zone—meaning that regardless of who captured the city, it would have to be handed over to the Russians immediately after the war ended. As Eisenhower would reflect years later, 100,000 lives seemed a steep price to pay for real estate that would have to be given back a few weeks after it had been taken. This led Eisenhower to make his most controversial decision of the war: Berlin would be left for the Russians.

On March 28, for the first (and only) time during the war, Eisenhower cabled a message to Moscow that began "Personal to Marshal Stalin." It assured the Soviet leader that American and British troops on the Western Front would not dash for Berlin, thus precluding a race between the Allies on the Eastern and Western fronts for the German capital. It further explained that Eisenhower believed the nearby Ruhr was a better target for the Western Allies—capturing the region would eliminate once and for all what remained of Germany's capacity to make war. Stalin messaged back, agreeing that his troops would lead the attack on Berlin but disingenuously claiming that rooting the Germans out of Czechoslovakia would be their first priority.

The British were apoplectic. Eisenhower had not consulted them before sending his cable, bypassing London because he knew they would oppose his decision and keeping Washing-

ton out of the loop to provide political cover for his bosses, General George Marshall and President Franklin Roosevelt. To appease London, Washington officially ordered Eisenhower to have no further direct contact with Moscow. But both Marshall and F.D.R. were in accord with Ike.

With many German cities now in Allied hands—Cologne had fallen on March 7, Coblenz on March 18, Mainz on the 21st—Eisenhower now trained his sights on the region of Germany that lies amid a triangle formed by three mighty rivers. The area east of the Rhine, north of the Ruhr and south of the Lippe, known to Germans simply as "the Ruhr," was the source of almost all the Third Reich's coal and steel production, most of its electricity and the lion's share of its industrial capacity—the last reserve of Germany's ability to produce materials needed to wage war.

Knowing that the war must end in a matter of weeks—perhaps days—after the Ruhr was lost, the Germans resolved to defend it as tenaciously as they would Berlin. The task was given to Army Group B, under the command of Field Marshal Walther Model, which consisted of more than 400,000 German troops spread over the 4,000-sq.-mi. area of the Ruhr.

U.S. SIGNAL CORPS

DO TREAD ON ME **A light tank from the U.S. 11th Armored Division passes through the streets of Lembach, Germany, where local citizens have rolled out a Spring, 1945 version of a red carpet**

HELP! Seconds before this picture was taken in the streets of Cologne on March 7, the U.S. tank at the right was hit by a German shell; the soldier on top of the tank was blown out of the turret, the only member of his crew to survive. The soldier at left is running to his aid. Cologne Cathedral is visible in the background

On the Allied side, Eisenhower sent two Allied armies to strangle the Ruhr in a bear hug: General Courtney Hodges and the First Allied Army to the south; the Ninth Allied Army, under the command of British Field Marshal Bernard Montgomery, to the north. Within 24 hours of Ike's telegram to Stalin, the First Army had moved north of the Ruhr River and captured 700 sq. mi. of territory and some 16,000 prisoners.

Rather than coming together immediately, however, both the First and the Ninth Armies continued moving eastward, along the long sides of the triangle shaped by the Ruhr and Lippe rivers. Eisenhower was determined to encircle the Germans, and he was eager to make this "Ruhr Pocket" as

BARRIER Below left, in Gudingen, near Saarbrücken, U.S. troops risk their lives as they peek over a roadblock set by German troops—who are waiting at the far end of the street

DESPERATION German civilians carve meat from the body of a horse that was killed in combat as U.S. forces of the 10th Armored Division rolled into a small town outside Frankfurt

THE END Prominently displaying a large white flag of surrender, three German medical men are guided to an American area as fighting wanes in Coblenz on March 21

COMRADE! Celebrating a long-anticipated moment, U.S. and Russian troops join hands at the Elbe River in late April. It was a brief moment of amity before the onset of the cold war

large as possible before completing the massive envelopment.

By March 31, the 3rd Armored Division was leading the First Army's advance on the southern edge of the triangle. Commanded by the tough General Maurice Rose, the 3rd Armored had earned the nickname "Spearhead," because it had spent months at the tip of Allied advances in France, Belgium and now Germany. On this day, Rose had pushed the 3rd Armored more than 80 miles—the largest single-day advance for a U.S. unit in Europe during the war. Rose was leading this advance personally, as was his habit, riding in a jeep at the head of his column, near the town of Paderborn. Turning a corner at high speed, his jeep ran into the back end of a German Tiger tank. The teenage tank commander poked his head out of the turret and pointed his machine gun at Rose.

What happened next was later ascribed to rumors that the German boy somehow knew that Rose was Jewish, which is highly unlikely. What is known for certain is that Rose reached for his sidearm and the German boy fired, killing him instantly. What will never be known is whether Rose was attempting to draw his gun and fire on the German (which would have been entirely in character) or preparing to toss the pistol aside. Rose was the only U.S. division commander killed in the European Theater during the war; in his honor, Eisenhower renamed the ongoing battle the "Rose Pocket."

By April 1, the First and Ninth Armies had reached Lippstadt and linked together. The nearly half a million Germans trapped within were now completely surrounded but had not finished fighting. Ignoring repeated demands for surrender, German troops staged delaying actions in many of the Ruhr's numerous towns and cities. On April 5, Eisenhower ordered 18 divisions into the interior of the pocket, to begin clearing out German resistance. Nine days later, these troops pushed through to the city of Hagen, effectively splitting the German-held area into two separate and smaller pockets. Surrounded, shrinking islands of resistance were now being carved up almost at will by British and American troops. On April 18, the Germans finally capitulated. General George Marshall would later call the Ruhr battle "the largest pocket of envelopment in the history of warfare." In one stroke, the First and Ninth Armies took more than 325,000 German prisoners—more even than had been captured by the Russians at Stalingrad.

Eisenhower kept his word to Stalin and resisted the temptation to march on Berlin. Stalin, slightly less ethically meticulous, reneged on his promise to Ike, ignored Czechoslovakia and hurled two Soviet armies into the German capital. The price for this prize turned out to be almost as high as Eisenhower's staff had predicted: more than 70,000 Soviet troops died in the struggle for the city.

While the German army made the Russians pay for every block of Berlin with thousands of lives, Hitler's troops in the West essentially gave up after their defeat at the Ruhr. The final advances by British and U.S. troops met little opposition. Eisenhower sent the 101st Airborne Division south toward Hitler's mountain retreat at Berchtesgaden. This was nearly as mesmerizing a prize as Berlin; moreover, some intelligence reports indicated that Hitler might try to flee the capital and stage a dramatic last stand at his Berghof high in the Alps.

Eisenhower's remaining armies advanced toward the Elbe River, the border of the Russian occupation zone agreed upon at Yalta. The first U.S. troops, from the Ninth Army's 2nd Armored Division, reached the Elbe on April 11. For the next two weeks, more American and British units caught up with this advance and took up positions along the west bank of the river. Finally, on April 25, a small U.S. patrol on the east bank of the river came across a lone Russian soldier on horseback, galloping several miles ahead of his unit. The next day, American and Russian division commanders Emil F. Reinhardt and Vladimir Rusakov officially greeted one another at the village of Torgau. Germany was cloven—and long would remain so.

The Allies' elation was matched by the Germans' disgrace. Five days before Reinhardt and Rusakov shook hands at the Elbe, Field Marshal Model could not bear to surrender. Instead, he simply told his troops that they were free to stop fighting if they so desired. That is exactly what they desired, with the exception of a small number of SS and Hitler Youth detachments, who paid for their fanaticism with their lives. Then Model went for a walk in the forest near his field headquarters at Duisberg. He may have been considering that without the Ruhr, Germany could no longer fight. Or pondering what would become of his Fatherland (or himself) at the hands of the Allies after the war. Or wondering what he would tell Hitler, who had ordered him to hold the Ruhr at all costs. Whatever Model was thinking, as he walked, he unholstered his pistol and fired a single shot into his brain. ∎

Heart of Darkness

Across Germany and its long-occupied neighbors, Allied soldiers begin liberating Hitler's prisoners—and uncover horrors that still appall us

SIXTY YEARS AFTER HORRIFIED SOLDIERS OF THE U.S., British and Russian armies first entered Adolf Hitler's vast chain of concentration and death camps, the details of the Holocaust remain difficult to confront. Yet confront them we must.

When Allied commanders saw the conditions within the camps, their immediate impulse was to force the residents of nearby towns to march through them, to see with their own eyes the unspeakable crimes committed in the name of German culture. That impulse—to bear witness—continues to animate our response to the camps. Survivors like Elie Wiesel have made it their life's work to document these depravities; writers and artists have grappled to express and understand them in a host of forms: prose and poetry, paintings and films, even graphic novels. Museums of the Holocaust document the tragedy for future generations. Yet for sheer immediacy, it

is hard to surpass the accounts of the TIME reporters who accompanied the first soldiers into the camps. The reports that follow are all excerpted from TIME's April 30, 1945, issue. "For 12 years the enemies of totalitarianism had told the world of these horrors," the editors wrote in introducing them. "They were past belief. But the evidence of the camps was as irrefutable as death, as monstrous as degradation."

Bergen-Belsen *FROM THE BERGEN-BELSEN CAMP, CORRESPONDENT George Rodger reported:*

As Winston Churchill addressed the British troops on the banks of the Rhine on March 26, I heard him say: "We are now entering the dire sink of iniquity." These seemed strange words and I did not understand the full meaning of them until today, when at Belsen I witnessed the ultimate in human degradation. There the 6-sq.-mi. barbed wire enclosure in the

SHADOWS: Starving prisoners greet their liberators at the Ebensee camp in Austria, which was entered by the U.S. 80th Infantry Division on May 7, 1945

heart of a rich agricultural center has been a hell on earth for 60,000 men, women and children of a dozen nationalities who were being gradually starved to death by SS guards under a brutish, pig-eyed leader, Captain Krämer. During the month of March, 17,000 people died of starvation, and they still die at the rate of 300 to 350 every 24 hours.

The magnitude of suffering and horror at Belsen cannot be expressed in words and even I, as an actual witness, found it impossible to comprehend fully—there was too much of it; it was too contrary to all principles of humanity—and I was coldly stunned. Under the pine trees the scattered dead were lying, not in twos or threes or dozens but in thousands. The living tore ragged clothing from the corpses to build fires over which they boiled pine needles and roots for soup. Little children rested their heads against the stinking corpses of their mothers, too nearly dead themselves to cry. A man hobbled

up to me and spoke to me in German. I couldn't understand what he said and I shall never know, for he fell dead at my feet in the middle of his sentence.

The living lay side by side with the dead, their shriveled limbs and shrunken features making them almost indistinguishable. Women tore away their clothing and scratched the hordes of lice which fed on their emaciated bodies; rotten with dysentery, they relieved themselves where they lay and the stench was appalling. Naked bodies with gaping wounds in their backs and chests showed where those who still had the strength to use a knife had cut out the kidneys, livers and hearts of their fellow men and eaten them that they themselves might live.

Over all this the SS guards, both girls and men, had watched coldly and unmoved. I saw them too—fat, fleshy and inhuman. Now they have a different role in the camp. Under British

"You are now entering the dire sink of iniquity."
—Winston Churchill, to British soldiers

guard they are made to collect the dead and drag them to a mass grave. From dawn to dusk the SS girls and men alike hold in their arms the bodies of the men, women and children whom they killed, and British Tommies, roused for once to a burning fury, allow them no respite. It is their just reward. Perhaps it can all be summed up in the croaking words that came from a pitiful pile of rags and bones that lay at my feet: "Look, Englishman, this is German culture."

■Buchenwald *FROM THE CAMP AT BUCHENWALD, TIME CORRE-spondent Percy Knauth reported:*

In Buchenwald today I saw death reduced to such a state of ordinariness that it just left me numb and feeling nothing, not even sickness at my stomach.

Propaganda is propaganda and in this war we have had more than our share of atrocity stories, but Buchenwald is not a story. It is acres of bare ground on a hillside where woods and fields are green under warm spring sun. It is miles and miles of barbed wire once charged with electricity and guard-ed by machine-gun towers built of creosoted pine logs. It is barracks after barracks crowded with 21,000 living, breathing human beings who stink like nothing else on earth and many of whom have lost the power of coherent speech.

Buchenwald is a fact which has existed, on a small scale at first, for eleven years, and it is a fact which will stink through the years of history as long as generations of mankind have memories. Buchenwald is something of a showplace now,

nine days after it was liberated, and there are certain things you have to see. There were two ovens there, each with six openings. It was a clean room with no smell. The ovens were not clean. In some of them there were still charred remains, a grinning, blackened skull, a chest from which the flesh was still not fully burned away, skeletons half melted down. The ovens were cold now but in recent weeks before the Ameri-cans came their clean bright flame consumed between 150 and 200 people daily.

We passed into another yard fenced in by a high wooden wall. There was a pile of bodies there, stacked more or less the way I stack my firewood back home, not too carefully. There were men and some of them were naked. They looked strange. Their mouths were open as though in pain and little streaks of blood flowed from their noses. "Some kind of hem-orrhage," said a medical corpsman. "Hell, those guys died of starvation," said another G.I. He stared and stared and couldn't get that thought out of his mind, repeating it over and over. "Those guys just starved to death. They just starved."

It was easy to see that they were starved. There was just nothing on them, nothing but yellowish or brownish skin stretched tightly over bones and cavities. Buchenwald did not have a diet, really. There was some form of soup once a day and

Murder, Inc.

One of the first eyewitness accounts of a German death camp appeared in TIME's *Sept. 11, 1944, issue, after the magazine's Moscow correspondent, Richard Lauterbach, toured the Maidenek camp outside Lublin, Poland, days after it was liberated by the Red Army. Here is Lauterbach's report:*

It was Sunday and the sun was hot. The Polish girls who wore their best embroidered dresses to Mass and the men of Lublin chatted on street corners without a furtive, over-the-shoulder look. We drove out along the Chelm road about a mile from the town. Dmitri Kudriavstev, Secretary of the Soviet Atrocities Commission, said: "They called this 'the road of death.'" Kudriavtsev has an even, soft way of talking. You could not guess that he has pored over more horrors in the past three years than any living man.

Our car halted before a well-guarded gate. "This is Maidenek," Kudriavtsev said. I saw a huge, not unattractive, temporary city. There were about 200 trim, grey-green barracks, spaced for maximum light, air and sunshine. I had to blink twice to take in the jarring realities: the high double rows of electrically charged barbed wire; the kennels which once housed hundreds of gaunt, man-eating dogs.

We got out to inspect the bathhouses. Said Kudriavstev without emotion: "They came here first for a shower. Then the Germans said: 'Now you have had your wash. Go in there.'" He led us into one of four gas chambers. It was a solid grey concrete room, about 20 ft. square and 7 ft. high. A single large steel door sealed the entrance hermetically. There were three apertures, two for the pipes which brought in the gas, one, a thick glass peephole, protected by steel netting. It took about seven minutes for this "Zyklon B" to kill the occupants, as many as 250 at a time. Kudriavstev was explaining: "The gas affects all parts of the organism. It is quicker when the body is warm, washed and wet."

I took notes calmly, feeling little emotion. It was all so cold and bare. Kudriavstev was still explaining: "On one day, Nov. 3, 1943, they annihilated 18,000 people—Poles, Jews, political prisoners and war prisoners."

STRIPPED Bodies stacked at Buchenwald. At the Maidenek camp, a TIME correspondent found, shoes were valued while human life was cheap

REMAINS The ovens in the crematorium at the Maidenek camp were similar to those at Buchenwald, above, which still held human remains when U.S. troops entered the camp

The crematorium might have been a big bakeshop or a very small blast furnace. Here the Nazis carted the bodies, straight from the gas chambers. They cut them up scientifically. They put the chunks on iron stretchers, slid them on rollers into the five greedy mouths of the coke-fed ovens. They could disintegrate 1,900 people a day. "There was great economy," said Kudriavstev. "These furnaces also heated the water for the camp."

We heard about a young Polish girl who had refused to undress for a shower. The degenerate sadistic [German] who ran the crematorium ordered her shoved into the furnace alive. Her hair burned quick and bright. Then she crisped up like bacon on an over-hot skillet.

Near the ovens were the remains of a room with a big stone table. Here gold fillings were extracted from the teeth. No corpse or piece of a corpse could be burned without a stamp on the chest: "Inspected for gold fillings."

Back in the camp we saw a room full of passports and documents. Papers of Frenchmen, Russians, Greeks, Czechs, Jews, Italians, Serbs, Poles. Records left behind by some of the 1,500,000 of 22 nationalities who were brought here.

We came to a large, unpainted warehouse. Not suspecting, I stepped up and went inside. It was full of shoes. A sea of shoes. Not only shoes. Boots. Rubbers. Leggings. Slippers. Children's shoes, soldier's shoes, old shoes, new shoes. The sea of shoes was engulfing. In one place the sheer weight had broken the wall. Part of the wall had fallen out, and with it a cascade of shoes. Kudriavstev said: "There are 820,000 pairs here and 18 carloads of the best were shipped to Germany."

Standing on the sea of shoes, Maidenek suddenly became real. The barbed wire had barbs which ripped flesh. The ashes on the big cabbages were the ashes of the brothers of the worn but pretty peasant women who had spoken to us that morning at Mass.

"The loudspeakers from the camp kept screeching Strauss waltzes," a Polish woman in Lublin said to me. *The Beautiful Blue Danube* can never be beautiful to us again." She paused and repeated the words so many Poles and Russians had said that day: "I hope you Americans will not be soft with the Germans."

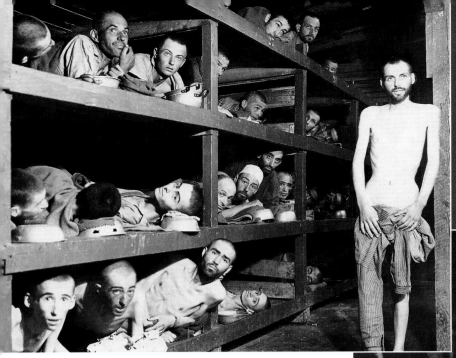

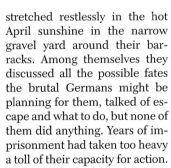

some bread. The amount doesn't matter: it was not enough to sustain life. I saw hundreds of Buchenwald's 21,000 (there had been 48,000 but more than half had been evacuated to the interior of Germany) who were as starved as the corpses in the crematorium yard. You cannot adequately describe starved men; they just look awful and unnatural. There was nothing but their bones beneath the tightly stretched skin, none of the roundedness, the curving and the flat places, the swelling muscles which men usually have. They walk or creep or lie around and seem about as animate as the barracks and fence posts and the stones on Buchenwald's bare, hard-packed earth, and when they are dead they are corpses and then gone.

Buchenwald is beyond all comprehension. You just can't understand it, even when you've seen it. It is beyond understanding to see human beings with brains and skillful hands and lives and destinies and thoughts reduced to a state where only blind instinct tries to keep them alive. It is beyond human anger or disgust to see in such a place the remnants of a sign put up by those who ran the place: "Honesty, Diligence, Pride, Ability ... these are the milestones of your way through here."

■ **Erla** *AT THE ERLA CAMP, THE SS guards prepared to massacre the prisoners as the U.S. Army approached. The prisoners knew what was coming, but most of them were too weak to try to escape, although a Czech prisoner had short-circuited the electric fence. From Erla, TIME reporter Bill Walton pieced together the atrocity from the stories of the few survivors:*

All day Tuesday the SS guards made their preparations. All day the prisoners moved weakly around their barracks or stretched restlessly in the hot April sunshine in the narrow gravel yard around their barracks. Among themselves they discussed all the possible fates the brutal Germans might be planning for them, talked of escape and what to do, but none of them did anything. Years of imprisonment had taken too heavy a toll of their capacity for action.

Shortly before noon the guards herded the few remaining able-bodied prisoners into the barracks for the weak and ill, saying that a noon meal would be served there. Two hundred and ninety-five men were crowded into that barracks—40 ft. by 120 ft.—jammed in and the doors locked after big tubs of soup had been brought in.

Once the doors were locked the SS men began to work with furious speed. First they nailed army blankets over every window. Then they hauled up huge cans of highly inflammable acetate. The 13 guards were all ready, armed with every weapon in their bursting arsenals. At a signal all sprang into action.

The low murmur of worried conversation turned to cries of fright when the guards unlocked the two doors and hurled in acetate, dousing the tinder-dry buildings and splashing over the prisoners crowding close to the only routes of escape. In one split second the acetate ignited and burst into a roaring inferno. Cries of fright turned to screams of terror and of mortal agony that were soon drowned by the leaping flames and the bursting of hand grenades tossed into the open doorways.

At least 100 flaming men clawed their way through the exits, packed with crazed, dying men. Through spattering gunfire from SS machines pistols and bazookas, most of the men staggered blindly for the nearby latrine even though it too was aflame. In a last gasp of agony they threw themselves into the excrement-filled trench where SS guards shot them and clubbed them to death, their bodies sinking slowly into the filth.

A few others got as far as the low, 3-ft.-thick band of barbed wire beside the electric fence before they were shot or died of burns. So awful was their agony that they paid scant attention to the angry prongs of barbed wire and wiggled under even though it ripped their flesh to ribbons. A handful, protected by the mad confusion, got over the fence, hastily stripped off their burning clothes, and started running eastward across the flat plowed field. On the other side of the field was a tank also retreating eastward. Hitler Youths, manning that tank, turned their guns toward the blazing barracks and mowed down the naked prisoners running and falling and rising to run again across the open field. Only four made it to safety. ∎

J'ACCUSE! A Russian slave laborer at the Mittelbrau-Dora camp identifies a German officer who, the prisoner told U.S. troops, was one of the most brutal guards in the camp

FREE AT LAST! Prisoners at the Dachau concentration camp outside Munich, Germany, cheer their liberators. The first of Hitler's political prisons and a template for others, it was founded by Heinrich Himmler, then Munich's police chief, in March, 1933; it fell to the Allies on April 29, 1945

A Time to Pray

Soldiers who might never visit a church in their civilian lives found themselves kneeling in prayer during the war; famously, there are no atheists in foxholes. With one's death no longer an abstract notion to be faced decades away, but rather an everyday companion, young soldiers found solace in prayer—and in the bravery of the unarmed chaplains who tended to their spiritual needs, even in the cannon's mouth

■ **FIELD SERVICE** Above, a Roman Catholic chaplain says Mass for soldiers of the 89th Infantry Division, part of General George Patton's Third Army, on March 15, 1945. The men are preparing to cross the Moselle River

■ **ALL HANDS ON DECK** At left, British sailors observe Sunday services on the forecastle of H.M.S. *Scylla,* anchored off the coast of France not long after the invasion of Normandy; other vessels from the enormous D-day armada are visible in the background

■ **SHRINE** At right, on Dec. 29, 1944, soldiers of the U.S. 82nd Airborne Division pause to pray at a roadside crucifix in the Belgian countryside

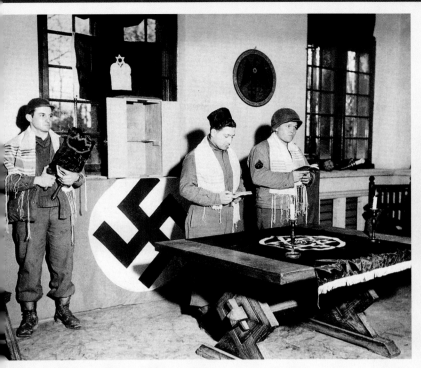

EASTER PARADE Their cathedral a garage, U.S. troops are joined by German civilians in celebrating Easter Sunday Mass in Bessenbach, Germany, in April 1945

CLEANSING Left, PFC Abraham Mirmelstein, Captain Manuel Poliakoff and Corporal Martin Willen conduct Sabbath services in Schloss Rheydt, the former home of Dr. Joseph Goebbels, Hitler's propaganda chief

Berlin Armaggedon

As U.S. and British armies stand off, two Soviet generals drive their troops into Berlin to finish off Adolf Hitler's Third Reich

O N APRIL 1, 1945, JOSEPH STALIN SAT IN HIS KREMLIN study facing his two top battlefield commanders, Marshals Georgi Zhukov and Ivan Konev. "Well, then," began the man whose massive purges in the 1930s had devastated the officers corps of the Red Army, "who is going to take Berlin—we or the Allies?" Both generals knew what Stalin wanted to hear, and what the price might be for telling him anything else. They shouted over each other that Russian troops would capture the capital of Hitler's Reich, with each general insisting that his forces would get there first. Stalin smiled, for few things made him happier than stoking the rivalry between these commanders. (Had it not been for the desperate situation he faced after Germany's invasion of Russia, the paranoid Stalin would never have allowed either to become so powerful.) He then looked down at an operational map showing the deployment of Zhukov's and Konev's forces along the Oder and Neisse rivers, stretched across a front more than 250 miles long. At its closest point, this front was no more than 60 miles from Berlin. The Soviet general staff had drawn a line on the map, marking a boundary between the two armies. The line put Berlin squarely within the path of Zhukov's forces, while sending Konev's troops to the south of the city. Still smiling, Stalin picked up a pencil and began erasing this line at a point on the River Spree, south of Berlin. The implication was clear: once either general reached this point, the next move was up to him—and may the best man win. Before dismissing his generals, Stalin added that it would be fitting to subdue Berlin by April 22, Lenin's birthday.

The generals were shaken; they had come to Moscow to ask Stalin for an operational pause on the battlefield, during which they would firm up the front, resupply their troops and prepare for an orderly advance on Berlin in May. Instead, they were ordered to draft plans for a new offensive within 48 hours. Stalin also withheld from his generals the cables he had exchanged with SHAEF commander Dwight Eisenhower days earlier, which stipulated that the Americans and British would encircle the Ruhr and then drive south into Bavaria, leaving Berlin for the Russians. Stalin taunted the rivals with intelligence reports (probably fabricated) that the Americans were planning a massive attack on Berlin by paratroopers and gliders. If the Russians were to beat the Allies to the capital, the luxury of time was

DEFEAT Soviet tanks, warplanes and troops swarm toward Germany's capital building, the Reichstag, in the final hours of the Third Reich

out of the question. Both the Soviet armies would now have to push forward with all possible speed, regardless of the cost.

The cost would be considerable. Preparing for his last stand, Hitler had removed the militarily inept SS chief Heinrich Himmler from command of the Army Group Vistula. In his place, the dictator had appointed general Gotthard Heinrici, a veteran defensive specialist from the Eastern Front. Hitler's strategy, if it could be called that, was to exact from Stalin a higher price for Berlin than he would be willing or able to pay. By halting the Soviet advance, Hitler believed, he would force ei-

In the early morning hours of April 16, the battle lines along the two German rivers—the Oder to the north, the Neisse to the south—roared with the reports of more than 40,000 Russian heavy guns. Three thousand truck-mounted Katyusha rocket launchers (nicknamed "Stalin Organs" for their cluster of launch pipes and distinctive whine) soon joined the ghoulish chorus. As Russian troops surged across the two rivers, German tanks, artillery and heavy machine guns fired into their ranks at point-blank range.

The opening lap of the race to Berlin went to Konev. By the

> "The Russians will suffer the greatest defeat, the bloodiest death in their history, before the gates of Berlin." —Adolf Hitler

ther Moscow or London and Washington to seek a peace with Berlin, leaving himself both alive and still in power.

Stalin's 2.5 million troops were on the cusp of victory after a 1,000-mile journey from Moscow to Berlin. The belief that they could be turned back a few miles from their goal by 250,000 German soldiers is a measure of Hitler's distance from reality. His troops had little ammunition, less fuel and no hope of assistance from the air. Nor could they expect to be reinforced from the rear: there was no conventional rear remaining in Germany, only front.

end of the first day, Zhukov's troops were repelled by Heinrici's Army Group Vistula at the Seelow Heights, an area of high ground between Berlin and the Oder. When Zhukov cabled these results to Moscow, Stalin wired back that he was ordering Konev to drive directly for the center of Berlin. The next day, Zhukov resorted to brute force. Using tanks as battering rams followed by human waves of infantry charging on foot at German strong points, the Russians advanced. The carnage continued for two more days. Finally, on April 19, the road to Berlin was open.

HASTE Left, Soviet troops dash through the streets of Berlin. More than 70,000 Russians are believed to have died in the battle for the city

VICTORY Right, after hearing a false report that his troops had hoisted a flag over the Reichstag, General Zhukov decided to make the rumor true. He sent a unit to take the building, and after a long firefight, soldier Meliton Kantaria raised a homemade flag, brought from Moscow for this moment by Soviet cameraman Yevgeny Khaldei

ODE TO JOY Below, poet Yevgeni Dolmatorski (on tank at left) recites to troops near Berlin's Brandenburg Gate

Meanwhile, Konev's army had slowed, as the Germans facing the southern advance put up a dogged resistance. The Hitler Youth boys proved especially willing to sacrifice themselves, often standing in the open before oncoming Russian tanks and firing their *Panzerfausts*, primitive bazookas.

On April 20, the race to Berlin ended in a tie, as both Zhukov's and Konev's troops entered the city's suburbs. The center of the city was now within Russian artillery range, and Hitler, for the first time in the war, could hear the sound of Stalin's guns. The process of completely surrounding the city took another five days, during which both Zhukov and Konev sent large troop detachments racing past the city to meet U.S. and British forces further west, at the Elbe River.

On April 26, the final siege of the encircled city began. Defending the stronghold of the Reich were fewer than 100,000 soldiers—if the term can be stretched to include boys not yet old enough to shave and men too old to walk easily up a flight of stairs. Frantically, Hitler ordered that troop detachments outside the city fight their way in and relieve his position. Most of these units were themselves surrounded, and some of them no longer existed, except in Hitler's mind.

When the final Russian push into Berlin's central government district began on April 27, the Germans trapped within the city struggled with all the crazed gallantry that Hitler demanded. Each room of each building became a battleground, and the grisly savagery that had defined the struggle between Russia and Germany from the beginning reached new heights. Upon hearing that Russian troops were advancing through the city's subway tunnels, Hitler ordered them flooded—notwithstanding that hordes of German civilians and wounded soldiers had taken shelter there. Thousands drowned. Russian troops didn't bother to distinguish between German civilians and the irregular soldiers of the Hitler Youth and *Volkssturm* (whose "uniform" was often only an armband); they machine-gunned thousands of noncombatants.

Finally, on April 30, Russian troops battled room-to-room past the last German elements holding out in the Reichstag building and hoisted a Soviet flag over it. As joyous Russians stood in front of the shattered building, looking up at their flag, they did not yet realize that they were standing only a short walk away from a bunker located 50 ft. below the ground—the site chosen by Adolf Hitler for his personal apocalypse. ■

Witness in the Bunker

Sixteen-year-old Armin Lehmann found himself in Adolf Hitler's secret hideout during the final 10 days of the dictator's life. This is his story

WHERE DID YOU FIGHT?" THE GRAYING MAN ASKED the young boy. "In Silesia, southeast of Breslau, my Führer," the 16-year-old proudly answered. The stooped figure, lost in his overcoat, smiled then raised his hand and patted the youngster's shoulder as he whispered hoarsely, "Another brave boy."

It was April 20, 1945—Adolf Hitler's 56th birthday—and the boy, Armin Lehmann, was part of a delegation of Hitler Youth who had been decorated with the Iron Cross for bravery in combat. "After he had walked down the line and greeted each of us," Lehmann remembers, "Hitler made a short speech. He

said that Germany was like a patient whom doctors believed was going to die. But Hitler said this patient does not have to die—he can be saved with a miraculous new medication, which was being developed just in time to save him. The only question was whether the patient had a strong enough will to hang on until the medicine arrived. The medicine that was going to save Germany was a secret new 'wonder weapon' that was just a few days from being deployed on the battlefields. But until it was, we had to fight on with an iron will."

"I believed him completely," says Lehmann, now a 77-year-old retired travel executive living in Oregon, who distanced

But in 1945, only seven years later, "he had aged decades," Lehmann says. "The difference was unbelievable—like day and night. He was hunched over. The flesh seemed to hang from the bones of his face, and he had black circles under his eyes. His hand trembled so badly that he was gripping the lapel of his overcoat to make it stop."

Moments after leaving Hitler, the entire group of 16-year-old Hitler Youth fighters was assigned to the suicidal battle against the Russians. It was then that an officer discovered Lehmann did not have the driver's license necessary to operate the vehicles that would take the group to the front lines. (True to form, the authoritarians who had pillaged most of Europe, murdered millions of innocents and were now facing the prospect of their own annihilation could not countenance the breach of regulations required to put an underage driver behind the wheel of a truck.) "Thank goodness," Lehmann says now. "As far as I know, the rest of the group was killed." Lehmann was pulled out of the detachment and given a new assignment: he would serve as a messenger between Hitler's underground bunker and nearby government offices.

"Because some of the radio and telephone lines into the bunker had stopped working," he remembers, "Hitler Youth leader Artur Axmann was ordered to detach a group of couriers to the bunker. Our job was to run from the communications room inside the bunker to offices above ground, where the lines were still working. Most of the time, we took messages to the radio and telephone centers of the Reich Chancellery, which was directly upstairs, or the party headquarters, across the street."

For the next 10 days, Lehmann would witness firsthand the swirling vortex of personalities and events that converged upon Hitler's subterranean lair for the final days of Nazi Ger-

"If we leave the world stage in disgrace, we'll have lived for nothing."
—Adolf Hitler, to Joseph Goebbels

DOOMED This picture of Hitler at a ceremony honoring Hitler Youth members is commonly cited as having been taken on his 56th birthday, April 20, 1945. However, Armin Lehmann, who was present at the April ceremony, believes this photo was actually taken in March, at a similar event. Whatever the date, it is the last picture of Hitler alive. The location is the garden of the Reich Chancellery, just above the bunker

many. For some of the players in this drama, Lehmann would develop an instant dislike. "[Heinrich] Himmler was standing beside Hitler when we were presented to him," he recalls. "He was what in German is called a 'cream face.' He had very soft skin and wore small glasses. He did not look at all to be the warrior type. He was more of a schoolteacher type. He looked to me like a softy."

But for others in Hitler's entourage, Lehmann formed an instinctive affection. "At one point, I ran downstairs and into the bunker with a message I had been told was very important," he remembers. "I hadn't eaten or slept for several days, and there was a cart in front of me, containing sparkling water, juices and fresh sandwiches." The boy knew better than to touch the food. But then, "a blond woman with a kind smile and a soft voice told me to help myself. This was how I met Eva Braun. I was so nervous that I dropped the first glass I picked up and it shattered, making a terrible mess. She just smiled gently at me and told me to take another."

In January 1945, in the wake of his failed Ardennes offensive on the Western Front, Hitler had returned to Berlin after an absence of several years. By this time, both of the field headquarters at which he had spent much of the war—the Eagle's Nest, near the German border with Belgium, and the

himself from his past for decades but finally told his story in his memoir, *In Hitler's Bunker* (Lyons Press; 2004), and who spoke with TIME for this book. "Even at that moment, with Berlin surrounded and Russian shells falling all over the city, it didn't occur to me that we could possibly lose the war."

Yet Lehmann found the encounter sobering. "I had seen him speak in Breslau, in 1938," Lehmann says. "Then, he had looked tall and strong—like a leader. He had impressed me as a captivating person who created an atmosphere, an energy, that enveloped everybody around him. Even in a large hall, his eyes had a hypnotic effect. He seemed in complete control."

Wolf's Lair in East Prussia, near the Russian border—were uncomfortably close to the advancing armies of his enemies.

Germany's capital was a city for which Hitler had little love —nor had aristocratic Berlin society ever fully embraced the unpolished Austrian corporal. No matter: with time running out, Hitler had few options. He would have been more comfortable in his Alpine retreat at Berchtesgaden, but for political reasons this was out of the question. "How can anyone tell a nation to continue fighting if the order comes from a weekend chalet?" he had protested to his entourage.

One reason Hitler had avoided going to Berlin after mid-1943 was that the city was increasingly being reduced to rubble by Allied bombers. Because of this, a complex of bunkers that had originally been constructed in 1936 beneath Hitler's Reich Chancellery building was expanded in 1943. The addition was buried 50 ft. below the garden of the Chancellery, beneath a concrete slab 10 feet thick. It was designed to withstand direct hits from the most powerful bombs in the U.S., British and Russian arsenals.

The older, less deeply buried section of the complex came to be known as the *Vorbunker* ("front bunker"), while the newer, deeper wing was called the the *Führerbunker* ("leader bunker"). The old and new sections of the shelter were con-

INSIDE Photographer William Vandivert took this picture of a young Russian soldier standing amid a disorderly jumble in the bunker. Undated, the photo was taken at least several days following Hitler's suicide; only Russian troops and photographers were present for the city's fall

SIGHTSEERS A Russian soldier shows British troops the trench where—he claimed—the bodies of Hitler and Eva Braun were burned in the Reich Chancellery garden after their suicide

SEAT OF POWER Winston Churchill, who famously preached "In victory, magnanimity," eschews his better tendencies to indulge in a well-earned bit of gloating. Visiting a conquered and occupied Berlin on July 1, 1945, he went to the Reich Chancellery and sat in a chair believed to have been used by Hitler in the *Führerbunker*

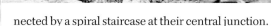

nected by a spiral staircase at their central junction.

By late March, the Allied carpet bombing of Berlin had become so frequent and accurate that Hitler abandoned his offices and apartment in the Chancellery and took up residence full time in his underground warren of windowless concrete rooms, the walls of which were always damp with condensation. And, as always, his entourage of sycophants and paladins followed him down the steps.

"On my first visit to the bunker, late on April 20," Lehmann recalls, "Axmann came with me to introduce me to the security chief and explained that I should be issued a pass. By the following day, however, the security people had come to know me.

INSIDE THE BUNKER

dolf Hitler's underground bunker was located 50 ft. beneath
garden at the Reich Chancellery building. The older
ection (Vorbunker) was built in 1936; an addition
Führerbunker) was built in 1943. Constructed by
he civil engineering firm Hochtief, experts in
he use of steel-reinforced concrete, the
unker was shielded by a 10-ft.-thick
oncrete slab overhead

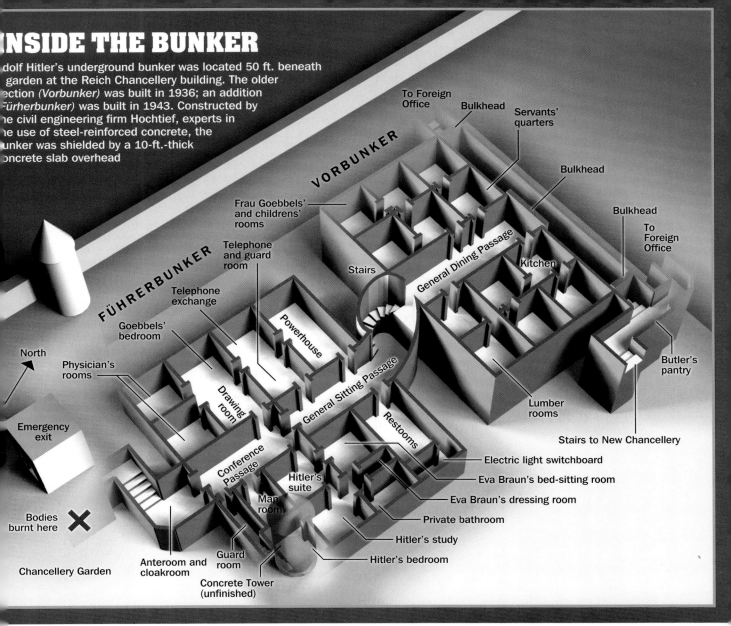

Hitler's bodyguards started calling me 'Der Junge'—the young man. My immediate impression of the bunker was that it reminded me of an air raid shelter. Particularly because of the sounds of the ventilating equipment and the diesel engines used as generators. It also had the same smell as an air raid shelter—the smell of damp concrete. Although it was not a luxurious facility, some of the staff had tried to make it less oppressive. They brought some of the nice furniture downstairs from the Chancellery, and put carpets on the floors and hung pictures on the walls."

FROM HIS FIRST DAY AS A MESSENGER IN HITLER'S BUNKER, Lehmann understood that it was a world apart. Occasionally, a conference room door would open and the boy would glimpse Hitler inside. Although the dictator was often conferring with his generals, Lehmann was sometimes surprised to see Hitler poring over architectural models of the Austrian city of Linz—Hitler's hometown, for which he had grand plans. "Berlin was literally crumbling, and the bunker itself was shaking from Russian artillery," Lehmann recalls,

"and yet he was poring over blueprints and making adjustments to plans that he must have know would never be built."

On his second day in the bunker, Lehmann encountered another of Hitler's fawning familiars: Martin Bormann, the chief of the Nazi Party bureaucracy. "Although he was always a sycophant around Hitler," Lehmann recalls, "Bormann was astonishingly arrogant in his dealings with everyone else. When he saw me walking into the bunker with a message, he didn't know who I was. But he wouldn't lower himself to ask me directly. Instead he asked one of the guards, speaking about me as if I weren't there."

On April 22, Lehmann met Nazi propaganda chief Joseph Goebbels. "He arrived with his wife Magda and their six children," Lehmann recalls. "He announced that he was moving into the bunker with his family." While the wife and children settled into bedrooms in the Vorbunker section, Goebbels closeted himself with Hitler and Bormann in the Führerbunker. Earlier in the day, Hitler announced to his entire staff for the first time that he believed the war was lost and he intended to kill himself, rather than fall into Russian hands. But

"TILL DEATH" This undated photograph was found among Eva Braun's personal photo albums following the war

Goebbels and Bormann (who had no desire to die in Berlin and were intent on persuading Hitler to flee to his Berchtesgaden retreat while it was still possible) rallied their leader's spirits.

Of Goebbels, Lehmann recalls, "he had a club foot and I think he was always trying to make up for this deformity by sounding intelligent and commanding. He spoke always like he was giving orders—in a rapid, staccato voice. But even if he didn't succeed in making himself charismatic, Goebbels did look better than most people in the bunker—he didn't appear to be tired or worn out."

BY APRIL 25 HITLER HAD APPARENTLY DECIDED THAT HE would not leave Berlin—or his bunker—alive. The rescue missions he had ordered hadn't materialized. "I intend to continue fighting as long as there is a single soldier with a single bullet under my command," he said bitterly. "And when the last soldier deserts, I will shoot myself." In a calmer moment, he said to Goebbels, "It's the only chance to restore my personal reputation … If we leave the world stage in disgrace, we'll have lived for nothing."

The only orders Hitler had left to give were for every unit to continue fighting to the last man; his only goal was to stave off the inevitable as long as possible. On April 28, he was told that Russian soldiers would be coming down the steps into the bunker no later than May 1—and probably much sooner. On this day, Eva Braun (who had decided to share Hitler's fate) walked up the stairs to the Chancellery garden to look at the sun one last time. Hitler followed, but when a Russian artillery shell exploded in the garden, he turned back without a word.

In the last 48 hours of Hitler's life, the decorum that the dictator had always insisted upon in his household began to break down. Many of the bunker staff were drunk. Officers smoked in Hitler's presence—behavior strictly forbidden in other times. When Hitler's secretary, Traudl Junge, ventured upstairs to retrieve some office supplies from the Chancellery, she was shocked to see SS guards having sex with young women in the building's ornate reception rooms.

On April 29, the day Hitler married Eva Braun, Lehmann saw the Führer alive for the last time. "I was standing in the main hallway, waiting for a reply to a message I had just brought in," he recalls. "An SS officer was asleep on the floor next to where I was standing. A door opened from a conference room, and Hitler walked out, directly in front of me. At that instant, a Russian shell landed directly above us. The bunker shook, and plaster dust fell from the ceiling onto both of us. I was so startled by the explosion and by seeing Hitler that I forgot to salute. But he didn't notice. He just walked past, as if he didn't see me—or anything. He was deep in thought.

"Although I had been in and out of the bunker dozens of times, I hadn't seen Hitler for a few days," Lehmann says, "and even in that short time, his appearance had deteriorated again. He had the appearance of a ghost, and also now looked as if he had jaundice. When the shell hit, he raised his arm to steady himself … it was shaking so badly that it took him a moment to find the wall. Then he walked past me and was gone."

The next day, April 30, Hitler committed suicide, along with Eva Braun. She took poison. Whether he also swallowed cyanide, fired a pistol into his temple or perhaps did both is still a matter of some dispute. The Goebbels family soon followed. Later that day, Lehmann returned to the bunker to deliver another batch of messages. "The ground near the entrance was smoking," he remembers. "And one of the SS guards told me that this was where they had burned Hitler and Eva Braun's corpses."

Afterward, "Bormann became even more arrogant," Lehmann says. "Before killing himself, Hitler had promoted him to chief of the Nazi Party. So Bormann, who was now drunk, demanded that Axmann gather all of the remaining Hitler Youth in Berlin to serve as his personal bodyguard and escort him out of the city. Axmann refused, which probably saved the lives of those of us who had survived to that point. After that conversation, I never saw Bormann again."

As the last inhabitants of the bunker fled into the chaos of the Russian advance, Lehmann linked up with other Hitler Youth. They tried to march west, with the hope of surrendering to the Americans instead of the Russians. But as they began their march, Lehmann was hit by shrapnel from an exploding shell; temporarily paralyzed, he was partially buried beneath the rubble of a collapsed building.

"When I awoke, two days later," he says, "a female Russian doctor who spoke perfect German asked me whether I was a fascist. I told her no, and they shipped me back to Breslau. After the paralysis passed, I found out that my family were in the American area of occupation. So I walked for days to get to the border, then swam across a river to escape the Russian zone."

"When I was debriefed," Lehmann recalls, his voice growing softer, "the American who questioned me was a Jewish officer who was fluent in German. He showed me newsreel documentaries about the liberation of two concentration camps—Bergen-Belsen and Buchenwald. I was sick to my stomach— less from the pictures than from the thought that I had played a part in this. It was so unbelievable. I searched for an explanation as to how this man, who had seemed like the savior of Germany, was actually the biggest criminal in history. Sixty years later, I am still looking for an explanation." ∎

The Lives and Deaths of Hitler's Accomplices

Many of those in Adolf Hitler's inner circle had been at his side since the the failed Munich Beer Hall Putsch of 1923. Two of them were in the bunker when Hitler died; three committed suicide; only two ever stood trial for their crimes

Hermann Göring

The larger-than-life leader of Germany's air force was one of the few top Nazis who faced Allied justice after the war. The erstwhile World War I flying ace ultimately lost favor with Hitler as the Luftwaffe was overpowered by the U.S. and British air forces; he was expelled from the party in 1945 and arrested. Taken into custody after the war, he was sentenced to die at the Nuremberg war-crimes tribunals, below, but enjoyed a last laugh: he swallowed a hidden capsule of poison and died the night before he was to be hanged, left.

Heinrich Himmler

The chief architect of Hitler's gruesome, far-flung archipelago of concentration and death camps, Himmler was an early Nazi who participated in the Beer Hall Putsch. As armies began closing in on Germany, Hitler placed the militarily unqualified Himmler in charge of the Western Front in 1944, then of the Eastern Front in 1945. Hampered by overpowering Soviet superiority in men, weapons and fuel, Himmler was unable to hold off Stalin's armies and was replaced. In April, 1945, Himmler attempted a peace feeler to the Allies seeking some form of German capitulation; when Hitler learned of this, he ordered Himmler arrested. Himmler fled and was seized by British troops in Bremen. Before he could be questioned, he swallowed cyanide and died, at top.

Dr. Joseph Goebbels

Hitler's master imagemaker enjoyed a title steeped in cynicism— or self-delusion: he was the Reich's Minister of Enlightenment and Propaganda. After graduating from the University of Heidelberg, Goebbels joined the Nazi Party in 1922, where his quick intelligence and way with words helped him climb the ranks. Beginning as the editor of the Nazi newspaper, he was appointed Gauleiter of Berlin in 1926 and was named the head of the Nazi propaganda organization in 1929, four years before Hitler came to power. A fervid believer in Hitler and his cause, Goebbels stayed with the Führer to the end; his wife and six children moved into rooms in the bunker. After Hitler and Eva Braun committed suicide, as Russian troops closed in on central Berlin, Goebbels and his wife had

Hitler's physician administer morphine injections to the children, then crushed cyanide capsules in their mouths. Then the Minister of Enlightenment and his wife killed themselves, either by poison or by the gun of a willing SS guard; the exact means is still unclear.

Martin Bormann, Rudolf Hess

Hess, right, was Hitler's close friend; he took part in the 1923 Beer Hall Putsch, and Hitler dictated *Mein Kampf* to him as they served time for the deed. In May 1941, Hess flew a plane to Scotland on a one-man peace mission but was imprisoned. After the war, he was tried and sentenced to life in jail; he committed suicide in 1987. Boorman, left, once Hess's aide, became Hitler's top deputy during the war. In the bunker, he witnessed Hitler's marriage to Eva Braun and their suicide, then fled, either escaping or dying in the attempt. Over the years, stories of sightings of the lone "escaped" Nazi circulated, but in 1972 a Berlin work crew dug up a set of bones that were identified as Boorman's.

In the Ruins of the Reich

Hitler is dead, Berlin has fallen, and the war should be over. But at the last minute, Germans play for time—and deliverance from the Russians

AT LAST, IT WAS OVER—OR NEARLY OVER. AS MAY 1, 1945 dawned, Adolf Hitler and much of his inner circle lay dead in the flaming ruins of Berlin. Most of those who hadn't committed suicide with their leader were now on the run or in hiding. But a handful of the Führer's accomplices remained to inherit the disaster he had wrought.

Hitler's last testament, dictated less than an hour before his death, named the head of the German navy, Admiral Karl Doenitz, as his successor. Hitler divided other posts among those who supported him to the end, naming Joseph Goebbels Chancellor and Martin Boorman the new chief of the Nazi Party. But both men had died within hours of Hitler, so Doenitz was now the closest thing Germany had to a leader.

Finally free of Hitler's spell, Doenitz quickly realized that the only task that remained for him was to end the war as quickly as possible. But he wished to do so on his terms, rather than those of the Allies. So Doenitz commanded the troops facing the Russians to continue to fight, while ordering those on the Western Front to surrender immediately. His hope was to avoid the bitter pill of "unconditional surrender" that had been the shared goal of the U.S., Britain and Russia since 1943. Another consideration was also behind Doenitz's maneuvers: above all, he wanted to clear the way for the largest possible number of Germans, both civilians and military personnel, to move west and fall into the hands of the British and Americans, from whom they could expect to receive more humane treatment than from the Russian troops, who had proved to be fixed on revenge and rape. Doenitz was partially successful: his delaying gambit allowed an estimated 1.8 million German troops who would otherwise have fallen into Russian hands to surrender to U.S. and British troops.

Surrender—or, maddeningly, a series of surrenders—followed. Berlin formally capitulated on May 2, as did German forces in northern Italy. The next day, hoping to continue to

TOURISTS: In late July, women of Britain's Auxiliary Territorial Service take a stroll through the shattered Court of Honor in the Chancellery building

direct events for as long as possible, Doenitz moved his headquarters in northern Germany from Plon to Flensburg, several hundred miles from both the Eastern and Western fronts. From here, he directed German forces still fighting in Holland, Denmark and the northwestern sector of Germany to lay down their arms on May 4. Resistance in the mountains of southern Germany stopped May 5, and Nazi troops in Austria laid down their arms two days later.

During this time, Doenitz and his new "Cabinet" went through the farcical motions of governing a nation that had effectively ceased to exist. Each morning, they were greeted by an honor guard (still armed with rifles and live ammunition), after which Doenitz would convene a Cabinet meeting with the Third Reich's new leaders. Among them were Albert Speer, Hitler's former Armaments Minister, who would later recall of these meetings that there was almost nothing to discuss. At one point, Heinrich Himmler showed up and volunteered to participate in the new government. He was asked to leave and disappeared into the chaos of the Nazi apocalypse.

One of the few orders Doenitz issued that had any effect was to forbid the *"Heil Hitler"* greeting among Germany's military and restore the traditional military salute. But while Germany played for time, the patience of Allied leaders wore thin. Testing the well-known tensions among the victors,

Doenitz sent a delegation to Eisenhower's headquarters at Rheims on May 5 to propose that the Germans continue fighting the Russians, with U.S. and British support. Eisenhower refused even to consider such an idea.

The following day, Doenitz sent a different delegation to Rheims, proposing essentially the same arrangement. This time, Eisenhower told the German representatives that if they didn't surrender unconditionally that very day, the Allies would renew air raids and bomb what was left of Germany into submission. Reluctantly—and after communicating with Doenitz once again—the emissaries acceded to Eisenhower's terms. At 2:41 am on May 7, the instrument of surrender was signed, stipulating that Germany would cease fighting on all fronts within 24 hours.

Determined not to accord undue courtesy to people he regarded as criminals, Eisenhower refused to enter the room in which the surrender ceremony took place until after the German delegation had signed the document. When the unsmiling Eisenhower finally did walk in, the Germans saluted. Not returning their salute, Eisenhower coldly asked, "Do you understand the document of surrender you have signed?" When the Germans answered yes, Eisenhower and his aides turned and left the room without another word.

The following day, May 8, was officially declared V-E day,

but even then, the last act was not finished: the Russians were furious that the document signed by the Germans did not replicate the exact text that had been agreed upon by Roosevelt, Churchill and Stalin at the Yalta conference. Seizing upon this momentary discord, the Germans announced that they considered the May 7 surrender "not final" and once again began trying to maneuver themselves between the Russians and the Western Allies. So another surrender ceremony (this one in Berlin) was organized for May 9. By that time, the shooting had stopped, the victors had begun to look homeward, and the vanquished had begun to face their reckoning. As an odd historical footnote, however, Russians celebrated V-E day on May 9, while the other Allied nations filled their streets with parades and ticker tape on May 8.

On May 9, the Germany army issued its last report and final orders. They read, in part, "On the orders of the Grand Admiral, the Wehrmacht has stopped the fight which had become hopeless. The struggle lasting almost six years is accordingly at an end."

Less grandiose, but far more eloquent, was the brief text of the last message sent from the Supreme Headquarters of the Allied Expeditionary Force to Washington. In its entirety, it read, "The mission of this Allied Force was fulfilled at 0241, local time, May 7, 1945. Eisenhower." ∎

CHAIN GANG In September 1945, women Berliners were still forming lines to remove rubble from the streets of the city; they were paid for their labor by occupying Soviet authorities under an inviting, if brutal, rubric: "Those willing to help will eat more"

COMRADE KILROY WAS HERE Russian troops left their calling card in Berlin's Reichstag in the form of graffiti. When the building was restored in the 1990s by British architect Norman Foster, some of the graffiti were preserved, a reminder of its storied history

DONE! Holding the pens used by the Germans to sign the surrender documents, Dwight Eisenhower forms Churchill's V-for-Victory sign. Behind the pens is Ike's chief of staff, General Bedell Smith; between the two Americans is Ike's British aide, Kay Summersby

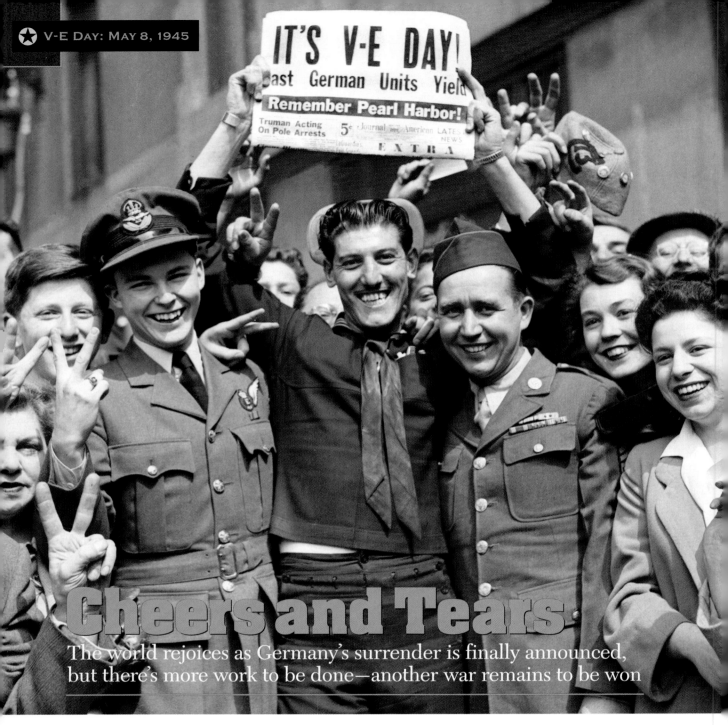

IT'S V-E DAY!
East German Units Yield
Remember Pearl Harbor!
Truman Acting
On Pole Arrests 5¢ Journal American LATES NEWS
EXTRA

Cheers and Tears

The world rejoices as Germany's surrender is finally announced,
but there's more work to be done—another war remains to be won

HARRY TRUMAN AWAKENED AFTER HIS FIRST NIGHT OF sleep in his new home, the White House; the morning was chilly and gray. He entered the Oval Office, accompanied by his family, aides and Cabinet members. It was to be a day of celebration, but the festivities were a bit more earth-shaking than the President's 61st birthday, which just happened to be this day, May 8, 1945. At 9 a.m. he went on the radio, delivering in a quiet, clear voice the speech that had been prepared for a week, awaiting this moment: "This is a solemn but a glorious hour. General Eisenhower informs me that the forces of Germany have surrendered to the United Nations. The flags of freedom fly over all Europe."

Truman's message, while welcome, was a bit of an anticlimax. Nine days before, Americans had begun to celebrate

after the Associated Press broadcast a peace bulletin, but the party stopped abruptly when the news turned out to be false. The news—correct news, this time—that Germany had unconditionally surrendered to the Allies had percolated across the world the day before Truman's speech, yet it had not been followed by an official statement from any of the Big Three Allied powers, nor by a news bulletin. In fact, the U.S. government had slapped the A.P. with an embargo when it tried to release the story of Germany's surrender.

On that Monday, May 7, some 500,000 people had gathered in Times Square by the afternoon, waiting for the news flash announcing peace in Europe to scurry around the famed "zipper" sign on the old New York *Times* Tower, but after five hours Mayor Fiorello LaGuardia's unmistakable voice barked

over a loudspeaker, "Go home … or return to your jobs!" In the harbor, a police launch sped to investigate a rumor rippling through the crowd that a German submarine had surfaced, flying a white flag. The "enemy sub" turned out to be a U.S. Navy vessel, with the sailor's laundry hung out to dry.

Tuesday was different, as TIME reported in its May 14 issue: "The people began to get the self-conscious feeling that they were witnessing history. In Manhattan, as if someone had pulled a giant lever, the windows went up and paper tumbled in torrents, soon after the President's first words were heard. For minutes, a diapason of booming whistles from the gray ships in the North [Hudson] River seemed to drown out everything. Then, as if they might burst unless they let it off, people began to shout."

NEW YORK CITY Sailors, soldiers and civilians join the huge throngs in Times Square. "I only wish President Roosevelt had lived to see this day," said Harry Truman

CHICAGO A priest leads students at a Roman Catholic school, St. Columbkille, in a flag-waving celebration

The cheers were echoed across the Atlantic. In London, effigies of Hitler were hoisted on lampposts; guards regiments paraded through the streets; pubs were packed; and G.I.s on furlough seized the opportunity to stage peace offensives upon willing British lasses. Jovial crowds milled about outside the gates of Buckingham Palace, shouting for an appearance by the King. He did not oblige, but when three servants stepped onto the balcony to take in the throng, the crowd

LONDON Winston Churchill told rejoicing Britons: "My dear friends, this is your hour ... We were the first, in this ancient island, to draw the sword against tyranny"

MOSCOW Jubilant crowds hoist a soldier in Red Square, where V-E day was celebrated on May 9, as Stalin was hesitant to accept the German surrender signed with U.S. and British but not Soviet generals

PARIS France's great World War II celebration was Liberation Day, Aug. 25, 1944, but V-E day offered another chance for U.S. soldiers and French mademoiselles to solidify alliances

OKINAWA These glum, drenched Americans can't join in the party. Yet the war in the Pacific, which at this time promised to drag on for years, would be over in three months

gave them a welcome fit for a royal. Winston Churchill, however, was happy to address the crowds, and the old bulldog reminded them of their finest hour, the bleak summer of 1940. "There we stood, alone," he said. "Did anyone want to give in?" The crowd roared "No!" "Were we downhearted?" "No!"

In Paris, which could never top its day of liberation in August of 1944, the Eiffel Tower was illuminated with spotlights, and the Seine glittered with the reflection of fireworks. In Rome, snake dances wound through the streets. In Stockholm, magnums of champagne dangled outside office windows, an invitation for passers-by to quaff. In Jerusalem, people congratulated each other in English, Hebrew and Arabic, and the Tower of David and old city walls were bathed in floodlights.

Joy! Yet the rapture was modified, for there was still work to be done. As President Truman had reminded his listeners in his White House announcement: "We must work to finish the war. Our victory is but half won. The West is free, but the East is still in bondage to the treacherous tyranny of the Japanese. When the last Japanese division has surrendered unconditionally, then only will our fighting job be done." ∎

"The lights went out and the bombs came down. But every man, woman and child in the country had no thought of quitting the struggle. London can take it." —Winston Churchill

NO PLACE LIKE HOME:
The first of 34,000 Londoners evacuated to Leicester began returning to St. Pancras Station on Aug. 4 on "homeward special" trains

To Victory in the

GUADALCANAL Marines land on the island in the Solomons in August 1942, in one of the first U.S. offensives of the war. Taking the island required six months of constant fighting, at a cost of some 6,000 Marines wounded and dead and the loss of eight major U.S. Navy ships

PACIFIC

THE PHILIPPINES After holding off a superior Japanese force at Bataan, U.S. forces surrendered on April 9. The Japanese sent the POWs on a 60-mile "death march" from Mariveles to San Fernando, left

SINGAPORE Japanese troops cheer the fall of the city-state; the British surrendered after a week's fighting. Prime Minister Winston Churchill called it "the worst disaster and largest capitulation in British history"

HAWAII: Right, the battleship USS *Arizona* begins to sink during the Dec. 7 attack on Pearl Harbor. Japanese planes sank 3 battleships, capsized 1 and damaged 4 more. Three light cruisers and 3 destroyers were severely damaged, and 92 Navy planes and 77 Army planes were also lost. The Japanese lost only 28 fighter planes and 5 midget submarines

Japan Rising

Emerging from the jungles of Burma in May 1942 after a harrowing 22-day retreat on foot, U.S. General Joseph Stilwell defied headline writers in America who were proclaiming him a hero. "I claim we got a hell of a beating," Stilwell declared, "And it's as humiliating as hell."

The acerbic general was speaking of the U.S.-British-Chinese collapse in the face of a smashing Japanese advance in Southeast Asia, but he might as well have been describing the past four months in the entire Pacific, a period in which the U.S. and Britain were utterly humiliated by Japan's well-armed, well-disciplined and well-led war machine.

The series of setbacks began with Japan's highly successful surprise attack on the giant U.S. naval base at Pearl Harbor in Hawaii on Dec. 7, 1941. By day's end, 18 U.S. ships were sunk or severely damaged, more than 2,000 Americans were dead, and the Pacific fleet was crippled. The only saving grace: by sheer luck, some of the U.S. Navy's biggest aircraft carriers weren't berthed at the harbor that day. The same day, Japanese planes destroyed more than 100 U.S. airplanes, including half the B-17 bombers in the region, on the ground at Clark Field on Luzon Island in the Philippines.

In the weeks that followed, U.S. and British territories toppled like dominoes before the Japanese juggernaut. On Dec. 25, the British colony at Hong Kong fell; on Feb. 15, 60,000 British surrendered at Singapore. In the Philippines, 78,000 Americans surrendered at Bataan on April 9, and the garrison at Corregidor fell on May 6. Together, these were and remain the greatest military surrenders in U.S. history. As with Stilwell in Burma, the battle in the Philippines ended with America's chief Army general, Douglas MacArthur, driven to ignominious retreat— he fled in a small PT boat.

By May 1942, the Empire of the Rising Sun was ascendant all across the Pacific. Stilwell, MacArthur, America and Britain had taken a hell of a beating.

MIDWAY The smoking hulk of the Japanese heavy cruiser *Mikuma* lists to port; it was among the five major Japanese ships sunk by U.S. planes at the Battle of Midway, widely considered the most decisive conflict in U.S. naval history

Fighting Back

Branding Japan's attack on Pearl Harbor "a day which will live in infamy," President Franklin D. Roosevelt pledged in the same address that "the American people in their righteous might will win through to absolute victory." Sadly, the President's strong words belied his weak hand in the Pacific. America's Navy was battered, and its Army base in the South Pacific, the

Philippines, was also under attack. When the U.S. managed to retaliate for Pearl Harbor with a daring bombing raid on Tokyo on April 18, 1942, led by Army Air Force Lieut. Colonel Jimmy Doolittle, the coup was hailed as a major victory. But F.D.R. and his military advisers knew that the gambit was the strategic equivalent of slapping a Band-Aid on a hemorrhage.

In truth, America was reeling. Yet fate,

luck, courage and alert intelligence work would combine in the spring and summer of 1942 to bring the U.S. two immensely significant victories in the Pacific.

Japan's series of triumphs bred euphoria in its admirals and generals—"victory disease," they would later call it. Rather than pausing to consolidate their enormous gains across the Pacific, they now pushed on toward New Guinea,

THE CORAL SEA U.S. sailors abandon the exploding and sinking U.S.S. *Lexington* on May 8, 1942; almost all hands were rescued. Despite the loss of the big aircraft carrier, the battle stopped the Japanese advance in the South Pacific

the Solomon Islands and Australia.

Early in May a Japanese fleet steamed for Port Moresby, New Guinea, in the Coral Sea—Japan's staging point for an invasion of Australia. It was engaged by two big U.S. aircraft carriers, the U.S.S. *Yorktown* and *Lexington*, which had been alerted of the move two weeks earlier thanks to the breaking of Japanese radio codes by U.S. intelligence units. In a gripping battle fought by airplanes launched from aircraft carriers that never made visual contact, the U.S. turned back the Japanese but lost the *Lexington*. Although the Battle of the Coral Sea was technically a victory for the imperial navy, it stymied Japan's advance, halting the empire's momentum for the first time.

One month later, the U.S. Navy reversed that momentum, as two U.S. task forces combined to deal the main Japanese fleet a devastating defeat at the Battle of Midway, westernmost of Hawaii's inhabited islands. The U.S. lost the *Yorktown,* yet the Japanese lost four big carriers, 3,000 men (including 100 of its best pilots) and 322 planes. Japan would never regain its dominance of the Pacific skies. In one month, the tide of battle in the Pacific had turned.

◼ Uphill Battle

Japan's exhilarating skein of victories in the Pacific was finally halted at the Coral Sea and Midway, but the Allies faced a severe challenge in winning back the ground they had lost.

America entered the war woefully unprepared. The Army and Navy were desperately short of men and machines. Moreover, the U.S. was fighting two massive wars at once, and F.D.R. and his top military advisers agreed that defeating the Germans in Europe was more immediately imperative than beating the Japanese in Asia.

Progress in the Pacific was further hindered by interservice squabbles. With generals and admirals battling to take command in the region, Roosevelt made a Solomonic decision: Army General Douglas MacArthur would take charge in the South Pacific, while Navy Admiral Chester Nimitz would be given leadership elsewhere.

Slowly, America and its allies began to challenge the Japanese. Two counteroffensives were mounted in the months after Midway. Admiral Nimitz sent Marines onto the island of Guadalcanal in the Solomons; General MacArthur sent a ragtag force into New Guinea. Both campaigns would be ultimately successful, though at an enormous cost in Allied lives.

The year 1943 brought scant Allied progress. But the silence was deceiving: in the factories on the home front, American workers were churning out the planes, tanks and landing boats that would carry its troops to victory.

Finally, late in 1943, the U.S. mounted twin offensives that dictated the final pattern of the war. In November Nimitz sent the Marines into the Gilbert Islands at Tarawa Atoll in the central Pacific, again paying an exorbitant price for victory. Meanwhile, MacArthur's U.S. Army troops, with the welcome assistance of Australian units, battled entrenched Japanese units to extend the Allied foothold in New Guinea.

TARAWA U.S. Marines landed at Betio and Makin, two islands on Tarawa Atoll in the Gilbert Islands, in late November 1943. On Betio the 2,500 Japanese troops and some 2,000 captive laborers were so well entrenched it took 35,000 Marines four days to take the island, at a cost of 1,500 men

BOUGAINVILLE Above, U.S. Army troops shielded by a tank secure an area on the island in the Solomons in March 1944, five months after the first U.S. landing. Australian troops took over much of this campaign; some Japanese units held out, not surrendering until August 1945

THE MARIANAS At left, a Japanese bomber, trailing fire, streaks toward the escort carrier U.S.S. *Kitkun Bay* in the Battle of the Philippine Sea. After some 375 Japanese airplanes were felled in the "Marianas turkey shoot," U.S. Navy planes rained damage on the fleeing Japanese ships

■ The Allies Take the Offensive

As 1944 dawned, the U.S. was increasingly dominant in both the seas and skies of the Pacific. With more soldiers, pilots, planes and ships pouring into the theater every week, U.S. military strategists firmly believed they would eventually triumph over the Japanese, but they couldn't predict when, or exactly how, the war's end would come. Victory, they knew, would command a high price, for the Japanese warrior culture, Bushido, demanded that every army must fight to the last soldier, and every soldier must fight to his last breath. By now—on Guadalcanal and Tarawa, in the air and at sea—tough Japanese soldiers, pilots and sailors had proved that their devotion to Bushido was firm.

The pattern in the Pacific Theater was now set: moving west across the central Pacific and northwest from the South Pacific, the Allies would struggle to advance, island by island, upon the Japanese mainland, and the Japanese would dig into entrenched positions and fight to the last man for every inch of soil. With each hard-won victory, U.S. bombers drew closer to Japan's cities.

In the central Pacific, Admiral Nimitz continued the island campaign begun at Tarawa in late 1943, sending Marines ashore in the Marshalls at Kwajalein and Eniwetok in early 1944, then into Guam and Saipan in the Marianas during June and July. In the Battle of the Philippine Sea off the Marianas on June 19, the imperial navy tried to block the U.S. advance, but U.S. planes and gunners downed some 375 Japanese airplanes and sank three carriers, further crippling the Japanese fleet.

In the South Pacific, another prize beckoned. General MacArthur's troops extended their control over New Guinea, leapfrogging up the northern coast of the island in a series of amphibious landings covered by airpower. Each victory brought MacArthur closer to his cherished goal, an invasion of the Philippines, which would allow him to fulfill his 1942 vow: "I shall return."

SITUATION REPORT: JULY 1944

U.S.S.R.

LAKE BAIKAL

SEA OF OKHOTSK

OUTER MONGOLIA

MANCHURIA

Peking

KOREA

SEA OF JAPAN

JAPAN

Tokyo

**U.S. bombs
4/18/42**

CHINA

TIBET

EAST CHINA SEA

**Britsh surrender
12/25/41**

INDIA

FORMOSA
(Taiwan)

Hong Kong

**Battle of Philippine Sea
U.S. naval victory
6/19/44**

PACIFIC OCEAN

BURMA

SIAM

**U.S. surrenders
5/6/42**

MARIANA ISLANDS

Wake

Saipan

**U.S. invades
6/15/44**

FRENCH INDOCHINA

Corregidor

Guam

Saigon

SOUTH CHINA SEA

PHILIPPINES

CAROLINE IS.

MARSHALL ISLANDS

MALAYSIA

PALAU IS.

Sumatra

Singapore

Borneo

**Allies capture
1/2/43**

**Allies invade
11/1/43**

Ta

Celebes

NETHERLANDS EAST INDIES

Java

NEW GUINEA

Buna

Bougainville Island

SOLOMON ISLA

New Georgia

Guadalcana

**British surrender
2/15/42**

Port Moresby

CORAL SEA

NEW HEBRI

**Allies invade
8/7/42**

**Japanese control
5/20/42**

**Battle of Coral Sea
U.S. stops Japan's Navy
5/7-8/42**

NEW CALED

AUSTRALIA

**Allies control
6/21/43**

INDIAN OCEAN

BERING SEA

Alaska (U.S.)

Aleutian Islands

NORTH PACIFIC OCEAN

Allied territory
July 26, 1942

Japanese-occupied territory
July 26, 1942

Neutral territory
1942

Taken from Japanese
by July 1944

Midway

**Battle of Midway
U.S. naval victory
6/4-5/42**

Hawaii (U.S.)

Pearl Harbor

**Japan strikes
12/7/41**

**Allies control
3/1/44**

**Allies invade
11/20/43**

LBERT
ANDS

SAMOA ISLANDS

SOUTH
PACIFIC OCEAN

SKULL SESSION At the critical strategy meeting in Hawaii, Admiral Nimitz refers to a giant map of the Pacific, while General MacArthur, F.D.R. and Admiral William Leahy look on. Later, F.D.R. chose the Philippines as the next objective

Three Men, Two Strategies

In July 1944, President Franklin D. Roosevelt met in Hawaii with his two top commanders in the Pacific—the Army's General Douglas MacArthur and the Navy's Admiral Chester Nimitz— to plan the final stages of the war against Japan.

For 30 months now, MacArthur and Nimitz, both brilliant, headstrong leaders, had agreed on only one thing: there should be a single commander for all American and Allied forces in the Pacific. Each had proposed the right man for the job—himself. Early in the war effort, F.D.R. and his top military advisers had brokered a compromise; the Army and the Navy would each get its own Pacific war to fight. The resulting division of labor, men, supplies and objectives had satisfied no one. Now a critical choice of America's next steps in the war had to be made.

Japan's empire was reeling: its heady, high noon of victory had lasted less than six months, from Pearl Harbor to the Battle of the Coral Sea. A few weeks later, at the Battle of Midway, the sun had begun to set on Tokyo's ambitions, and throughout 1942 and 1943, the shadows had lengthened at Guadalcanal, Tarawa and Burma. The current year had brought no relief to the would-be rulers of the Greater East-Asian Co-Prosperity Sphere. The Marshall Islands had been retaken before the end of February; in June, only a month before the Hawaii conference, Japan had lost three more carriers, almost 500 aircraft and hundreds of veteran pilots at the Battle of the Philippine Sea off the Marianas chain.

What may have seemed to the Japanese to be a carefully choreographed apocalypse was, in reality, two quite separate wars. From the south, MacArthur was leading an amphibious island-hopping campaign that had driven the Japanese from New Guinea and now was threatening the Philippines. From the east, Nimitz was commanding an advance on the seas and the islands stretching across the central Pacific from Midway into Japan's home waters.

What next? In Hawaii, F.D.R. heard the two men out. MacArthur argued for invading the Philippines; Nimitz proposed bypassing the Philippines and invading Formosa.

Again, the President divvied up duties. In August, he decided that the Philippines would indeed be the next objective, but that Nimitz and the Navy would take the baton after that and lead the final push into Japan's home islands. For MacArthur, the moment must have been bittersweet. His triumphal return to the islands would mark one of the high points of his life, but it would also effectively mean the end of his war. Nimitz, however, was thrilled: the war he had wanted to fight ever since Pearl Harbor was finally about to begin.

"I Have Returned"

General Douglas MacArthur and a mighty U.S. force land on Leyte,
and the U.S. Navy wins one of the war's most decisive battles at sea

AS THE LANDING CRAFT BOBBED UP AND DOWN IN THE
surf on the morning of Oct. 20, 1944, the occupants
grew increasingly tense. They were within sight of
the shore of Leyte Island, which only hours before
had been the scene of an amphibious assault second in size
only to the D-day landings in Europe four months earlier.
Gunfire still crackled on the beach, and personnel carriers
were still disgorging men and supplies. But the senior officer
aboard the landing boat wasn't concerned about stray bullets.
He had waited more than two years to set foot once again
upon Philippine soil, and he felt that his personal honor and
his professional future were poised on the next few moments.

Onshore, however, all was chaos. The harried Navy controller at Leyte's Red Beach sector, where the 24th Infantry
Division had landed at dawn, was trying to keep order among
the endless stream of boats moving toward the beach while
wounded were being brought down to the waterfront and
evacuated. Told that a landing craft carrying VIPs would take
precedence over this knot of vessels, and that he would have
to clear the beach to await its arrival, the anonymous traffic
director bellowed, "Let 'em walk!"

So it was that the landing craft bearing General Douglas
MacArthur back to his "second homeland," the Philippines,

**LOOKING UP As a landing barge
approaches the beaches of Leyte,
all eyes turn to the skies, where
U.S. and Japanese fighter planes
are locked in combat**

was forced to run aground a dozen yards from shore and disgorge its passengers into knee-deep surf. Several biographers have attributed the look of grim determination that photographs show on the general's face at that moment to his fury at the Navy controller who had seemingly botched MacArthur's carefully choreographed return to the islands. Yet when the vainglorious general later saw newsreels of his landing on Leyte, he was so stirred by the sight of himself wading heroically ashore that he ordered his staff to arrange for all subsequent island embarkations to begin offshore, so he could walk through knee-deep water onto the beach.

Just as he mastered the photo-op long before the term was coined, MacArthur knew the value of a good sound bite. "I shall return," he had famously vowed 31 months before, when, under direct orders from Franklin D. Roosevelt, he had abandoned the fortress of Corregidor and its 12,000 men, beating an ignominious retreat in a torpedo boat. Now he declared into a radio microphone, "People of the Philippines ... "I have returned ... The hour of your redemption is here."

That redeeming hour, for both the Philippines and MacArthur, had been set in motion at a secret conference in Hawaii three months earlier, to which Roosevelt had summoned the two feuding warlords of the Pacific Theater, Mac-

DIRECT HIT Kamikazes made their first appearance at Leyte. Above, struck by a suicide pilot, the U.S.S. *St. Lo* explodes in flames. The small escort carrier sank within 30 minutes; all hands were rescued

Arthur and Navy chief Admiral Chester Nimitz. The Navy wanted to bypass the Philippines entirely and instead target Formosa, Nimitz told FDR, noting that the island could serve as a steppingstone to China and then to Japan itself.

MacArthur's argument was less strategic than personal. He maintained that the U.S. had a moral obligation to rescue the many thousands of American prisoners being held in the Philippines under deplorable conditions and to liberate the occupied Filipinos. In the last week of August, Roosevelt made his decision: MacArthur would return to the islands.

But where should he land? The obvious answer seemed to be Mindanao, headquarters of the largest Japanese garrison. But in early September, the pugnacious U.S. naval commander Admiral William F. ("Bull") Halsey had conducted an exploratory raid through the waters of the central Philippines. Much to Halsey's surprise and mild disappointment, he encountered almost no resistance. He had stumbled upon a secret overlooked by U.S. intelligence analysts: the Japanese Navy, increasingly short of ships, aircraft and fuel, was leaving large stretches of ocean almost entirely unpatrolled. This discovery argued for a landing on the large island of Leyte, which offered several advantages: it was lightly defended, boasted a large natural harbor, contained several airfields and could serve as a base for subsequent actions against both Mindanao Island to the south and Luzon Island to the north.

The U.S. force targeting Leyte was one of the mightiest invasion teams ever assembled: the Sixth Army, more than 200,000 men strong, was backed by the Fifth Air Force and two Navy fleets with a combined total of 35 aircraft carriers, 12 battleships, 28 cruisers and 150 destroyers, along with more than 700 landing craft and support vessels. When the U.S. Eighth Army joined the Sixth Army a few days after the invasion, their combined manpower would exceed the forces used to invade North Africa and Italy.

YET ON OCT. 20, EVEN AS U.S. TROOPS BEGAN TO LAND ON Leyte's beaches near Tacloban, Dugan and Tanuaun, a more consequential action was shaping up at sea. The Battle of Leyte Gulf was (and remains) the largest naval engagement in the history of armed conflict. It began three days after MacArthur's land forces touched the shore at Leyte and raged over an area the size of France for 96 hours. By the time

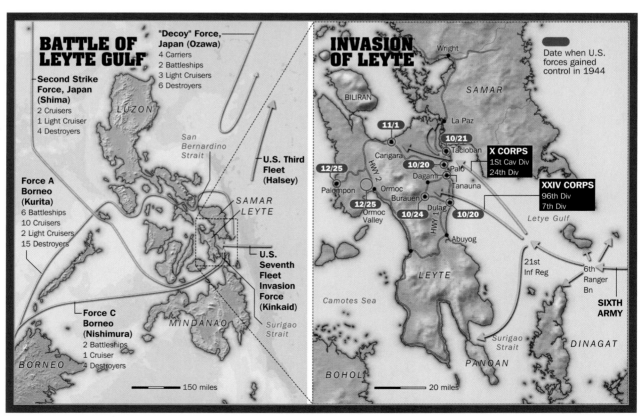

it was over, the Japanese navy had effectively ceased to exist as a meaningful fighting force.

The Japanese had taken MacArthur at his word: while maintaining only a light force in the seas around the islands, they had long been planning a strategy that would dispatch reinforcements to defend them against his return. The Japanese hoped to ambush MacArthur's troop transports, and the gunboats escorting them, on the approaches to the beach.

For this mission, Japan's naval chief, Admiral Soemu Toyoda, dispatched four armadas to the Philippines: two from Japan's home waters to the north, commanded by Admirals Kiyohide Shima and Jisaburo Ozawa, and two from Borneo to the south, under the command of Admirals Takeo Kurita and Shoji Nishimura. This was the bulk of the ships the Japanese navy had left after three years of war with the U.S., but the defense of the Philippines was vital: the island chain controlled the sea lanes between Japan and dozens of other islands from which the Japanese took essential supplies of rubber, oil and steel. Toyoda had no choice: he risked all to protect the Philippines.

On Oct. 23, Admiral Thomas Kinkaid, commander of the Seventh Fleet, learned of the forces approaching from Japan, and he steered his flagship, the U.S.S. *Nashville*, toward the waters north of the Philippines. His mission was to link up with Halsey's Third Fleet—16 fast carriers and six new battleships—and intercept the numerically superior Japanese force.

Knowing "Bull" Halsey's reputation for impulsiveness, Toyoda was preparing a trap for him. But before he could spring it, the battle was joined. On Oct. 23, moving toward the rendezvous with Halsey, submarines escorting Kinkaid's Seventh Fleet stumbled upon Kurita's Japanese task force headed north from Borneo. The subs sank two of the cruisers and damaged a third, but the Japanese fleet did not stay to engage them. The next day, planes from Halsey's carriers tracked the same force and sank one of its battleships. Still, Kurita's fleet from Borneo pressed on toward its rendezvous point at the San Bernardino Strait north of Leyte.

The following day, Oct. 25, Kinkaid's fleet discovered elements of Shima's flotilla sailing south from Japan. This unit had attempted a feint, sailing past Leyte, after which it planned to hook back northward and sail through the Surigao Strait. In this narrow strait the Japanese fleet ran directly into the battleships and carriers of Kinkaid's fleet. The U.S. ships executed a textbook naval maneuver known as "capping the T," in which they formed a crossbar to the stem created by the Japanese column. In such a position, the U.S. ships, with their broadsides facing the oncoming Japanese, were able to fire almost with impunity at the enemy vessels, whose bows pointed directly at the Americans—an angle from which naval guns

JAWS A pair of U.S. Coast Guard LSTs unload supplies on a Leyte beach. The troops onshore are building sandbag piers to speed up the process

are almost useless. Thus began a pitched 48-hour battle; when it ended, almost the entire Japanese fleet had been sunk.

Now Toyoda sprang his trap. The bait he dangled was Ozawa's fleet, just arriving from Japan's home waters. In the fog of battle, it looked impressive, but this task force consisted of obsolete battleships and sagging aircraft carriers stripped of their planes. With this "prize," Toyoda hoped to lure the impulsive Halsey—who liked to quote Admiral Nelson's maxim that "no captain can do very wrong if he places his ship alongside that of an enemy"—away from the San Bernardino Strait.

Halsey took the bait. Hearing sightings that a second armada was moving in from Japan, he rashly ordered his fleet into pursuit, leaving the crucial San Bernardino Strait guarded only by Kinkaid's force, the weaker of the two U.S. units. Now Kinkaid would have to continue the fight against the first of the fleets from Japan's home waters and still intercept the two Japanese fleets sailing from Borneo. With both U.S. task forces fully engaged, the troops still landing on Leyte would be left with little naval cover.

At dawn on Oct. 25, at Cape Engano, Halsey finally caught up with Ozawa's phantom flotilla. In less than a day, his guns and planes sank the entire fleet. But it was an empty triumph: while Halsey had been chasing his quarry, the remnants of Shima's fleet sailing from Japan and the two task forces steaming north from Borneo had converged on Leyte. Brushing past Kinkaid's outnumbered ships, they set upon the token U.S.

naval force guarding the rear of MacArthur's landing troops.

It was a one-sided battle, but the U.S. ships fought a desperate holding action. American destroyers charged directly at much larger Japanese battleships, at times veering so close that the Japanese ships couldn't lower their guns sufficiently to aim at them. This enabled the Americans to launch torpedo attacks at point-blank range. Handfuls of lightly armed planes from the small escort carriers assigned to the invasion beaches engaged swarms of Japanese fighters. For 24 hours, the Americans took heavy casualties, but they held out, preventing the Japanese from getting past the naval flotilla and assaulting MacArthur's forces on the beaches.

Then, in an example of how luck can change history, Kurita was given faulty intelligence, which led him to believe that Halsey's fleet was less than an hour away from his position. Unwilling to risk the Imperial Navy's last ships, he broke off the assault and retreated. In what seemed like a miracle to the American defenders, Japanese ships poised to finish them off and rout the invasion forces mysteriously disengaged and fled.

Kurita's retreat was futile: Halsey's and Kinkaid's fleets linked up behind the retreating Japanese ships and gave chase. In another 12 hours, almost all of Kurita's fleet had been either disabled or sunk. By twilight of Oct. 27, the Battle of Leyte Gulf had cost Japan four carriers, three battleships, 16 cruisers, 9 destroyers and as many as 10,000 sailors. The Empire of the Rising Sun, whose control of the Pacific skies had been destroyed

at the Battle of Midway more than two years before, was now effectively finished as a fighting force on the sea.

ONE EFFECTIVE TACTIC, A LAST-DITCH IMPROVISATION, remained in Japan's arsenal: kamikaze pilots first appeared during Leyte Gulf. And only one effective strategy remained: to delay the U.S. advance for as long as possible by digging in deeply on every island and fighting to the last man. And that's just what they did on Leyte. Sosaku Suzuki, the Japanese army commander, chose not to sacrifice his men on the beaches. Instead, the Japanese retreated to more defensible positions on high ground to face the invaders.

By the time night fell on A-day (the designation given to the invasion), U.S. troops had pushed several miles inland and captured an airfield. The following day, the 1st Cavalry Division secured Tacloban, the largest city on Leyte. By Nov. 1, U.S. troops held the northern end of Leyte Valley and the port of Carigara and were driving toward the highest peak overlooking the landing beaches, Catamon Hill, a Japanese observation and artillery post. In two days of round-the-clock fighting, the Americans overran 53 pillboxes, 17 fortified caves and dozens of other Japanese defensive positions and occupied Catamon Hill.

The U.S. task grew tougher when the Japanese managed to bring more than 34,000 additional troops onto the island; they holed up in the Ormoc Valley, on the west coast. As two U.S. forces set out to assault their positions in a pincer movement, they ran into a typhoon that obstructed them with falling trees and mudslides. The Ormoc Valley wasn't fully subdued until an amphibious tank unit leap-frogged down the coast and attacked the Japanese from behind.

Days later the port of Palompon, the last harbor on Leyte still in Japanese hands, fell to the Americans, leading MacArthur to announce on Dec. 26 that the Battle of Leyte was over. He was right, if a bit premature; isolated pockets of Japanese resistance would harass U.S. units through the end of February. But Leyte was now securely in American hands and would shortly be the staging ground from which new operations, against Luzon and Mindanao, would begin. The U.S. was now firmly in control in the war in the Pacific. ∎

BANG! Top left, soldiers hold their ears as a "Long Tom" fires. The target is a convoy of Japanese trucks on the Carigara front on Leyte's north end

WELCOME Above, heading through the city of Tacloban, soldiers of the U.S. 1st Cavalry Division stop to accept thanks from excited Filipinos

SETTING SUN The fighting dragged on for weeks on Leyte; at right, soldiers celebrate the capture of a Japanese position—and flag—in December

"Leyte was to be the anvil against which I hoped to hammer the Japanese into submission in the central Philippines."
—Douglas MacArthur

Promise Fulfilled

Douglas MacArthur left the Philippines as the beaten general of a beaten army. He returned as commander of the world's mightiest seaborne power

I N THE CAPTAIN'S CABIN OF THE 77-FT. PT-41 he lay on the tiny bunk, beaten, burning with defeat. Corregidor was doomed and with it the Philippines, but one leading actor in the most poignant tragedy in U.S. military history would be missing when the curtain fell. Douglas MacArthur, Field Marshal of the Philippine Army, four-star general in the U.S. Army, had left the stage. It was the order of his Commander in Chief.

As he lay on the bunk General MacArthur was already trying to plan for a swift and overwhelming return. The cockleshell craft pounded noisily south through the swells of the Sulu Sea. The general was seasick; his wife chafed his hands to help the circulation. They could travel only by night; by day Japanese aircraft ruled the skies and they had to skulk in covers. At last the PT put in at Mindanao; a battered Flying Fortress took the MacArthurs on to Australia.

That was in mid-March 1942. The MacArthur who flew into Australia then was the picture of what had happened to the U.S. in the Pacific. He had been West Point's First Captain, and one of its greatest students. He had been the Rainbow Division's commander in World War I, later the Army's youngest Chief of Staff, and always the professional soldier's notion of what a professional soldier should look like. Now he was rumpled and untidy and probably for the first time in his life he looked his age. He was 62.

But he was not really beaten. In Adelaide he made the promise that the U.S., bewildered and shaken by the Japs' victorious campaign, heard with renewed hope: "I came through—and I shall return."

Last week, on the flag bridge of the 10,000-ton, 614-ft. light cruiser *Nashville* stood a proud, erect figure in freshly pressed khaki. Douglas MacArthur had come back to the Philippines, as he had promised.

He had slept well, eaten a hearty breakfast. Now with his corncob pipe he pointed over the glassy, green waters of

Leyte Gulf, where rode the greatest fleet ever assembled in the Southwest Pacific. Around him were hundreds of transports, shepherded by an Australian squadron and MacArthur's own Seventh Fleet, reinforced with jeep carriers from Admiral Chester Nimitz's vast armada of seagoing airdromes. On the horizon loomed the majestic battleships of Admiral William F. Halsey's Third Fleet—some of them ghosts from the graveyard of Pearl Harbor. Beyond the horizon steamed the greatest concentration of waterborne air power in war's history—Vice Admiral Marc Mitscher's fast carrier groups.

There was not a Japanese surface craft in sight. Only one enemy plane ventured out to attack. It dropped one bomb harmlessly into the sea. The *Nashville* bore shoreward. The first landings, on Homohon and on nearby Dinagat, were only the preliminaries in MacArthur's vast and meticulously planned schedule of operations. His first major goal was Leyte, in the heart of the islands, where devoted Visayan guerrillas had been heard calling by secret radio for help a year ago.

This was what Douglas MacArthur had long advocated, with an intensity that seemed wholly justified because he believed he had been ordered out of Corregidor only in order to lead a counterinvasion soon. Now at last he was striking his massive blow, far behind the enemy's main positions, where the enemy neither expected it nor had organized himself to resist it effectively.

Five hours after the first wave of Army infantrymen dashed across the shell-pocked beaches, General MacArthur and his party filed down a ladder from the *Nashville's* deck into a landing barge. With him were men who had left Corregidor with him 31 months ago. When the barge grounded in shoal water, he walked down the ramp and waded ashore. He was wet to the midriff, but the sun glinted on the golden "scrambled eggs" on his strictly individualistic cap as he faced a microphone. To Filipinos his first words were the fulfillment of a promise: "This is the Voice of Freedom." That was how the last Corregidor radio programs began. Said MacArthur: "People of the Philippines, I have returned. By the grace of Almighty God, our forces stand again on Philippine soil ... Rally to me ... Let every arm be steeled." ∎

THE EGOTIST MacArthur's vanity, well known during World War II, would be magnified by his postwar service as virtual ruler of occupied Japan. As leader of the U.N. forces during the Korean War, he tangled with President Harry Truman, who fired him

The Perils of Paradise

Undeniably, the war in the Pacific played out against an exotic background that would later be romanticized in James A. Michener's *Tales of the South Pacific* and Rodgers and Hammerstein's musical comedy adaptation, *South Pacific*. On the ground, though, the environment could be a brutal enemy. There was little romance in beriberi, malaria and fungus-borne "creeping crud"— or in the huge leeches that preyed on one and all

■ **LAUNDRY DETAIL** "I'm gonna wash that ammo right out in the air ... " After a flood, Marines on Guadalcanal in the Solomon Islands hang just-washed machine-gun cartridge belts out to dry

■ **SWIMMIN' HOLE** Above, Marines take a dip in a bomb crater after the tough battle for Okinawa; a wrecked Japanese plane is behind them. It's July 22, 1945; the war will be over in three weeks

■ **NO TIP** Corporal Glenn H. Tanner Jr. gets a trim from POW Nishi Nobuyuki, a barber in civilian life, on Okinawa

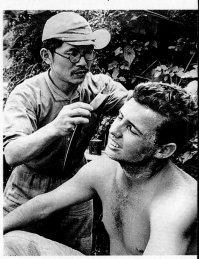

SWAMPED On Guadalcanal in 1944, PFCs Harold Williams, left, and lward R. Robinson return from a gravel-hunting mission. The two soldiers will use the rocks to build up a berm around their tent to ward off the floodwaters they're wading through

■ **LIFEGUARD** A Marine machine gunner stands watch against snipers while members of an engineering battalion bathe in a river on Guadalcanal in 1943. Guns were of little use against the natural predators that made life miserable. Leeches were common, and pulling them off left sores that would fester and rot; soldiers learned that touching a lit cigarette to the blood suckers would remove them safely

■**TIGHT SCRAPE** Soldiers and mud—they just seem to go together. Above, a hapless American at the Ryukyu air field on Okinawa pauses to improve his traction

■**NO STARS** Left, perhaps tardy in making reservations at any of Iwo Jima's finer dining establishments, two Army Air Force men settle for the homey Slop-Chute

■**BATTLE'S END** Exhausted after three continuous days of fighting in Okinawa's Awacha Pocket, two Marine gunners snooze in their foxhole, helmets at hand

■ **FRONT PORCH** Above, a unit of black U.S. soldiers has set up camp in a grass-roofed native hut on New Guinea. America's armed services were segregated in the war, but the constant interchange of black and white soldiers and the proud service of black troops would prove to be major factors in the assault on segregation in the U.S. that followed the war

■ **SETTLING IN** At left, with Papua New Guinea firmly under U.S. control by late 1944, camps began sprouting such features as laundry shacks, barber shops and mess halls

■ **DOG-TIRED** Right, using his helmet as a pillow, PFC John W. Emmons of Sheffield, Ala., beds down with a pal on Okinawa in 1945

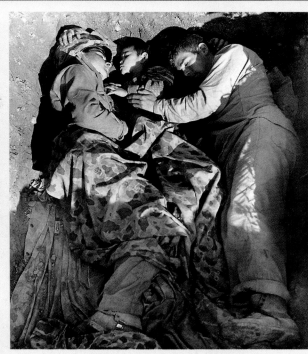

■ **STRANGE BEDFELLOWS** A pair of Marines share ponchos and sack time with a native boy outside the capital city of Naha on Okinawa, the last major island invaded by the U.S. in the war

■ **SINCERELY** Left, PFC Francis R. Chamberlain of Dallas, Pa., drops a missive into an improvised mailbox on Emirau Island. Occupied by the U.S. in March 1944, Emirau was used to launch bombing raids on the large Japanese air base at Rabaul

COMING IN! Weaving through a hail of antiaircraft fire, a Japanese "Jill" fighter carrying a torpedo bomb approaches the U.S.S. *Yorktown* aircraft carrier off the shore of Truk Island on April 29, 1944

Wings Across the Water

In a clash of seaborne military might, a new kind of ship, the aircraft carrier, merges aerial and naval power into a deadly floating weapon

FROM PEARL HARBOR TO HIROSHIMA, THE WAR IN THE Pacific began and ended in the air. Whereas the battle for Europe was decided on land, with pilots often grumbling that their missions relegated air power to the role of assisting the infantry, the campaign across the vast reaches of the Pacific Ocean was essentially a struggle for control of the skies. The taking and holding of land were primarily important as a means of acquiring airfields with long runways from which heavy bombers could be deployed. Indeed, as the U.S. advanced upon the Japanese homeland, Japanese-occupied islands unfit for bombers were sometimes bypassed entirely and left in enemy hands until the end of the war. The vessels most treasured by the admiralties of both sides were themselves a form of artificial land. This was the war that introduced to the world a fascinating new kind of mobile military machine: the aircraft carrier, a floating tarmac from which fighters and small bombers could be launched.

Pilots had begun trying to take off from boats in the early years of aviation: the first successful launch from a ship was in November 1910, when aviation pioneer Eugene Ely took off from a temporary platform on the bow of the U.S.S. *Birmingham.* Three months later, Ely became the first man to land a plane on a ship, when he touched down on the U.S.S. *Pennsylvania.* Between the wars, all the great naval powers built aircraft carriers, mostly because the Washington Naval Treaty of 1922 severely restricted the tonnage of battleships but placed no limits on carrier size. Even so, through the late 1930s, admirals around the world clung to the orthodoxy that the next war on the waves would be won or lost by cruisers, destroyers, and battleships—not the newfangled aircraft carriers that reduced the successors of John Paul Jones and Admiral Nelson to the role of aerial support staff.

This complacent belief that the future would resemble the past was shattered by two events, both of which occurred on

"Flying is hours and hours of boredom sprinkled with a few seconds of sheer terror." —Gregory ("Pappy") Boyington

the morning of Dec. 7, 1941. First, the devastating Japanese attack on Pearl Harbor was conducted almost exclusively from a fleet of six aircraft carriers. (A few Japanese submarines also took part, but they played no significant role.) At the same time, four other Japanese carriers launched strikes at British and Dutch targets across the Pacific. Using the largest and most modern carrier fleet ever assembled, the Japanese had seemingly brought three world powers to their knees.

Second, by a stroke of luck, the three American aircraft carriers then stationed in the Pacific—the U.S.S. *Enterprise*, U.S.S. *Lexington* and U.S.S. *Saratoga*—were at sea, away from Pearl Harbor, on the morning of Dec. 7 and thus did not share the fate of the 11 major American gunships (including the battleship U.S.S. *Arizona)* that went to the bottom that day. For better or for worse, American naval leaders would now have to build their war plans around aircraft carriers, however reluctantly, because these were the only tools they had left.

I T TURNED OUT TO BE FOR BETTER; INDEED, NECESSITY bred victory. Five months after Pearl Harbor, the first naval battle in history fought primarily by aircraft carriers took place in the Coral Sea, off New Guinea. In a further sign of how much war on the seas had changed, this was the world's first naval engagement during which neither side was able to see the other's ships. Although technically a narrow

One month later, at Midway, this loss of momentum was transformed into outright, catastrophic defeat. A combination of luck, skill, gutsy leadership by Admiral Chester Nimitz and strategic intelligence in the form of decrypted enemy radio intercepts sent four Japanese carriers—the *Soryu, Hiryu, Akagi* and *Kaga*, all of which had taken part in the attack on Pearl Harbor—to the bottom, taking with them hundreds of planes and more than 2,500 men. After Midway, the nation that had led the world in naval aviation was effectively finished as a force in the air. Japanese pilots would continue to fight through the end of the war but only in an increasingly desperate defensive role.

> "I don't mind being called tough, since I find in this racket it's the tough guys who lead the survivors." —General Curtis LeMay

win for the Japanese, who suffered slightly smaller losses than the Americans and British, it was in fact a Pyrrhic victory from which Japan would never recover. The Battle of the Coral Sea prevented a planned invasion of Port Moresby, just north of the Australian mainland, and marked the end of Japanese expansion in the Pacific, halting for the first time what had seemed an unstoppable juggernaut of conquest.

This was not the war that Tokyo had wanted. Since at least 1907, Japanese naval planners had been refining a strategy for the coming war with the U.S. Their grand plan called for devastating America's Pacific fleet with a surprise attack, then luring any ships that remained into Japan's home waters, where they would be shredded in an apocalyptic battle. But the U.S. Navy (which, to be fair, had been preparing strategies

for possible war with Japan since 1897) would not be lured into a climactic sea battle. Instead, American planners settled on an "island hopping" strategy that emphasized control of the air above all else.

In the early years of the war, the Japanese followed a policy that focused on land-based garrisons and asserted control of the shipping lanes with aircraft carriers, submarines and heavy battleships. Midway finished Japan's bid for control of the skies above those islands and shipping lanes. Another turning point came in October 1944, in the Battle of Leyte Gulf, where Tokyo lost four more aircraft carriers, three heavy battleships, six cruisers and 9 destroyers, ending the Japanese navy's role as an effective fighting force. Between these two milestones, in 1943, U.S. factories began churning out the machinery of war. By July 1945, Japan would have only 4,000 aircraft left in its possession (with just one-fifth of those still operational), while American commanders in the Pacific Theater had slightly more than 22,000 planes in the air.

Along the way, specific advances in aircraft design hastened the rollback of Japan's conquered empire. In early engagements in 1942, the Mitsubishi "Zero" fighter outperformed anything in the American arsenal. By 1943, the Navy Hellcat, a fighter specifically designed by Grumman to fly faster and farther than the Zero, and to make sharper turns in dogfights, was blasting Japanese fighters out of the sky.

AS THE WAR PROGRESSED, THE SKIES OVER THE PACIFIC filled with a staggering array of specialized aircraft: torpedo bombers and reconnaissance planes, intelligence gatherers, weather watchers and submarine hunters; giant, cargo-hauling PBY Flying Boats and tiny Piper Cubs used by artillery spotters. In the U.S. fighter class alone, a menagerie of beasts took wing: the F6F Hellcat and F7F Tigercat, the P-36 Hawk and P-39 Airacobra, the P-51 Mustang, P-61 Black Widow, P-70 Nighthawk and P-75 Eagle. American kids could recite the litany of bombers: the B-17 Flying Fortress, the B-24 Liberator, B-25 Mitchell and the mighty new long-range craft, the B-29 Superfortress.

Hollywood Goes to Tokyo

The picture below offers a fascinating footnote to the U.S. air war. Even before Pearl Harbor, the Army Air Force approached Hollywood producer Jack Warner and asked him to make a series of short films to be used for instructional purposes. When the war began, the First Motion Picture Unit started cranking out films treating every aspect of wartime aviation, including such titles as *Operation of the Bomb Sight, Land and Live in the Jungle* and *Recognition of the Japanese Zero*.

Later in the war, the unit created the detailed set below, which showed Tokyo and its environs at scale; it covered an entire sound stage. The camera then was moved across the set, replicating a bombing run, and the film was sent to Okinawa and used to brief B-29 crews. Thus pilots knew the geography of their targets before taking off—and workers at the studio knew the time and location of bombing runs weeks before the pilots.

NATIONAL ARCHIVES

ACTION! Kept under wraps until after the war, the Tokyo set was enormous. The two workers at right provide a sense of its scale

If the aircraft carrier was the scalpel that gradually trimmed the tentacles of Japan's empire in the Pacific, the hatchet that was intended to sever the enemy's head was the long-range bomber. Based on land and able to carry up to 10 tons of bombs as far as 5,000 miles at speeds greater than 350 m.p.h., these mammoth fighting machines, it was hoped, would deliver the knockout blow to Japan that would end the war. (In fact, many military historians in retrospect believe that the strategic bombing of both Germany and Japan—like the extensive German bombing of London—was not as effective a weapon as the proponents of air power had predicted.)

Pre-eminent among the long-range bombers was the B-29 Superfortress, which began rolling off American assembly lines in 1944 and was deployed exclusively in the Pacific. The plane's first raid was in June 1944: 47 B-29s took off from Chengtu, China, and hit the Imperial Iron and Steel Works at Yawata. It was the first time American bombers had violated the skies over Japan since the surprise Doolittle Raid against Tokyo in the months after Pearl Harbor.

After the Battle of Leyte Gulf, Japan was cut off from the territories it had conquered in the first months of the war and from which it still desperately needed vital raw materials, like oil. Control of the seas had also been wrested from Japan's grasp, leaving its home islands all but defenseless from the air. The empire was now ripe for the strategy that U.S. Strategic Bombing Commander Curtis LeMay, who transferred to the Pacific from the European Theater in late 1944, bluntly described as "bombing them into submission."

By March 1945, U.S. forces had advanced close enough to Japan that Tokyo, Osaka, Nagoya, Kobe, Kawasaki and Yokohama were within range of American heavy bombers. Over

time, as his bombers returned unscathed from their raids against the Japanese homeland, LeMay abandoned the Air Force's recently developed doctrine, based on experience garnered in the Allied sorties over Germany, of bombing by day from high altitude. Instead, he sent his B-29s over Japan by night at 5,000 to 8,000 ft., rather than 35,000 ft. Secure in his dominance of the skies, he also ordered the crews to remove defensive gun turrets and their operators, increasing each plane's capacity to carry bombs by more than five tons. The bombs themselves were designed to set a match to Japan's famous wood-and-paper architecture.

The first firebomb raid against Tokyo, which began on

Nose Art

There is nothing like a dame, according to the authorities cited by Oscar Hammerstein in *South Pacific*. And there is certainly no dame on earth with the exaggerated proportions of the lovelies painted on the noses of World War II planes, a contemporary take on the figureheads that graced the bow of wooden ships. A 1945 caption for the picture at right of Marine PFC Randall Sprenger ("the Michelangelo of the Marianas") notes that he lamented the absence of a live model for his creation.

U.S. MARINE CORPS

March 9, 1945, reduced almost 17 square square miles of the city to ashes. In fact, the destruction of Tokyo would become so complete that the bombing raids were discontinued after May 1945: there were no military targets in Tokyo left to strike. On the ground, as Japan's Foreign Minister Mamoru Shigemitsu would later recall, "day by day, Japan turned into a furnace from which the voice of a people searching for food rose in anguish."

EVEN BEFORE THE BATTLE FOR OKINAWA BEGAN IN APRIL 1945, U.S. air power had destroyed nearly every man-made structure on the island and killed almost every living thing that had not taken shelter belowground in fortified bunkers. In the prelude to the invasion, U.S. bombers also sank the *Yamato*, the largest battleship ever constructed and one of Japan's last remaining heavy gunboats. Such victories were won at a high price. During the battle for Okinawa, more than 700 American planes were shot down.

Navy and Marine pilots also played a crucial role at Okinawa, which to this day remains the largest sea-air-land battle in history. Strafing and bombing Japanese positions at close range, they facilitated the difficult American advance. The Japanese retaliated with waves of attacks by suicidal kamikaze pilots, who scored their greatest blows against U.S. ships in this battle.

By June 1945, when the Allies had succeeded in driving the Japanese from Okinawa, they controlled runways less than 300 miles from Kyushu, the southernmost of Japan's four main islands. Now there was no spot anywhere in Japan that would be safe from U.S. bombers. The island nation was virtually undefended by sea or air, and the road was open for a gruesome, if apparently necessary, final air campaign: sustained, round-the-clock saturation bombing that would either bring the country to its knees or pave the way for an American invasion of Japan itself.

The future seemed unimaginably bloody. Anticipating a cataclysm and the role that every Japanese citizen would play in it, Shigemitsu wrote that "the clarion call was accepted. If the Emperor ordained it, they would leap into the flames." Indeed they might have, but an unforeseen weapon would make such sacrifices unnecessary. On Aug. 8, at Hiroshima, the flames would come to the Japanese, borne from the skies. ■

Pappy's Flying Circus

BOYINGTON'S BOYS "Pappy," third from right on the ground, enjoyed gilding his reputation as a drinker, brawler and misfit

The formal name of the Marine fighter unit known to history as "the Black Sheep Squadron" was VMF-214. Initially called the Swashbucklers, these gutsy pilots flew Wildcats and then Corsairs from a succession of island bases across the Pacific. In a single 84-day period stretching from late 1943 to January 1944, the Black Sheep flyers totaled 197 engagements, shooting down dozens of Japanese aircraft, attacking enemy shipping routes and staging strafing and bombing runs against ground installations.

Contrary to the 1970s TV show based on their exploits, the Black Sheep were not a crew of misfits, though their leader, Lieut. Colonel Greg ("Pappy") Boyington, was a born rebel. Rather, these flyers were among the most professional and highly qualified pilots in the Marine Corps. In the last months of 1943, Boyington scored 22 confirmed kills of Japanese aircraft, tantalizingly close to the record of 26 held by Eddie Rickenbacker, the No. 1 U.S. ace of World War I. On Jan. 3, 1944, Boyington was shot down during a dogfight over Rabaul, although not before taking three Japanese fighters with him. Boyington survived, but he was captured and remained a POW for the rest of the war.

Flyboys and Flattops

The U.S. Navy operated three different classes of aircraft carrier during the war. The biggest, designated fleet carriers, or CVs, displaced some 24,500 tons; they carried 100 planes and a crew of almost 2,700. These *Essex*-class carriers were the largest ships of any kind in America's fleet. The smaller, light carriers, or CVLs, displaced 11,000 tons and carried 30 planes and a crew of 1,500. The smallest class was the escort carrier, or CVE, which displaced 7,000 to 17,000 tons and carried 36 planes. The first two classes were lightly armored and highly mobile; the CVEs were more heavily armored and thus less mobile. During the critical Battle of Leyte Gulf, U.S. CVEs weathered the first attacks by Japanese kamikaze pilots in the war and managed to hold off the battleships of the Japanese navy, saving the invasion force still disembarking on Leyte Island

■ **OUCH!** Above, when the U.S.S. *Bennington,* a CV, ran into a monster typhoon on June 5, 1945, giant waves driven by winds of 115 m.p.h. bent its flight deck like a paper clip. The ship was repaired and fought on

■ **THAT WAY** At left, his pants rippling from prop wash, a crewm directs a plane to take off aboard the U.S.S. *Enterprise.* The big CV was one of only eight carriers in the U.S. fleet on Dec. 7, 1941

■ **HINGED** Top left, facing page: a torpedo bomber has its wings folded up to help conserve space aboard the *Enterprise*

■ **GEARING UP** Top right, facing page: pilots are briefed in the ready room of the *Enterprise,* which became the most decorated U.S. ship of the war

■ **SQUEEZED** At right, airplanes are crowded onto the flight deck of an aircraft carrier in a task force bound for the invasion of Iwo Jima in 1944

■DOWN UNDER Top, sailors resembling stagehands in a play prepare to move a fighter off the elevator that has brought it from the flight deck on the *Enterprise* to the hangar level beneath. As the big carrier became increasingly obsolete in the years after the war, attempts to raise funds to preserve it as a memorial fell short; the historic ship was scrapped in 1958

■GO! Above, a flight deck crew races to meet a plane that has just landed on a carrier in 1942; censors withheld the ship's name. Spared the fate of the *Enterprise,* four other carriers that saw service during the war—the *Intrepid, Hornet, Lexington* and *Yorktown*—are now museums

■HOLDING Left, a plane revs up on the flight deck of the *Enterprise,* awaiting the signal to take off. The runway on the big CVs was 802 ft. long; the smaller CVL carriers had shorter flight decks, at 552 ft.

■ESCAPE Above, Ensign (j.g.) Fraifogl of Mansfield, Ohio, abandons his Hellcat fighter on the flight deck of the U.S.S. *Ticonderoga* in 1944. One of his auxiliary fuel tanks came loose and was ignited when a propeller hit it

■LIFELINE Right, with its ships on duty far from shore, the U.S. Navy perfected the art of refueling at sea. In this picture, seamen aboard the tanker U.S.S. *Kaskaskia* are doused by heavy seas as they connect fuel lines

■MOVING TARGET Here's the view from the air as the pilot of a Curtiss "Helldiver" scout bomber prepares to land aboard a carrier in 1944. The two flyers have slid back their canopies to get a better look at the runway

Death's Divine Wind

Striking from the sky and dying, exultantly, for their cause, dive-bombing kamikaze pilots breed terror, damage ships and delay the Allied advance

I WAS SITTING IN THE COCKPIT, WAITING TO BE CLEARED for takeoff," recalls Will Souza. "A dozen or so planes were bunched up on the back end of the flight deck, near the fantail, when suddenly, every gun on the aft of the ship opened up." On Nov. 25, 1944, Souza was a 24-year-old torpedo-bomber pilot stationed aboard the carrier U.S.S. *Essex* off the Philippines. The crew of the *Essex* had heard about but had yet to encounter a Japanese tactic initiated the month before: planes loaded with explosives would dive straight into American ships, killing the Japanese pilot but also inflicting horrific damage on his target. "I knew something serious was up," Souza remembers, "because everything was firing: 20- and 40-mm guns, then 5-in. cannons. A

second or two later, the gunner in the back of my plane began firing, something we never, ever did before takeoff."

Souza knew that only one thing could provoke such a frenzied fusillade. "I braced myself," he says, "then heard a tremendous roar right over our plane." Looking up, he saw "the underside of a Japanese fighter pass directly over my head. The belly of his plane was no more than 30 ft. over the canopy of mine." Souza's eyes followed the Japanese plane as it descended at high speed onto the flight deck of the *Essex* and slammed into the deck near the carrier's "island" superstructure, which housed its bridge.

"There was a tremendous explosion," he recalls. "I was close enough that the heat burned the inside of my throat."

Belowdecks, Gerald Thomas, another torpedo-bomber pilot, was sitting down to lunch in the officers' wardroom. "We had hit a convoy of Japanese ships that morning," he recalls. "I was going to fly again later that day but was trying to relax for a few minutes before heading to the preflight briefing. Suddenly, I heard a tremendous burst of gunfire from the flight deck, one level above me, and a few seconds later I heard a deafening whine that kept getting closer and louder."

Thomas, now 84 and a retired president of the University of New Mexico, recalls that at the moment of impact, "the whole ship seemed to shudder. I could hear the sound of tearing metal, and the paint started peeling off the walls. Within a minute, the wardroom was completely filled with smoke."

On the flight deck above, Souza could see a gaping hole in the runway where the Japanese plane had crashed. "There was fire and smoke everywhere," he says. "I could see that we weren't going to be able to take off, and then I heard the cannons and machine guns open up again behind me, which meant that another plane was coming in. I was sitting in an airplane full of gasoline that was loaded with several thousand pounds of bombs, and surrounded by a dozen other planes just like it. So I killed the engine and got the hell out of that plane. As I was running across the deck, I could see a second Japanese plane hit by our gunners. It fell into the water about half a mile from the back of the ship.

"I was headed over to a stairwell on the port side," Souza recalls, "which would take me down to the ready room, when more than a dozen people came pouring out of the hatch and started running to the starboard side. Then I looked up and realized why—a third Japanese plane was coming in." This one was also shot from the skies by the *Essex* gunners before it could reach the ship. "When I got to the ready room," Souza remembers, "there was nobody there, but a phone on the wall was ringing. I picked it up, and a sailor from seven decks below wanted to know what the hell was going on." Within minutes, Souza says, "wounded sailors started to wander into the ready room. There was one who was pretty badly burned over the upper part of his body, so I applied first aid."

Thomas, who also made his way to the ready room, recalls helping organize an impromptu first aid station as more and more wounded sailors made their way there. On the flight deck, engineers were busy welding steel plates over the damage left by the first Japanese plane. As other members of the crew fought fires, manned guns and repaired damage, the pilots busied themselves with helping tend to the wounded. "The policy was that pilots were too important to risk with anything but flight missions," Thomas recalls. "So we did what we could while awaiting further orders."

The frantic activity aboard the *Essex* was in service of a sin-

gle goal: to get the planes and their pilots, the most valuable commodity in the Pacific war, off the vulnerable carrier and into the air. That way, if the carrier went down, the planes could still land on another ship or one of the nearby islands.

Souza, now 85 and a retired executive living in California, recalls, "It was less than 20 minutes after the first plane hit that an order came over the speakers: 'Pilots, man your planes!' That's how long it took them to repair the flight deck," he says, the amazement still evident in his voice. Souza, Thomas and dozens of other pilots hurried topside and began scrambling into their TBM "Avengers." Less than 10 minutes later, they were airborne and forming up to strike Japanese targets on Luzon and in the San Fernando Bay. "As we took off," Thomas recalls, "we were hoping the *Essex* would still be around when we got back."

THE TACTIC OF SACRIFICING PILOTS TO CRIPPLE U.S. ships was developed by Vice Admiral Takijiro Onishi, commandant of Japan's First Air Fleet. Preparing for the Battle of Leyte Gulf, Onishi was faced with the task of holding off an overwhelming U.S. onslaught with fewer than three dozen aircraft. At a staff meeting in the weeks before the battle, he commented, "I don't think there would be any other certain way to carry out the operation than to put a 250-kg bomb on a Zero and let it crash into a U.S. carrier."

The informal name for these suicidal flyers was kamikaze, or "divine wind," originally a reference to the unexpected typhoons that miraculously saved Japan twice from Mongol invasions, in 1274 and 1281. Although this term would be adopted by Americans, the actual Japanese name for these units was *tokubetsu ko geki tai,* "special attack squads."

The first kamikaze pilot was Lieut. Yukio Seki, a 23-year-old ace who said of himself that "Japan's future is bleak if it is forced to kill one of its best pilots." On Oct. 25, 1944, he led a formation of nine pilots who, to the utter surprise of U.S. sailors, hurled themselves into the carrier U.S.S. *St. Lo,* which sank in less than 30 minutes. Afterward, Emperor Hirohito asked his staff, "Was it necessary to go to this extreme?"

In the view of the Japanese general staff, it was. By the fall of 1944, American and British progress across the Pacific had brought Allied long-range bombers within striking distance of Japan itself. Both sides reckoned that an invasion of the Japanese home islands was less than a year away. But the Japanese military, increasingly deprived of aircraft carriers, large battleships, new airplanes (as well as the oil needed to run all three) and most other necessities of modern naval warfare, had fewer and fewer tools with which to fight. Moreover, the idea of laying down one's life for Emperor and homeland resonated deeply with followers of Japan's ancient warrior code, Bushido. If the war was lost—and by the autumn of 1944,

ATTACKED! Crewmen of the U.S.S. *Bunker Hill* fight the flames caused by two dive bombers that struck the aircraft carrier within 30 seconds of each other on May 11, 1945; more than 370 Americans were killed and more than 260 wounded in the attack off the island of Kyushu during the battle for Okinawa

more and more Japanese realized it was—then individual honor could be redeemed by an act of heroic self-sacrifice.

As with the ancient Romans, suicide with honor is a distinguishing feature of Japanese culture; it is known as seppuku. One pilot who declined to volunteer for a kamikaze mission wrote to his young wife that it was for their sake that he had chosen not to sacrifice himself. She promptly drowned their three children and then committed seppuku, leaving a note telling the pilot that he was now free to die for the Emperor.

Japan's military leadership quickly refined the kamikaze technique, switching to younger, less experienced pilots and equipping them with damaged or obsolete aircraft, thus sparing its better men and machines. The results were stunningly effective. Between October 1944 and the war's end, dive bombers sank three U.S. aircraft carriers and damaged more than 15 others so badly that they were taken out of action for months at a time. In the 11-week battle for Okinawa, kamikaze attacks accounted for most of the 32 U.S. ships sunk and the more than 200 that were seriously damaged. By the spring of 1945, kamikaze pilots were the only element of Japan's military machine that was helping delay the Allied advance toward the home islands. When the war ended, more than 5,000 Japanese suicide pilots had died (most of them shot down before hitting their targets), but they had managed to kill as many as 7,000 U.S. and British servicemen. They had also terrorized their enemies. "You could outrun a submarine," Thomas recalls, "outgun an enemy ship, shoot down Japanese fighters. You might even be able to rake a torpedo with fire in the water. But there was almost nothing you could do about a plane that was deliberately trying to slam straight into you."

Before climbing into the cockpit for his last mission, a kamikaze pilot would engage in a Shinto ritual of purification, which culminated with the drinking of the *wakare no mizu sakazuki*, the "farewell cup of water" (in fact, sake). Pilots who flew south from Japan would pass and salute Mount Kaimon, sacred ground that ranks second only to Mount Fuji in Japanese affection. Pilots flying east would cross Kikaijima Island, where they would drop flowers from their planes. Local legend maintains that vast beds of cornflowers and groves of cherry trees bloom each spring where these flowers fell.

In the twilight hours of Nov. 25, 1944, Will Souza, Gerald Thomas and their fellow pilots had completed their bombing mission over San Fernando Bay and were flying east. With the sun setting behind them over the dwindling empire of the Rising Sun, they scanned the water ahead for their damaged carrier. "Just as the sun was going down," recalls Souza, "she appeared on the horizon." In spite of repeated attacks throughout the day by young pilots who were told that at the moment they died, "all the cherry blossoms at Yasukuni shrine in Tokyo will smile brightly at you," the *Essex* was still there. ∎

"Dear Parents: Please congratulate me. I have been given a splendid opportunity to die. This is our last day."
—**Kamikaze pilot Isao Matsuo, May 1945**

Shipmates

Sailors of World War II may have been working on the most advanced vessels the world had ever seen, but their downtime still bore a briny whiff of old-time seafaring life, including the men's fascination with tattoos and the observance of centuries-old romps upon the crossing of the equator. The big aircraft carriers, like the U.S.S. *Enterprise,* were floating cities that supported 80 to 90 aircraft and a crew of as many as 2,900 men

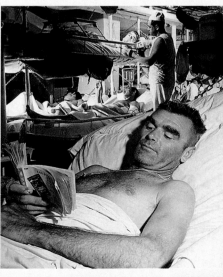

■ **NEEDLEWORK** Above, a sailor decorates a friend's arm aboard the aircraft carrier U.S.S. *New Jersey* in 1944

■ **STRATEGISTS** Far left, a pair of sailors might as well be in a country store as they enjoy a game of chess in one of a Coast Guard ship's storerooms

■ **SICK BAY** Left, PFC Clifford Jameson of West Brook, Mo., recuperates aboard a hospital ship, the U.S.S. *Solace,* in 1945

DON'T ARGUE WITH THE REF As the Coast Guard transport U.S.S. *Arthur Middleton* steams toward Okinawa in May 1945, a boxing ring has been set up, and early arrivals perch on ringside seats aboard a pair of cargo booms. The savvy referee is Coast Guard Commander Jack Dempsey

■ RITE OF PASSAGE
Observing a centuries-old "Father Neptune" custom, a sailor who has never crossed the equator before runs the gauntlet and takes his share of mock abuse from the old salts among the crew

■ YULETIDE If this small packet is drawing lots of attention, that's because it's a mail bag being passed from a destroyer to an attack transport ship—and it's only three days before Christmas 1944

■ STARCHY At right, sticklers for formality, officers of the U.S.S. *Enterprise* don dress whites for a wardroom dinner. The placid scene is a bit misleading: during the war, the big carrier's planes and guns downed 911 enemy planes, while her bombers sank 71 ships and damaged 192 more

■ **NEW DEAL** Above, steward's mates relax in January 1945 on the night before the invasion of Luzon, perhaps after serving a dinner in an officers' mess like the one shown below

■ **DEFENSE!** At left, pilots and crews on the light carrier U.S.S. *Monterey* square off for a game of hoops in the ship's elevator well. The athletic gent jumping at left was better known on the gridiron in college; he is future President Gerald R. Ford

Beneath the Waves, a Silent Service

Though Japan began the war with a series of stunning victories across the Pacific, it wasn't able to reap the full benefits of its new empire—the natural resources of the nations it had conquered. Long before U.S. planes, battleships and troops began attacking Japanese-held lands across the Pacific, U.S. submarines—the "silent service"—were strangling the Empire of the Rising Sun from beneath the waves.

Just as America's Pacific carrier fleet survived Pearl Harbor by a stroke of luck (all the flattops were at sea on Dec. 7, 1941), the subsurface fleet was saved by

a similar miracle: in their zeal to attack Battleship Row, Japanese bombers ignored the naval base's submarine pens.

That was a fatal mistake. President Franklin Roosevelt immediately ordered the Navy to begin "unrestricted warfare" against all Japanese shipping. Within weeks, U.S. submarines were on the far side of the Pacific, firing the first shots in a relentless, highly successful campaign to deny the Japanese oil, steel, rubber, food and every other vital commodity that they were now shipping from conquered territory to their home islands.

Adopting the "wolfpack" strategy with

which German U-boats had nearly starved Britain into submission earlier in the war, three or more U.S. subs—assisted by intercepted and decoded Japanese radio traffic—would stalk an imperial convoy for days at a time, until each ship was sunk or the subs ran low of fuel or torpedoes. Later in the war, innovations like radar (for hunting ships on the surface) and sonar (for finding enemy targets from beneath the waves) made the stealthy killers even more lethal.

The 288 U.S. subs deployed during the Pacific war sank nearly 5 million tons of Japanese merchant shipping (more than

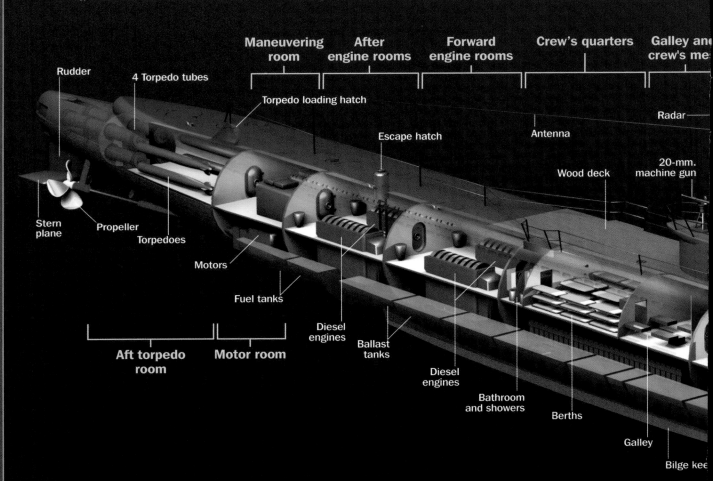

U.S. Balao Class Submarine

Crew . . . . **72 (8 officers, 64 men)**
Length . . . . **307 ft.**
Beam . . . . **27.5 ft.**
Hull . . . . **7/8 in. high-tensile steel**
Surface speed . . . . . **18 knots max, 13.5 knots cruise**
Submerged speed . . **20 knots max, 4 knots cruise**
Operating depth . . . . **640 ft.**
Collapse depth . . . . . **900 ft.**

half of the total lost by Japan), along with another 700,000 tons of enemy naval vessels, including eight aircraft carriers, 11 cruisers and one battleship. Those are the major kills: a more complete tally would include 43 destroyers, 23 submarines and 189 minor vessels. All told, submarines accounted for more than one-third of all the Japanese naval tonnage sent to the bottom during the course of the war.

By late 1944, U.S. seamen whose uniforms sported a twin-dolphin badge (the traditional insignia of the submarine service) were sinking Japanese ships at a rate of more than 50 each month—and also rescuing Americans from "the drink." A total of 504 U.S. pilots (among them future President George H.W. Bush) were rescued by U.S. subs, as were hundreds of sailors whose ships had sunk.

Submarines were invisible but far from invincible. Of the 14,750 officers and men who served on U.S. subs, more than 3,500 were killed in action—a loss rate that made submarine service the most dangerous single duty in the war.

The workhorse sub against Japan was the *Balao* class: with 119 vessels in service, this design accounted for more than 4 of every 10 subs that saw action in the Pacific. Longer than a football field (at 307 ft.), a *Balao*-class sub could carry a crew of 80 men or more for as long as 75 days without resupply, remaining submerged for up to 48 hours at a time.

There was no room for luxury on a *Balao*-class sub. The crew shared 30 beds (they were used in shifts), two toilets and two sinks. Officers and enlisted men alike worked 18-hour days in temperatures that often topped 100°F. Everyone was allowed one shower per week—which explains why, on these subs, even the enlisted men ranked. ■

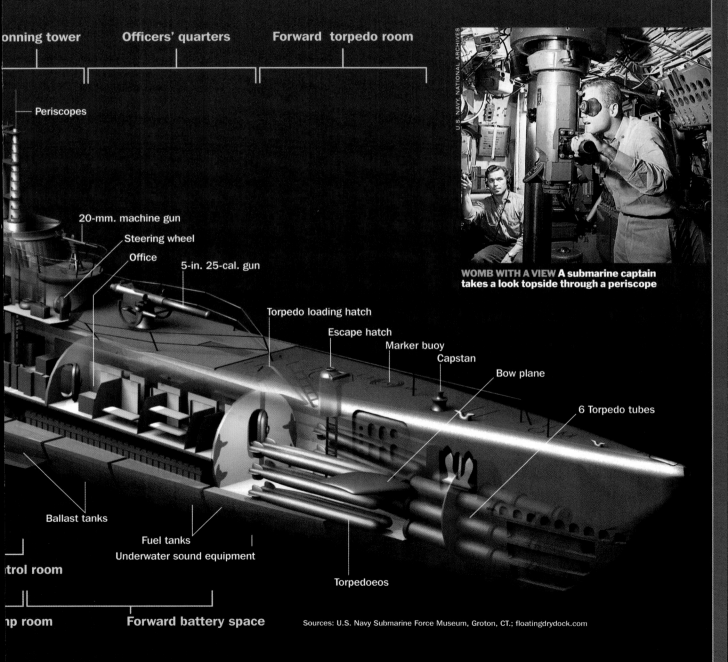

WOMB WITH A VIEW A submarine captain takes a look topside through a periscope

onning tower   Officers' quarters   Forward torpedo room

Periscopes

20-mm. machine gun

Steering wheel

Office

5-in. 25-cal. gun

Torpedo loading hatch

Escape hatch

Marker buoy

Capstan

Bow plane

6 Torpedo tubes

Ballast tanks

Fuel tanks

Underwater sound equipment

Torpedoeos

trol room

p room   Forward battery space

Sources: U.S. Navy Submarine Force Museum, Groton, CT.; floatingdrydock.com

"A ship is always referred to as she because it costs so much to keep one in paint and powder."

—Chester Nimitz

A Question of Balance

Thrust into command only days after Pearl Harbor, Chester Nimitz turned the ailing Pacific Fleet into a striking force that was fast, elusive and deadly

AT HIS NEW, SEABEE-BUILT HEAD-quarters on Guam, Chester William Nimitz sat at a shiny new desk. He wore khaki shorts and an open-necked shirt with the five stars of a fleet admiral on the points of his collar. He was waiting. Radio Tokyo went off the air, came on again, screaming about the approach of U.S. planes. Then the Navy signal was flashed: Vice Admiral Marc Andrew ("Pete") Mitscher's attack on Tokyo—600 fighter planes launched from the main striking force of the U.S. Pacific Fleet, steaming only 200 to 300 miles offshore from the Japanese capital—had begun.

Nimitz reached for his pen, gripped it in a hand gnarled by rheumatism (from submarine service a quarter of a century ago) and wrote in a neat, upright hand, "This operation has long been planned, and the opportunity to accomplish it fulfills the deeply cherished desire of every officer and man of the Pacific Fleet."

The disciplined language of the communiqué was scarcely an emotional outburst. But in those words Nimitz had allowed himself to unbend, for the world at large, more than at any previous time in his three years under the immense burdens of duty as Commander in Chief, Pacific Fleet.

Within an hour after the Japanese struck at Pearl Harbor, Nimitz had impressed his superiors as a man well suited for the Pacific command. He had been summoned to Secretary of the Navy Frank Knox's office on the second "deck" of the barracks-like Navy Department on Washington's Constitution Avenue. Nimitz, then a rear admiral and chief of the Bureau of Navigation, was the calmest man present. Soon, Knox went to President Franklin D. Roosevelt to decide the appointment of a new Commander in Chief, Pacific Fleet. A year before, Knox had submitted two names: Husband Edward Kimmel and Chester William Nimitz, in that order. Roosevelt had picked the first name. This time, said Knox, he would be satisfied with the second. The President agreed. Nimitz initially demurred. But he accepted his orders, and started west in civilian clothes, under the pseudonym of "Mr. Wainwright," by rail to San Diego and thence by air to Pearl Harbor.

In the first bleak days at Pearl Harbor, one of Nimitz's main tasks was to balance the fleet, set it on course for Tokyo and keep it there. Nimitz became to the fleet what a gyrocompass is to a ship. Unlike some admirals, he had never gone to Pensacola in middle age to take a course in aviation which would qualify him to wear wings. But he listened attentively while his flying officers—"Bull" Halsey, Forrest ("Fuzz") Sherman, Aubrey W. Fitch—argued the case of the carrier-cruiser task force. Nimitz was convinced. He sent Halsey out on the hit-run raids that buoyed the fleet's morale, and the nation's, early in 1942.

In the Coral Sea came history's first "battle beyond the horizon," in which carriers sent aerial artillery to strike at each other across hundreds of miles of water. Nimitz lost the *Lexington* but saved Australia and New Zealand. For the Battle of Midway, Halsey was ailing and unavailable. Nimitz sent Raymond Ames Spruance out first with two carriers, then Frank Jack Fletcher with the *Yorktown*. As senior, Fletcher took overall command, but when the *Yorktown* retired from the fight, crippled, Spruance carried on. The victory ended the Jap threat to Hawaii, the Panama Canal and the U.S. itself. It was the turning point of the Pacific war. In announcing the triumph, Nimitz punned, "We are about midway to our objective."

Nimitz was now 60; he had acquired the sureness of a man experienced in great responsibility. He composed differences among his staff by telling ribald stories. He broke young-officer ice by thrusting out his hand and saying, "My name's Nimitz." He was photographed dancing with a hula girl at an enlisted men's recreation center in Waikiki—and foresightedly sent the first print to Mrs. Nimitz at Berkeley, Calif. He posed happily for a goofy picture with a goony bird at Midway.

It was Nimitz who welded the carriers and cruisers of the war's early task forces into new and far more deadly task forces with battleships, when the new, fast battleships became available. As more and more ships, more and more planes reached the Pacific, Nimitz directed ever bolder strokes toward Japan. It was, he said, "simple arithmetic—subtraction for them and addition for us." This naval arithmetic has brought him to Japan's front yard. ∎

GUTSY Nimitz threw everything he had into the Battle of Midway in 1942, and the U.S. victory ended Japan's Pacific advances

GUERRILLAS AND MULES
Merrill's Marauders move through the jungle in the campaign that successfully drove the Japanese from north Burma in 1944

Off the Beaten Path

The theater was vast, the missions impossible, the supplies meager and the personalities eccentric in the Pacific war's complex Asian sideshow

ONCE UPON A TIME IN THE EXOTIC, REMOTE LANDS OF Southeast Asia, empires clashed in a conflict whose bizarre aspects, according to TIME reporter T.H. White, included: "maharajahs, dancing girls, warlords, headhunters, jungles, deserts, racketeers, secret agents." Its events were just as odd: "American pilots strafed enemy elephants from P-40s ... The Chinese Gestapo ferreted out beautiful enemy spies in their own headquarters ... Chinese warlords introduced American army officers to the delights of the opium pipe ... Tigers killed American soldiers."

Here, against a backdrop of towering Himalayan mountains and impenetrable rain forests, reckless Allied outfits like Chennault's Flying Tigers, Wingate's Chindits and Merrill's Marauders—led by charismatic military rebels who might have been refugees from one of T.E. Lawrence's desert reveries—staged daring strategic gambits. Here dashing volunteer pilots flew planes with tiger shark's teeth painted on their noses, while the Bible-quoting British guerrilla leader Charles Orde Wingate staged surprise attacks on the Japanese, and gritty U.S. General Joseph Stilwell led more than 100 Allied soldiers and civilians on a legendary jungle evacuation.

Well, that's the romantic view of World War II in the China/Burma/India Theater (CBI). And while there is plenty of truth in the legends, the real story of the CBI Theater is about as picturesque as a monsoon mudslide—or the giant leeches that preyed on soldiers of both sides, leaving bloody sores that refused to heal. For Japanese, American and British soldiers, the environment was the real enemy. Battles were fought by soldiers enfeebled by disease, and far more men died from cholera, dysentery and malaria than from enemy fire.

As for the cast of characters: Lieut. General Wingate, the leader of Britain's legendary Chindits, may charitably be said to have stayed out in the noonday sun a bit too long. Claire Chennault, the skillful U.S. aviator who led the Flying Tigers, was, in military slang, a glory hog. Chinese Nationalist leader Chiang Kai-shek presided over a corrupt, unfocused movement that would be toppled by Mao Zedong and his communist guerrillas only four years after the war ended.

Yes, there were heroes here: Brigadier General Frank Merrill and his Marauders won major victories against impossible odds. Wingate's Chindits played havoc behind Japanese lines. Stilwell, one of America's finest generals, was hamstrung by the conflicting agendas of the Chinese, British and U.S. in Asia; in the end he was unceremoniously recalled from his post, even as the goals he worked for were attained.

The far-flung CBI Theater is best viewed through the frustrating career of General Stilwell, a highly capable West Point

graduate who was one of the U.S. Army's finest tacticians. He first visited China in the 1920s, as a young veteran of World War I, and he grew to love the Chinese people for their high-mindedness—and hate them for their indolence. He felt much the same about his counterpart in China, Chiang Kai-shek, leader of the Kuomintang (Nationalist) movement. With his U.S.-educated wife, Chiang sought to unify, modernize and westernize China, against enormous odds. In the years following the Japanese incursion into Manchuria in

PARTNERS U.S. General Joseph Stilwell, right, worked closely with Chinese Nationalist leader Chiang Kai-shek and his wife long before World War II broke out, but he would ultimately clash with the pair. If the trio seem giddy in this picture, it's because they have just learned of the successful Doolittle bombing raid on Tokyo in April 1942

1931—as the Japanese empire advanced to control much of eastern and southern China—the two had been lionized in the U.S. as America's allies and China's saviors, not least in the pages of TIME, whose co-founder Henry Luce was born in China, the son of Protestant missionaries.

Stilwell, widely considered one of the U.S. Army's best tacticians and trainers of men, had been George C. Marshall's choice to lead the Allied invasion of North Africa, following which he would probably have been offered the chance to lead the invasion of Europe. But Stilwell's knowledge of Chi-

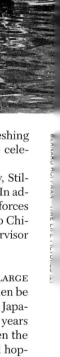

BIG MUDDY Above, a unit of Merrill's Marauders cross a river in Burma. Many Marauders were veterans of earlier campaigns in the South Pacific islands

THE BOSS Marauder leader Major Frank Merrill (later a Brigadier General) was a West Point graduate who endured the "walkout" retreat from Burma in 1942

na made him the perfect choice to be the top U.S. commander on the Asian mainland, and in January 1942, Marshall asked him to head up the U.S. CBI command. The European posts would eventually be given to General Dwight Eisenhower.

In the CBI Theater, Stilwell's overall goals were to support China and help the British defend their colonies in India and Burma. But when he reported for duty in February 1942, the Japanese were already invading Burma and sweeping the ineffectual British before them, just as they had in Singapore and Hong Kong. Stilwell could have retreated from the city of Shwebo in a U.S. C-47, but he chose to stay until the Japanese were at his doorstep. In a courageous and resourceful 22-day retreat, he led 113 British and U.S. soldiers and Asian civilians through 140 miles of deep jungle to safety. When he arrived in India, American newspapermen in desperate need of good news portrayed his deeds as heroic, but the caustic "Vinegar Joe" threw water on that fire, declaring "I claim we got a hell

of a beating." Ironically, his refreshing candor made him an even more celebrated figure in the Allied press.

With Burma lost to the enemy, Stilwell faced enormous challenges. In addition to leading the U.S. Army forces in CBI, he was America's liaison to Chiang, serving as the Chinese leader's chief of staff, supervisor of Lend-Lease aid and chief trainer of his troops.

STILWELL'S ULTIMATE GOAL WAS TO TAKE BACK A LARGE portion of the Chinese mainland, which would then be used as a staging area for bombing raids over the Japanese homeland. (This was the Allied strategy in the first years of the Pacific war; it would be altered late in 1944, when the Allied high command agreed that a campaign of island hopping across the Pacific was likely to bring U.S. bombers into range of Japan much sooner.) As Stilwell saw it in 1942, if China was to be saved, it must be supplied. And with Japan controlling China's ports on the Pacific, Lend-Lease equipment was now reaching Chiang only via the trans-Himalayan airlift known as "Flying the Hump." Here the U.S. pilots of the Air Transport Command were flying the world's longest and most difficult supply route, some 600 miles from eastern India to Kunming in China, Chiang's capital in exile. The route skimmed the world's tallest peaks, amid extreme weather, bad terrain and Japanese fighter attacks. Protecting the Hump pilots were the celebrated volunteers of Chennault's civilian flying squad, the Flying Tigers.

Chennault was an Army Air Force captain who retired at age 47 in 1937 and soon became the chief air strategist for his friend Chiang. At Chiang's urging, Chennault managed to buy 100 obsolete P-40 Tomahawk fighters, painted their pointed snouts with the grinning, deadly teeth of a tiger shark and put out a call for U.S. pilots to fly them. The American Volunteer Group, a motley crew of soldiers of fortune, took to the skies over Burma during the Japanese invasion and became the sole bright spot in the Allies' losing battle, shooting down more than 297 Japanese planes while losing only four of their own. On July 4, 1942, the Flying Tigers were disbanded, and Chennault and his flyboys officially joined the U.S. Army Air Force, forming the China Air Task Force, whose primary mission was to guard the skies over the Hump.

WITH CHINA LANDLOCKED FROM THE OUTSIDE WORLD and only a trickle of supplies coming in over the Hump, Stilwell needed to open an overland route to Kunming. That meant taking back Burma and controlling the Burma Road, which led to China, and connecting it to a new road, the Ledo Road, which the Allies were building to connect Burma to India. Throughout 1942 and '43, Stilwell proposed plan after plan for an invasion of Burma, but the Chinese troops were not ready for battle, and he lacked sufficient machines and men. Winston Churchill, Franklin Roosevelt and George C. Marshall had bigger fish to fry than CBI's woes.

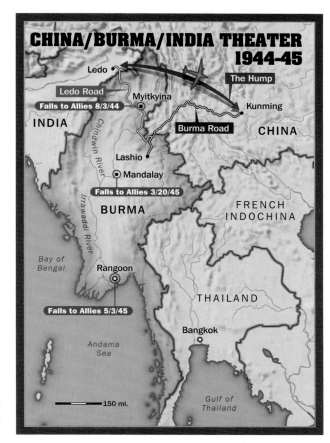

CHINA/BURMA/INDIA THEATER 1944-45

Ledo
Ledo Road
The Hump
Falls to Allies 8/3/44
Myitkyina
Kunming
INDIA
Chindwin River
Burma Road
CHINA
Lashio
Mandalay
Falls to Allies 3/20/45
BURMA
Irrawaddi River
FRENCH INDOCHINA
Bay of Bengal
Rangoon
THAILAND
Falls to Allies 5/3/45
Bangkok
Andama Sea
Gulf of Thailand
150 mi.

Wingate's Chindits: British Guerrillas in Burma

A pioneer of military units that stay mobile, work behind enemy lines and wreak havoc on enemy communications, transportation and morale, Orde Wingate was one of the last great military eccentrics of the British Empire. Son of a puritanical colonel in Britain's Indian army, Wingate attended the Royal Military Academy, studied Arabic and served in the Sudan. The deeply religious Wingate came into his own as an intelligence officer in Palestine in the 1930s, then a British protectorate, where he became a devoted Zionist and organized the "Special Night Squads" (guerrilla units that protected Jewish settlements) and helped train Moshe Dayan and other Israeli warriors of his generation. Unkempt, unorthodox and insubordinate, Wingate was often at odds with his

superiors; despite winning recognition in Ethiopia in 1941 for leading successful ambushes on Italian units, he became depressed and attempted suicide.

The British army gave Wingate one last chance. Winston Churchill loved his radical plan: "long-range penetration units" that would work behind Japanese lines in Burma. Christening his group the Chindits after a Burmese

mythical beast, Wingate led his 3,000 men through a harsh jungle training regimen in India that left many of them sick and exhausted. The Chindits moved into Burma in February 1943. Supplied by airdrops, they raised hell, blowing up railroads and ambushing Japanese units. In 1944 the Chindits teamed up with Merrill's Marauders to drive the Japanese from north Burma. Sadly, Orde Wingate did not survive to share the glory; he died in a plane crash in Burma in March 1944.

CONFAB Right, U.S. pilots meet with Wingate's Chindits behind enemy lines in 1945. Inset: Wingate in Burma, 1943

Moreover, Stilwell frequently clashed with Chiang, who, to be fair, faced immense challenges—from the Japanese invaders, from Mao Zedong's communist guerrillas and from power-hungry regional warlords whose fealty was negotiable. Utterly reliant on U.S. Lend-Lease aid, which Stilwell managed, Chiang lobbied continually for the general's removal, urging F.D.R. to replace him with Chennault, Stilwell's rival.

Rebuffed on all sides, Stilwell turned to the job he did best: training troops. Selecting several promising Chinese divisions, he drilled them mercilessly and scraped together enough matériel to make two very respectable fighting units of them, the "X Force" and "Y Force."

FINALLY, AS 1943 BECAME 1944, STILWELL AND THE BRITish were ready to launch an offensive in Burma. They would strike on three fronts: Stilwell would lead his Chinese troops down from the north toward the strategically vital city of Myitkyina on the Irrawaddy River, site of the only all-year, all-weather airfield in Burma. In central Burma, British Lieut. General Wingate and his Chindits (see sidebar) would stage a guerrilla campaign, disrupting Japanese communications and tying down troops. Meanwhile, an entirely new force in Burma, the 5307th Combat Unit (Provisional) would penetrate east of Stilwell and drive toward Myitkyina, forming a pincer with Stilwell's Chinese forces.

The 5307th unit, code-named Galahad, was formed after Stilwell convinced George Marshall at a 1943 meeting that the tool with which the Allies could wrest Burma from the Japanese was a guerrilla-style force operating behind enemy lines. Marshall agreed, and F.D.R. himself put out a request through the entire U.S. Army, asking for volunteers for "a dangerous

and hazardous mission" that would involve jungle training. Quickly, the quota of 3,000 men signed up for the unit; they were sent to India and trained by Wingate. Stilwell placed a trusted subordinate, Major Frank Merrill, in command. After spending some time with these jungle-hardened roughnecks, TIME correspondent James Shepley dubbed them "Merrill's Marauders," and the name stuck.

In late December 1943, two Chinese "X Force" divisions moved into north Burma along the Hukawng Valley. Stilwell joined them in late December, and directed them in taking the town of Yupbang Ga—the first time in Asia that Chinese soldiers had defeated the Japanese. Moving south, Stilwell's force reached the important city of Maingkwan and wrested it from the enemy.

Meanwhile, Merrill's units were moving east of Maingkwan, hiking over steep mountain passes, supplied only by airdrops. In the village of Walawbum the Marauders took on the tough Japanese 18th Division—conquerors of Singapore, Burma and Malaya—and dealt it a stinging defeat. By March 9 the Chinese troops and the U.S. Marauders were both moving south, heading for Myitkyina.

TIME-LIFE photographer Bernard Hoffman traveled with

the Marauders on this campaign and sketched their lives in an April 1944 dispatch, unpublished until now. "This is a typical Marauder outfit, having lived in the jungle for three months without rest, spending practically all its time behind and surrounded by enemy lines," he wrote. "Men have lived on 'K' rations mostly, depending on airdrop for food and supplies. Some are currently suffering from diarrhea and dysentery. Marauders moving fast and light have long since discarded mosquito nets and repellents as unnecessary weight. Well-kept arms and ammunition take priorities. Towels, toothpaste, toothbrushes, bedrolls, mess kits, raincoats and even clothing change is unknown. Majority are bearded, shaggy headed, sick. All are tough, tired, but rugged enough to ignore

troops joined them days later. Then, defying early Allied gains, the Japanese dug in, the monsoon rains came, and the battle for the river town bogged down into a long, miserable siege.

Finally, on Aug. 4, 1944, the last Japanese withdrew from the city; their leader, Major General Gezu Mizukami, committed seppuku, ritual suicide. Merrill's Marauders had weathered five major and 30 minor battles. With the Chindits and Chinese, they had driven the Japanese from north Burma—and work on the Ledo-Burma Road at last moved into high gear.

In 1945 the British took over most of the campaign in Burma, attacking from India across the Irrawaddy to Mandalay, which they captured in mid-March. They then pushed south to Rangoon, taking it on May 3. Burma was liberated.

> "[The CBI Theater] is a fabulous compound of logistics, personalities, Communism, despotism, corruption, imperialism, nonsense and tragic impotence." —TIME reporter Theodore H. White

personal discomfort. All are volunteers … I marched and bivouacked with them over more than thirty miles of jungle, crossing four hill ranges from 1,600 ft. to 3,000 ft. elevations … One officer bitten on crown by leech bled four days—leeches leave wounds defying coagulation. Personally collected twelve leechbites which infected. Monsoons are on and Marauders living in world of mud but morale good."

The Marauders went on to weather a grueling 13-day siege at Nhpum Ga, which they called "Maggot Hill"—it was their finest hour. They then struggled over a mountain range, regrouped and attacked Myitkyina on May 17; Stilwell's Chinese

In February 1945, a convoy of 113 U.S. vehicles made the first trip from Ledo in India to Kunming in China. The Burma-Ledo Road was open—under a new name. In an utterly hollow gesture, Chiang had christened it the Stilwell Road. Nor was Joseph Stilwell allowed to reap the fruits of his unstinting labors. Chiang had finally convinced F.D.R. to recall his acerbic foe; Stilwell left China in October 1944. Even more galling, thanks to Allied advances in the Pacific, the great roadway was no longer viewed as a vital lifeline to victory; like the CBI Theater itself, by 1945 it amounted to a scenic, forgotten detour from the main ocean arteries of the war in Asia. ∎

"I claim we got a hell of a beating. We got run out of Burma, and it is humiliating as hell. I think we ought to find out what caused it, go back and retake it." —Joseph Stilwell, 1942

A Crisis in China

Brisk and buttoned-up, Joseph Stilwell was one of the Army's smartest generals. But in Chiang Kai-shek he found an enemy he couldn't conquer

FRANKLIN D. ROOSEVELT STUFFED another cigarette into his long ivory holder. The White House reporters asked, "Anything you can tell us in the way of background on why it was necessary to call General Stilwell home?" The President flicked ash from his chalk-striped suit, answered:

General Stilwell has done extremely well … Generalissimo Chiang Kai-shek and General Stilwell had had certain fallings out, oh, quite a while ago; and finally the other day, the Generalissimo asked that somebody be sent to replace General Stilwell. And we did it …

Last week tart, taciturn Joseph W. Stilwell arrived in Washington from the Far East. He said nothing. His silence was eloquent. For few Americans knew China so well as he. Few understood so well as he the gravity of the crisis dramatized by his recall—its implications for the future fate of China, the U.S., the world.

Of all Americans Joe Stilwell should apparently be *persona gratissima* to the Chinese. He is a staunch admirer of China, a close friend of her people, a champion of her causes, a student of her culture. He is a rare "Old China hand" who knows the language so well that he can think in Chinese. And, as Chiang Kai-shek's first foreign Chief of Staff, Stilwell was the symbol of China's hope in the abiding aid and friendship of the U.S. [*West Point graduate Stilwell served in France in World War I and became fascinated by China in the 1920s as a military language student studying in Beijing.* —ED.] Between service stretches in China, Joe Stilwell taught infantry tactics in the U.S. He also raised a family—three daughters, two sons. But Joe Stilwell, honest, good-humored scholar, teacher and family man, was also known as an acidulous observer of the world of men. For his avuncular benignity, he was called "Uncle Joe." For his biting comments on dopes and humbugs, he was nicknamed "Vinegar."

In March 1942, General Stilwell went back to China, plunged immediately into the hopeless task of holding Burma against the Japanese. His famed retreat across Burma ("I

ELECTION ISSUE —

TIME
THE WEEKLY NEWSMAGAZINE

GENERAL JOSEPH W. STILWELL

TART Stilwell grew to despise Chiang Kai-shek; he dubbed the bald leader "Peanut." Vinegar Joe told F.D.R. that Chiang was "a tricky, undependable old scoundrel who never keeps his word"

claim we got a hell of a beating") did not shake his faith in the Chinese soldier. Generalissimo Chiang Kai-shek supported Stilwell, at first. So did his good friend, U.S. Army Chief of Staff General George C. Marshall. But on all sides, frustrations piled up. All of Joe Stilwell's vinegar personality couldn't bite a way through the conflicting confusions of U.S. foreign policy, Chinese domestic policy and Britain's Asiatic aims.

In his campaign to reopen a road to China through northern Burma, "Vinegar Joe," at 59, proved himself a crack field commander, a masterly tactician—and also a driving, red-tape-be-damned anti-diplomat. His men, Chinese and American, saw him frequently from their jungle foxholes. He jeeped across the tortuous terrain indefatigably, injected his high-octane personality into every advance.

But Joe Stilwell did not get along well with the British: Winston Churchill's policy in the Far East was consistently at variance with U.S. policy. He could not get enough supplies for the Chinese. The trickle of supplies that used to be hauled agonizingly over the Burma Road became a dribble when it had to be flown over the Himalayan "Hump." It is still a dribble.

Chiang Kai-shek believed that his government's most urgent need was more supplies. Instead of sending supplies, Washington proposed that General Stilwell be given command of all Chinese forces. The Generalissimo had earlier agreed to let Stilwell supervise U.S. Lend-Lease in China. Such a condition had been imposed on no other head of a foreign state. The implication was that Chiang could not be trusted with Lend-Lease. He had already accepted the proposal that Stilwell be given tactical command of China's armies. Then, seemingly in the discussion over the exact scope of Stilwell's command, he was pushed too far.

On Oct. 19 Joe Stilwell received his recall from Washington. Next day, over a formal cup of tea, he bade farewell to the Generalissimo. He declined the offer of a high Chinese decoration. He attended a final cocktail party with his staff, packed his dumbbells, captured samurai sword and traveling gear. Then he enplaned for the U.S. in the silver-painted transport known as "Uncle Joe's Chariot." Few men had been stouter friends of China. ∎

Off Duty

Waging war against a backdrop of some of the planet's most beautiful scenery had its advantages—namely, the moments when one wasn't waging war. Even TIME's 1945 account of a day in the life of Admiral Chester Nimitz at his headquarters on Guam carries an intoxicating whiff of tropical breezes: "Each morning, tanned from sunbaths, he walked a mile or so before breakfast; each afternoon he played tennis, or walked up and down Aiea Mountain, or hiked seven miles to a beach for a three-mile swim … "

■ **BREW** Above, Pacific duty offered rewards for reporters as well as soldiers. Here Frank Robertson of the Independent News Service, left, and Frank Smith of the Chicago *Times* assess captured Japanese beer on Leyte

■ **BANYAN BANJO** Far left, on Bougainville, PFC Jake Reynolds plays an instrument he pieced together from the wood of a banyan tree and used tin cans

■ **TOUGH ASSIGNMENT** At left, American nurses and soldiers clown around on an outrigger canoe in the surf off Tarawa Atoll in March 1944, months after the U.S. invasion of the atoll's two small islands claimed thousands of lives

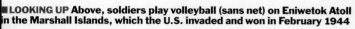

■ **LOOKING UP** Above, soldiers play volleyball (sans net) on Eniwetok Atoll in the Marshall Islands, which the U.S. invaded and won in February 1944

■ **DO-SI-DO** At right, a sailor gets a lesson in local dance customs from a South Pacific islander; the date and location of this picture are not known

■ **ANTE UP** Below, sailors from the Pacific fleet enjoy sunshine, palm trees and a game of cards at Geb Gab Beach on Guam, a U.S. Navy R.-and-R. camp

■ **GOT A LIGHT?** A soldier shares a smoke with a native; Lucky Strikes were preferre[d]

■ **NEWS** A G.I. reads **TIME**'s May 21, 194[5] issue (in a small military edition) on Okina[wa]

■ **AMATEURS** A trio of U.S. sailors don grass skirts and leis to entertain a local crowd on Agrihan in the Marianas chain. The island was occupied by the U.S. in June 1945, in an uncontested invasion

■ **WHERE THERE'S LIFE …** Indefatigable Bob Hope, the war's greatest ambassador to the troops, gets Allied soldiers laughing at a U.S. base on New Caledonia island in Melanesia in October 1944

■ **HIGH TIME** USO troupers kick off an impromptu show on a beach on Guam, a central Pacific transit hub. If the crowd's spirits also appear elevated, it may be because the month is November 1945, and soldiers were heading back to the U.S. after the war's end

■ **HUNGRY?** Army Lieutenant Richard Jones offers food to underfed local kids on Okinawa in 1945

■ **STOPOVER** At left, on Guam, Army nurses take a break from traveling; they're bound for duty at points farther west in the Pacific

■ **ENCHANTED?** Nurse Ida ("Chick") Vinquist of Minnesota and Major H.M. Licht of Illinois enjoy beach time on the Marianas

Mission to Manila

The U.S. lands the war's single largest invasion force on Luzon Island, but the Japanese, with no hope of escape, devastate the Philippine capital

I HAD BEEN IN THE FIRST WAVE TO LAND ON NEW GEORGIA in the South Pacific," recalls Alfred Cassella, "so I thought I knew what to expect." On the morning of Jan. 9, 1945, as he climbed down the nets on the side of his troop ship in Lingayen Gulf and into the amphibious landing craft waiting below, Cassella, then a 26-year-old infantry sergeant in the 43rd Division, tried to reassure the men under his command who had not yet experienced combat. "I told them to stay calm and move fast," he remembers. "The main thing was to get on dry land as quickly as possible, and then to move fast off that beach. Because anybody who stayed in the water or on the sand was going to die there.

"The weather was beautiful," says Cassella, now 86 and retired proprietor of a liquor store in New Britain, Conn. "A light breeze, gentle waves, and bright sunshine. The only clouds we could see were the smoke coming from the Navy's bombard-

ment of the beach. We could actually see huge shells flying over our heads, from ships farther out in the bay, and then exploding onshore. I thought, with the hell they were kicking up, we'd be able to walk right up that beach and not have to worry at all about the Japanese. Nothing could live through that."

On that day, Cassella and the 40 men under his command were assigned to the initial wave in one of the war's major invasions. The target was Luzon, the main island in the Philippines and site of the capital, Manila. As the naval barrage lifted and their landing craft began speeding toward shore, Cassella remembers, "all of the chatter died down, and each man was alone with his thoughts for a few minutes."

The landing craft slowed ever so slightly as it

entered shallow water, then scraped the sandy bottom with a dull thud—drawing to a halt a few second later as the front door lowered. "I was the first one out," Cassella says. "You technically aren't supposed to lead from the front in combat, but that was just my style. I knew my guys wouldn't hesitate to follow if I was shouting orders over my shoulder, instead of yelling at them from the rear. So I jumped down into waist-deep water and began wading toward shore." His men followed, holding their weapons and packs over their heads and moving as quickly as they could through the surf.

And then ... nothing. "It couldn't have been more different from New Georgia," Cassella recalls, sheepishly. "There was no fire on the beach at all. On New Georgia, whole companies had been wiped out by machine-gun fire as soon as the ramp was down, or even while they were still in the landing craft. But on Luzon, we didn't meet any opposition on the beach."

If Cassella thought that the entire Luzon campaign would be as effortless, he was wrong, and he bears the proof: to this day, he speaks in the gravelly voice of a man who has a bullet lodged in his throat that doctors have deemed safer to leave in place than risk removing. He calls it his souvenir of Luzon.

Cassella's first objective was to take his company off the beach and regroup at railroad tracks that ran parallel to the shore, several hundred yards inland. "The second wave came in right behind us," he says, "and they didn't get a scratch either. But just as we reached the tracks, the third wave land-ed—and that's when the Japanese artillery opened up." In the hills overlooking the beach, Japanese gunners who had pre-sighted their artillery onto the beach with minute precision began raking the sand with fire. "Our guys were getting de-stroyed," Cassella says. "We could hear them screaming."

Once he had formed his unit up at the railroad line, Cas-sella led his men through a large expanse of rice paddies to the foot of the hills from which the Japanese were firing. By nightfall, Cassella and his unit, Company I of the 169th In-fantry Regiment, had made it up to the top of the first line of hills facing the beach. The were told to dig in there and await further orders. "That's when the first Japanese counterattack came," he recalls. "They came out of caves and holes in the ground and would scream while they charged at us in waves."

On the hill that Cassella's platoon had taken, and dozens like

COMEBACK The battleship U.S.S. *Pennsylvania* leads a line of cruisers through the Lingayen Gulf in the Philippines as a vast U.S. armada assembles to support the invasion of Luzon

it overlooking the Luzon beachhead, rifle fire cut down as many enemy soldiers as dared to charge the U.S. positions head on. But the Japanese entrenched within bunkers and tunnels were far tougher targets. "We were one of the first units to have napalm," Cassella remembers. "It worked much better than ordinary flame throwers, because it would splash around inside a cave and stick to everything it hit."

The Japanese quickly learned to target Americans carrying this newfangled weapon. "Guys with napalm had to carry much larger tanks than soldiers with regular flame throwers," Cassella says. "So they moved slower and made a much bigger target. They did us a lot of good," he remembers, "but they never lasted long."

"I was always a big grenade man," Cassella says of the series of firefights that lasted another week, during which the hills overlooking the beach on Lingayen Gulf were cleared of Japanese defenders. "I always carried extra 'frags,' because that was the best way to clear out a Japanese position. The challenge was getting close enough to the enemy to use them."

FROM DOUGLAS MACARTHUR'S PERSPECTIVE, MANY LEVELS above that of a platoon sergeant like Cassella, the goal at Luzon was simple. Japan's air power had been destroyed at the Battle of Midway, in June 1942. The enemy's ability to fight on the seas had been seriously diminished months earlier at the Battle of Leyte Gulf. Now Luzon offered the chance to destroy Japan's ability to fight on land. If the Japanese army contingent garrisoned in the Philippines— some 430,000 troops, more than half of them based on Luzon

LUZON CAMPAIGN 1945

Philippine Sea

LUZON

Lingayen Gulf • San Fernando

Held by Allies 1/31/45

Held by Allies 3/15/45

Held by Japan 8/15/45

1st landings - 1/9/45

• Cabanatuan
• Clark Field

75 mi.

Manila

2nd landings - 1/29/45

BATAAN

Allies control - 3/4/45

CORREGIDOR

BICOL PENINSULA

South China Sea

MINDORO

3rd landings - 1/31/45

—could be eliminated, the third and last weapon in Japan's arsenal would be taken from the enemy. Moreover, MacArthur felt a personal obligation to liberate the Philippines, a task he had begun with the Leyte campaign, which had wrapped up only weeks before.

For the Japanese army commander in the Philippines, General Tomoyuki Yamashita, the stakes were equally high. The loss of the islands would cut Japan's Pacific empire in half, rendering every possession on the far side of the archipelago useless to Tokyo and vulnerable to Allied attack. But Yamashita also knew he could expect little support or reinforcement. So he broke Luzon's Japanese garrison into three forces (Shobu, Kembu and Shimbu Groups) and sent most of his troops in retreat to the island's mountainous interior, where the terrain would favor the defenders.

For his first stab into Luzon, MacArthur chose the beaches along Lingayen Gulf, where Cassella landed on Jan. 9, dubbed S-day by MacArthur's invasion planners. This area of sheltered beaches on the northwestern coast of the island would position U.S. troops close to the best roads and railways on Luzon, facilitating a speedy drive on Manila, MacArthur's primary objective. The 10 U.S. divisions MacArthur eventually hurled at the island would outnumber even the massive landing force that stormed Normandy on D-day and would mark Luzon as the largest campaign of the Pacific war. As of S-day-plus-three, more than 175,000 Americans had landed along a beachhead 25 miles wide.

American progress was steady in the first weeks of the campaign, but MacArthur was impatient to recapture the city

SCORCHED EARTH Almost three years after Corregidor fell to the enemy, American soldiers of the 503rd Parachute Infantry Regiment move through a blasted hillside landscape on the island. The date is Feb. 17, 1945; some 15,000 starving U.S. and Filipino soldiers had surrendered to the Japanese here after weathering a month-long siege on May 6, 1942

WELCOME! Tarawa it wasn't: a young American landing on a Luzon beach is greeted by exuberant Filipinos. The Japanese didn't contest most landings but moved inland and dug in there

"One gaunt, toothless, ragged woman had nothing to give. But she hobbled out to catch and kiss the hand of an embarrassed colonel. She sobbed: 'God bless the Americans.'" —TIME, Feb. 12, 1945

from which he had been driven in retreat three years earlier. Throughout January, he drove to the front lines almost daily, at one point exhorting the division commander of the 1st Cavalry, "Go to Manila! Go around the Nips, bounce off the Nips, but go to Manila!"

Determined to attack the city from several directions at once, MacArthur ordered new amphibious landings at other Luzon beaches on Jan. 15 and Jan. 31. For American troops landing at undefended beaches, the reception was unsettling. As bewildered U.S. infantrymen ran out of their landing craft, rifles at the ready, they were met by crowds of elated Filipinos singing *God Bless America.* Units diverted from these beaches onto the paved roads and rail lines leading into Manila often found them lined with cheering civilians.

In the hills and mountains above these beaches, where Yamashita had bivouacked the several hundred thousand troops of his Shobu, Kembu and Shimbu task forces, the story was very different. "We couldn't light a cigarette," Cassella remembers, "because it would instantly draw machine-gun fire. But we would look down at the roads, and see the 1st Cavalry driving toward Manila with their lights on. It was frustrating, because they wouldn't have been able to go near that road if the units in the mountains, like ours, weren't clearing out the Japanese positions covering them." American units stationed in the mountains were engaging, on average, in several fire fights each day—taking territory yards at a time and

paying a high price in blood. "Oh, well," Cassella says with a laugh. "We got the dirty deal, and they got the glory."

NOT QUITE: THE 1ST CAVALRY—AND OTHER U.S. FORCES that were converging on Manila from three directions by the first week in February—would soon get an unforgettable taste of Japanese resistance. Although General Yamashita was prepared to write the city off as indefensible, the Japanese naval commander in Manila, Admiral Iwabachi Sanji, felt that his honor and that of the Japanese Navy were at stake. He resolved to defy Yamashita and hold the Philippine capital to the last man.

On the outskirts of the city, the U.S. troops' rapid advance from the invasion beaches ground to a halt. The new tempo of the battle was highlighted by the resistance that U.S. soldiers met at the town of Imus, five miles south of Manila, on Feb. 3. After the town had been almost completely overrun, several dozen Japanese troops retreated into a stone house. Machine-gun fire and prolonged shelling by 75-mm howitzers failed to dislodge them. Finally, an American infantryman clambered onto the roof, poured gasoline through a hole made by the shelling and tossed in a phosphorous grenade. As the building burst into flames, the Japanese troops dashed out and were cut down by American riflemen. It was a victory, but the single firefight took almost an entire day.

Unaware that the prize so close to his reach still exceeded his grasp, MacArthur announced the next day that Manila's fall was imminent, and his staff began planning a victory parade. The plans were put on hold. Although American salients finally pierced into Manila on Feb. 5, the battle for the city quickly devolved into some of the bloodiest and most protracted street fighting seen anywhere in the course of the war. After savage house-by-house combat, U.S. troops eventually freed Santo Tomas University, which the Japanese had converted into a concentration camp that housed more than 4,000 POWs and civilians in horrifying conditions. During the battle for the capital, rampaging Japanese troops with no chance of escape set fire to hospitals, raped women of all ages, mutilated small children and babies and murdered an estimated 100,000 Filipino civilians. When the battle was over, Manila was a smoking ruin. Of all the cities ravaged in World War II, only Warsaw and Stalingrad would suffer more.

On March 4, the last Japanese stronghold within the city, the massive stone Finance Building, was subdued. Typically, the Japanese within had continued fighting until no one was left alive. "My country kept the faith," MacArthur told the people of Manila later that day. "Your capital city, cruelly punished though it be, has regained its rightful place—citadel of democracy in the East."

Manila's full military value could not be exploited until the Bataan Peninsula, on the western shore of the city's harbor, and the fortress island of Corregidor, from which MacArthur had fled in 1942, were won. Both objectives were finally taken—at great cost—as the last mopping up within Manila was completed. In the island's mountainous interior, the fighting would continue through the end of the war. But by the end of April, the fate of Luzon was clear. The island, and control of the Philippines, had been pried from Japan's grasp.

The victory came at a galling cost for both sides. Virtually all the 230,000 Japanese troops on Luzon were killed or wounded. Among the invaders, some 10,000 Americans were killed and more than 125,000 wounded, making the Luzon campaign one of the costliest of the entire war. One of the wounded was Alfred Cassella, who fought in the mountains until almost the very end. In one victorious firefight with a Japanese unit, he earned a rare battlefield commission, a promotion to second lieutenant. Just a week after donning his new bars, however, Cassella was targeted by a sniper, who fired the bullet that remains in his throat. It was his third combat wound, and this time the Army sent him home. "I got back to Connecticut in the middle of August," the veteran recalls. "And a few days later, the war was over." ∎

WASTELAND American troops advance past the ruins of the historic walled city section of Manila. Trapped Japanese troops terrorized the civilian population and devastated the Philippine capital before it fell

"The centuries-old walled city, the Intramuros, was a natural fortress. In one church, two machine guns were found beneath the altar."
—TIME, Feb. 19, 1945

Carl Mydans

Photojournalist Mydans and his reporter wife Shelley worked as a team for both TIME and LIFE. They began covering World War II in Europe, chronicling Hitler's drive into Poland and the fall of France. Assigned to the Pacific in 1940, they were stranded in Manila when the Philippines fell and spent eight months as captives in the internment camp at Santo Tomas University, then in a camp in Shanghai. They were repatriated in December 1943; four months later, Carl Mydans went off to cover the Italian front. When General Douglas MacArthur returned to the Philippines, the photographer went back to the Pacific to witness the liberation of the islands—and of the inmates still at Santo Tomas

■ **COMEBACK** General Douglas MacArthur wades ashore during the invasion of Luzon. His first wet trek, at Leyte, was an accident, but he repeated it, well aware that the result was a strong image

■ **SERVICE** At top right, American troops kneel as a Filipino priest says Mass outside the battered façade of St. Augustine, the oldest Roman Catholic church—and possibly the oldest European-style building—in Manila

■ **ALLY** At right, a Filipino boy sports a U.S. Army helmet and a cut-down uniform. Christened "Bobby," the youngster was adopted by the soldiers of the 33rd Infantry Division during the fighting on the island of Luzon

■STARVED Living skeletons, U.S. civilians Lee Rogers, left, and John C. Todd sit outside the Santo Tomas University camp. Rogers was a retired employee of the Cavite Navy Yard near Manila; Todd was a miner. Neither was a soldier. When Rogers entered the camp he weighed 145 lbs.; he weighed 90 lbs. when freed. Todd dropped from 172 lbs. to 102 lbs.

■RUINS On a street outside Manila, three Filipino girls hold their noses as they pass the body of a dead boy. TIME described Manila in March 1945 as "ten square miles of devastation"

■FREE Left, the liberated prisoners of the Santo Tomas University internment camp in Manila salute the first U.S. flag they have seen for 37 months. Carl Mydans was the first American to enter the camp, where he had been held captive. He was quickly recognized and given a hysterical greeting by 3,700 overjoyed inmates. "I was picked up bodily, full camera pack, canteen belt and all," he cabled to America, "and carried on the hands of the internees over their heads ... one loud din of endless voices all shouting and crying"

Prisoners of Japan

The war in the Pacific took place across scores of separate fronts, making it difficult to generalize about the treatment of prisoners of war. As a rule, though, the Japanese treated POWs very harshly, and with extreme brutality in many cases. Disease stalked the compounds: some 37% of American POWs held in Japanese camps died while imprisoned, compared with some 2% of those in German POW camps. In addition to POWs, the Japanese interned large numbers of civilians in camps in conquered nations like the Philippines

■ **CRAMPED** Above, the Aomori POW camp in Yokohama held 300 American, British and Dutch prisoners. After it was liberated on Aug. 29, 1945, its conditions were described by the U.S. Army as an "inquisitional form of barbarism"

■ **YULETIDE** At left, POWs celebrate Christmas on Dec. 25, 1943, at a camp at Cabanatuan in the Philippines. This picture was shot in secret on film smuggled into the camp

■ **MURDER** At right, in one of the most infamous images of the war, Australian Sergeant Leonard G. Siffleet, who was captured while on reconnaissance behind enemy lines on New Guinea, is about to be beheaded, although he was in uniform when taken. Two other POWs were beheaded with Siffleet on Oct. 23, 1943. The film was captured by U.S. troops in 1944. The Japanese commander who ordered the killings was tried and sentenced to death after the war

■**HUDDLED MASSES** At top, POWs shiver at a camp on Shikoku Island in Japan. News of prisoners often arrived in circuitous fashion; this picture was published in 1944 in the German magazine *Berliner Illustrierte Zeitung* as Axis propaganda; the caption read, in part, "Neither their apparel nor their demeanor speaks for victorious operations ..."

■**VICTIMS** Above, after the recapture of Rangoon, Burma, by the British, troops examine freed POW Corporal J. Usher, whose leg was amputated—without anesthetics—by Canadian surgeon and fellow POW Major McLeod, on his right

■**KP DUTY** Left, detainees work in the kitchen at the Stanley internment camp in Hong Kong, where some 2,800 civilians, mainly British, were moved in 1942, after the colony's fall

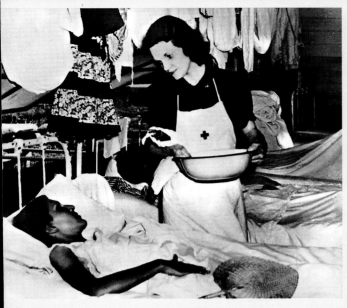

ON DUTY Navy Nurse Lieut. Margaret Nash attends an internee at Santo Tomas University in Manila. Nash was later moved to the POW camp at Los Banos, where she helped found an infirmary

SIGNS OF CHANGE Right, exuberant British, Dutch and American prisoners wave, cheer and hoist their national flags on their liberation day from the Aomori Camp outside Yokohama, Aug. 29, 1945

IN MEMORIAM Photojournalist Carl Mydans visited Camp O'Donnell on Luzon Island in the Philippines after its liberation in 1945 and recorded this image of a handmade cross marking a soldier's grave

SURVIVORS POWs freed from Camp Cabanatuan raise a cheer the day after their liberation. The camp once held as many as 8,000 POWs, but disease and the shipment of men to other camps reduced the number of prisoners

The Ghosts of Bataan

Avenging a defeat that had festered for three years, U.S. troops free the POWs who survived the infamous 1942 "death march" in the Philippines

I N ITS MARCH 12, 1945, ISSUE, *TIME* RAN PICTURES OF THE infamous Bataan death march, photographs taken almost three years before by Japanese troops and recently discovered by invading U.S. troops on Luzon. The pictures evoked stinging memories of one of the saddest events in U.S. military history—the brutal treatment of some 12,000 U.S. troops taken into Japanese custody following the Americans' surrender in April 1942 after a heroic stand on the Bataan Peninsula near Manila. The story of the 65-mile trek—during which thousands of Americans died—had been deemed so painful that the government withheld the story from the U.S. public; its details were not revealed until 1943.

Happily, U.S. troops on Luzon brought back more than images of the notorious march—they brought back some of the men who survived it, after a daring raid on the prison camp where they had been held, along with British and other Allied POWs, for most of the 34 months since their capture. These survivors called themselves "the ghosts of Bataan."

The POWs, 513 in all, were freed on Jan. 30, 1945, by 121 men handpicked from the U.S. Army's 6th Ranger Battalion and 286 Filipino guerrillas. Following directions provided by Filipinos, the unit marched through 25 miles of jungle behind enemy lines to reach the POW camp; along the way, they were given food and assistance by excited natives.

"Those Filipinos," one Ranger later told TIME-LIFE photographer Carl Mydans, "got a thing called bamboo wireless. Don't know how they work it, but they knew we were comin'. Everybody in every barrio was out there to meet us. It was a secret operation and we moved fast. In the first barrio we were given a few bananas. But by the time we reached the third, the whole village was out with roasted chickens wrapped in banana leaves for all of us. They were sure good."

When the Rangers and Filipinos arrived near the camp on Jan. 29 they prepared to strike—only to find that a full Japanese division was moving through the area. The assault was delayed 24 hours. The next day a Ranger near the camp's front gate fired a pistol shot; a second Ranger immediately shot and killed a Japanese sentry on a nearby guard tower. Throwing grenades ahead of them, the Rangers raced into the camp with knives drawn and quickly subdued the few Japanese guards inside. Sadly, many of the Americans the Rangers had come to set free were so malnourished and dazed after three years of imprisonment that they did not comprehend what was happening. But soon their joyous shouts joined those of their liberators: "They're Americans! They're here!"

That night, the men began tramping on foot toward the U.S. lines, with some of the freed prisoners so weak that they had to be carried by the Rangers. One POW died of shock, another when his heart gave out. Suddenly, Japanese troops from a nearby village attacked the column. They were quickly repelled, with the Filipino guerrillas taking the lead. As a Ranger later noted, "Don't forget the Filipinos. We broke into the camp, but the Filipinos got us through."

Photographer Mydans, traveling with another unit of U.S. soldiers, met the ragtag group the next morning, still five miles inside Japanese lines. "They were an exhausted column, Rangers and prisoners alike," Mydans reported, "but they were jaunty. They carried little with them. There was nothing from Camp Cabanatuan they wanted but their lives. As they approached our own lines their excitement increased. Some grabbed my arms, tugged them, and all in one way or another said the same thing, 'Christ, are we glad to see you!' and 'What guys these Rangers are!' and 'What an army!'

"Ambulances were coming in and trucks were throwing up sprays of dust. Everyone assembled about an old Filipino farmhouse. Fighter planes and Piper Cubs buzzed down over them like happy hornets. Some of the prisoners were in bad shape. Some were still mute. Some of these men were old friends of mine, but it was hard to recognize them. They had wasted away and their clothing was patched and weird."

Trucks and ambulances carried the POWs to an Army hospital, where the men were given immediate medical treatment. "The day was ending," Mydans reported, "and as I was making a last circuit in one of the hospital tents, I passed an

SIMPLE GIFTS Freed POWs each received Red Cross kits, which contained such luxuries as soap and a toothbrush

SUCCESS Below, the Rangers and Filipino guerrillas who liberated Camp Cabanatuan pose for Carl Mydans' camera

old fellow sitting by himself on a cot. He was dressed in a tattered shirt so patched that it was difficult to see the original fabric. I stopped and put my hand on his shoulder.

"'How are you, Dad?' I asked. He looked up and then burst into tears. He wept as I have seen no man weep. I sat down beside him and he took my hand and held it. We did not talk. Later I left him without either of us saying anything. As I walked away a young Marine sitting a few beds away beckoned to me. Pointing to Old Dad, he said with a catch in his own voice, 'That's the first time the old man has cried since he was captured.'"

∎

A Higher Power

Like the men they served, the chaplains of World War II—some 8,000 in the Army and 3,000 in the Navy—came from every denomination. No matter; with bullets flying, doctrine was expendable. Let the story of one Pacific chaplain, George S. Rentz, stand for all: when the Presbyterian minister's ship, the U.S.S. *Houston,* was sunk by a Japanese troop convoy in the Java Sea in March 1942, Rentz, a World War I veteran, led survivors clinging to flotsam in song and prayer. As his strength flagged, Rentz quietly placed his life jacket near a wounded sailor who had none and disappeared beneath the waves

■ REQUIEM Above, even as the clouds of battle still hover in the distance, a Coast Guard chaplain offers a Mass for the dead near a spot where fallen Americans have been buried. The service is taking place on Ie Shima, a small island in the Ryukyu chain, west of Okinawa. Among those who died in the battle for Ie Shima was the widely beloved American war correspondent Ernie Pyle, who was shot by a Japanese sniper on April 18, 1945. Pyle had come to the Pacific after reporting for years on the war in Africa, Italy and France

■ PEACE At left, U.S. Marines kneel as they receive communion on Iwo Jima

■ **ILLUMINATED** Above, sitting on sandbags in a canvas chapel, U.S. Navy Seabees hold candles during a communion service on an undisclosed island in the western Pacific in July 1945

■ **GOING IN** At left, Coast Guardsman Charles R. Roth leads his shipmates in prayer aboard an LST bound for Iwo Jima

■ **OLD-TIME RELIGION** Below, in a scene as old as the Bible, a tropical lagoon stands in for the River of Jordan as a Coast Guard chaplain, formerly a minister in Birmingham, Ala., baptizes one of the 30 soldiers a week to undergo the rite

Duel on Sulphur Island

U.S. Marines battle Bushido warriors, and a tiny scrap of land becomes
the scene of the war's most conspicuous displays of valor—on both sides

EVEN TODAY, BEN BERNAL, AN 80-YEAR-OLD RETIRED sheriff's deputy in Pima County, Ariz., still dreams about Iwo Jima. "I had been in combat on Kwajalein," he recalls, "and Saipan and Tinian. I had seen intense fighting in all those places. But Iwo Jima was different." Assigned to a scouts and snipers team with the 24th Regiment of the 4th Marine Division, the 20-year-old corporal was one of the first waves of U.S. troops to hit Iwo Jima's beaches on the morning of Feb. 19, 1945. His job: to race ahead of advancing Marine units and circle behind the Japanese front lines, where he would gather information and attack targets that couldn't be taken from the front, like snipers and fortified pillboxes.

"When we landed, the beach was mostly quiet," he recalls. "But it still scared the daylights out of us." What unnerved even combat-hardened veterans like Bernal was the otherworldly appearance of Iwo Jima, which translates from the Japanese as "Sulphur Island." Named for the mineral deposits that spill over its surface, Iwo Jima is, even in the best of times, a netherworld of volcanic ash, gagging smells (poison gases sometimes vent directly out of the ground) and barren life-

lessness. And February 1945 was not the best of times on Iwo Jima: the island's Japanese defenders had been digging in for more than six months, while U.S. naval and air units had been pounding the atoll for months, dropping almost 7,000 tons of bombs and firing more than 22,000 shells onto a teardrop-shaped spit of land smaller than Manhattan—all in anticipation of the invasion that had now begun.

"As soon as I was on dry land," Bernal recalls, "I knew Iwo was different from every other island landing we had made. Instead of sand, there was black ash, and we all sank up to our ankles in it. It was actually harder moving on land than it had been in the water." Stumbling up the beach and over the first seawall, he found that the Japanese had learned from earlier island campaigns. "They had mortars and artillery positioned in the hills and on Mount Suribachi [the island's dormant volcano], overlooking the invasion beach," Bernal recalls. "And they waited until more than 1,000 Marines were ashore before they opened up."

The Japanese began firing just as PFC Dewey Dossett, then a 20-year-old artillery observer with the 28th Regiment, 5th

Marine Division, was coming ashore." The ramp on our landing craft dropped forward," he recalls, "and one of the men standing in front took a bullet in the throat. He never even stepped off the ramp; he was killed instantly." Unlike Bernal, Dossett (now 79 and a retired architect living in Van Buren, Ark.) was experiencing combat for the first time. "We all ran forward, up the beach," he remembers, "but had to drop to the sand because of the heavy fire. We tried digging foxholes, but there was no sand on the beach, just this black ash." He and thousands of Marines who would follow him quickly learned that the island's granular, loosely packed ash made digging impossible. "The sides would just slide back down into the hole," he remembers. Pinned down on the beach for half the first day, Dossett's unit took eight casualties in the first hour. Dossett almost became the ninth. "I was taking cover in a shell hole," he remembers, "and more and more guys jumped in. After a few minutes, there were almost a dozen of us. And that seemed like too good a target for the Japanese the resist."

Not wanting to tempt fate, Dossett slid on his belly out of the hole and crawled forward about 25 ft. A few seconds later, he says, "there was a loud roar, and I was flying through the air. He scrambled back to the shell hole, which had taken a direct hit from Japanese mortar, and found a jumble of arms, legs and heads where his comrades had been. "A medical corpsman came over and asked their condition," Dossett remembers. "I told him they were all dead. But then a voice comes from under this pile of bodies, hissing, 'Don't say that! I'm not dead!' I helped the corpsman find the one guy who was still alive, but he died a few seconds later." Before the end of the third day, more than six of every ten men in Dossett's unit would be killed or seriously wounded.

Farther forward, as the Japanese fire began arcing over Bernal's head, he could hear the screams of men being hit on the beach behind him. "My orders were to keep moving," he

STAY LOW Moments after landing on Feb. 19, 1945, U.S. Marines attempt to move off the beach at Iwo Jima. The island's black ash beaches strongly aided the Japanese defensive position

says, "so when the Japanese fire started, I got down on my belly and started crawling toward the hills above the beach." Coming upon three Japanese at a makeshift gun emplacement, he shot them. A few hours later, Bernal linked up with his unit, which had moved off the beach and gone several hundred yards inland. "We were stalled in front of a series of pillboxes," he recalls. "Then my lieutenant came forward and said to three of us, 'Follow me.' We all admired him," Bernal remembers, "because he was a very unusual officer—he always led from the front. This time, he ran toward the first pillbox," Bernal says, awe creeping into his voice, "straight through the machine-gun fire. Somehow, he wasn't hit. Then he actually opened the door in the back, stepped in and emptied a full clip from his machine gun."

Certain that nobody inside could still be alive, the lieutenant stood at the door, waving Bernal and the rest of his squad forward. "But we didn't know about the tunnels that connected all these pillboxes," Bernal remembers, "and there actually were Japanese still alive inside." One of them walked to the door in which the lieutenant was standing and fired his machine gun into the officer's back. "It literally cut him up the middle," Bernal says, "in a line starting with his groin and moving up to his neck." Bernal and the remaining members of the squad charged the pillbox once again. "We got behind it and on top of it," he remembers, "and threw hand grenades inside. After they blew, we were sure nobody could be alive inside." But when Bernal walked through the door, "there was a Japanese soldier with his back pressed against the wall. I thought he was dead, but he reached for a hand grenade, so I unholstered my .45 and shot him in the chest."

WHAT BERNAL, DOSSETT AND THOUSANDS OF OTHER Marines were learning the hard way was that Iwo Jima's defenders had fortified this island like no other the Americans had yet invaded. Discovering that Iwo Jima's volcanic rock was soft enough to be carved with hand tools, they had dug more than 11 miles of tunnels deep beneath the surface of an island that is only eight sq. mi. in area. They had excavated hundreds of underground rooms, some of them more than 11,000 sq. ft. in area. The tunnels and subsurface bunkers were all connected to a network of more than 1,800 machine-gun nests, artillery and mortar emplacements and spider holes. Most of these positions had overlapping fields of fire and were heavily fortified. Earlier, the Japanese had discovered an unusual property of the island's volcanic ash: when mixed with cement, it formed a strong concrete that made for nearly impenetrable walls. With a handy supply of free ingredients for this goo close at hand, they had buttressed their bunkers with walls up to 10 ft. thick.

Recalling the preinvasion briefings, Dossett says, "They didn't know about those bunkers and tunnels. They told us this thing was going to be a walk in the park." But as the the second and third waves of Marines began landing on Iwo Jima, they were confronted by a ghastly sight that augured ill. As

Japanese fire took its toll on the first wave of U.S. troops, the water near the landing zone was filled with the dismembered remains of Marines who had never made it onto the beach. As their blood mixed into the surf, makos and hammerheads appeared; Marines in the second wave of troops arrived to see their fallen comrades being devoured by sharks.

I WO JIMA WAS ONCE THE ISLAND NEITHER SIDE WANTED. FOR most of the war, the Japanese had not bothered to garrison many troops there, apart from the personnel of a weather forecasting station. Nor did it figure significantly in America's Pacific strategy. But by February 1945 the situation had changed: earlier plans for an invasion of Formosa had been tabled, and General Douglas MacArthur's troops had won Leyte and were advancing on Luzon. U.S. Navy commanders—who had watched from the sidelines as General MacArthur and the Army were hailed for taking back the Philippines—were eager to resume their war. Faced with a two-month lull before the planned invasion of Okinawa, the steppingstone to Japan's home islands, they decided to pluck what must have seemed like a piece of ripe, low-hanging fruit: Iwo Jima. Thus was born Operation Detachment.

The Japanese realized before the Americans that Iwo Jima might be vital. Aware that its three airfields could be used to stage raids against Tokyo (less than 700 miles away), they started building up the island's defenses in mid-1944. They began by assigning a new commander, General Tadamichi Kuribayashi, to Iwo Jima. A descendant of samurai warriors, Kuribayashi had served as a military attaché in both the U.S. and

Canada and had concluded that America was "the last country in the world that Japan should fight." When he departed for Iwo Jima, he left his ancestral samurai sword at home with his wife and children, knowing he would never return.

Kuribayashi knew that the Japanese navy and air force had nearly ceased to exist, and that its army was being decimated on Luzon; he had no illusions about receiving help from outside Iwo Jima. Instead, he resolved to exploit the one element of the battle that would favor his cause: the terrain. He relentlessly drove the men under his command (who would number 22,000 by 1945) to dig tunnels, build bunkers and train in rearguard and delaying actions that eschewed suicidal banzai charges in favor of highly disciplined defensive tactics. "Each one of us," he commanded his troops, "must kill 10 of the enemy before we die."

American war planners were not unaware of Kuribayashi's efforts to transform Iwo Jima—but that's not to say they were well informed about his strength. U.S. intelligence estimates put the number of Japanese troops on the island at no more than 6,000 men. The plans for Operation Detachment called for Iwo Jima to be subdued within a week. And although three Marine divisions were assigned to take Iwo Jima, one of these (the 3rd Division) was to be held in reserve, so sure were the planners that Iwo Jima would be an easy victory.

Whatever the enemy's strength, U.S. Navy and Army Air Force brass were convinced that the island was worth taking. Because it was part of Japan's home territory, its capture would boost Allied morale while undermining Japan's. It would also deprive the enemy of three airfields that could be used to

"Among the Americans who served on Iwo island, uncommon valor was a common virtue."
—Admiral Chester Nimitz

"Henceforth, Iwo Jima would be a place name in U.S. history to rank with Valley Forge, Gettysburg and Tarawa."
—TIME, March 5, 1945

stage kamikaze attacks and of an early-warning station that alerted Tokyo to incoming air raids. Moreover, possession of those airfields would allow the U.S. to provide fighter escorts for the B-29 bombers that were now venturing into the skies above Tokyo. Finally, Iwo Jima could serve as an emergency landing strip for B-29s damaged while attacking Japan.

THREE DAYS INTO THE FIGHT FOR IWO JIMA, AMERICAN predictions of easy victory were tangling with reality and, like the suffering American troops, they were taking a beating. Dewey Dossett was still unable to do the job for which he had been sent in. "I was supposed to be an artillery observer, calling coordinates for targets back to the gun crews," he explains. "But we still didn't have any artillery or tanks ashore." This equipment, planned to land in the first three hours, was stymied by the sands on the beaches. Heavy guns sank into the shifting ash, while tank treads couldn't get any traction; they remained stuck on the beach until Japanese gunners on the flanks of Mount Suribachi could site in their artillery and pound them to pieces.

"Finally," Dossett recalls, "they brought in the kind of metal planking that was used to lay artificial runways for air bases. When they slapped these down on the beaches, they were able to drive tanks and howitzers over them." This made a world of difference for all the troops still pinned down by Japanese fire. "All we had to protect us up to that point was naval gunnery or air cover," Dossett recalls. "Those guys did their best, but they were firing from a long way off, so their targeting was very imprecise. They weren't able to do us much good." But with tanks moving up from the beach and heavy guns in position behind

BOOM! Marines hunker down after setting off a huge explosion in a cave connected to the vast, interconnected system of tunnels dug by the Japanese before the invasion

guns in position behind the front lines, "we were finally able to break out and begin advancing" Dossett says.

Four days into the fight for Iwo Jima, Ben Bernal was still sneaking around behind Japanese lines, looking for Japanese snipers and helping American sharpshooters find targets. "I saw a white flash," he says, "and then I was on my back." He had been hit by shrapnel from a mortar round. Bernal remembers that "I tried to get up, but my leg gave out." He couldn't call for medical help, because he was closer to Japanese positions than to fellow Marines. So he sat and waited, in quiet agony, until advancing American troops found him. He was given first aid by a Navy medic and evacuated to a hospital ship. For Bernal, the battle for Iwo Jima was over.

But for men like George Wahlen, then a 20-year-old Navy medic assigned to the 26th Regiment, 5th Marine Division, the battle was just beginning. "I came in with the third wave," he recalls now. "There were dead Marines everywhere. G.I.s who had lost their weapons or run out of ammunition were scavenging the dead for supplies." Wahlen's lieutenant was killed on the first day, after which his platoon sergeant took over. This sergeant was killed on the second day, after which another sergeant was given command. "On the third day," Wahlen recalls, "I was crawling forward, trying to find my unit, and I found a wounded Marine. When I asked him to show me where he was hit, he opened his jacket and his intestines spilled out. I gave him a shot of morphine and called litter bearers to evacuate him. I moved forward again and finally caught up with my unit just as orders came through to fix bayonets and get ready to move out."

By March 3, Wahlen's unit had advanced to the lower slopes of Mount Suribachi. On that day, in the face of withering fire,

his platoon overran four machine-gun nests but was finally pinned down by mortar fire and grenades coming from an unknown location. Reaching a group of five wounded Marines in a crater formed by a direct mortar hit, Wahlen finally spotted the hole from which the fire was coming. Because medics do not carry much weaponry, he borrowed a grenade from a wounded Marine, crawled toward the hole and dropped the grenade in it: mission accomplished. Moving from one wounded Marine to another on what he later found out was a broken leg, Wahlen treated 14 comrades that day, saving many of their lives. For his bravery, Wahlen—who is now an 80-year-old retired Army major (he signed up for a second military career after leaving the Marine Corps) living in Roy, Utah—was awarded the Congressional Medal of Honor.

The same recognition would go to 1st Lieut. Jack Lummus, albeit posthumously. On March 8, he personally led an assault on three machine-gun nests that were cutting his unit to pieces. A few minutes later, he was mortally wounded when a land mine blew off both his legs. As he lay bleeding, he continued to issue orders, urging his men forward through the gap in Japanese defenses he had created. Lummus, a talented college football player who played only a single game for the New York Giants before the war, joked to the field surgeon who struggled vainly to save him that "the Giants lost a mighty good man today." Lummus' commanding officer concluded a letter to the soldier's mother with the words, "We all lost a good man that day."

T HE NUMBER OF GOOD MEN AMERICA LOST ON IWO JIMA was staggering: 6,821 died, while more than 28,000 others were seriously wounded. The casualties were so numerous, and so unexpected, that the Pentagon ordered them kept secret until after the war. Iwo Jima is the single bloodiest battle in the history of the Marine Corps. Along with Wahlen and Lummus, 25 other American fighting men would earn the Congressional Medal of Honor for action there, more than for any other single engagement in U.S. military history.

American bravery was matched by the Bushido spirit of the Japanese. Cut off, surrounded and running short of supplies, Japanese troops increasingly saw an honorable death as the only exit. When they ran out of ammunition, officers would sometimes charge American tanks armed only with a samurai sword. Others would fashion spears out of bamboo or strap land mines to their bodies and charge American positions.

On March 22, Kuribayashi sent his last radio dispatch to Tokyo. "We are still fighting," he cabled. "The strength under my command is now about 400. The enemy suggested we surrender through a loudspeaker, but our officers and men just laughed and paid no attention." Later that day, Kuribayashi committed seppuku.

Of the 22,000 Japanese troops stationed on Iwo Jima when the Americans landed, only 1,083 were still alive when the island was declared secure on March 26. A few dozen stragglers continued to fight sporadically until December 1945, months after the war ended. The last two diehard soldiers, who had hidden themselves within Kuribayashi's tunnel network, didn't surrender until November 1949.

Even before the Japanese surrender, Iwo began to pay dividends for the Allies. On March 4, 1945, *Dinah Might*, a B-29 bomber crippled in action over Tokyo, touched down on Iwo Jima. In the months that followed, 2,250 other U.S. planes that would otherwise have ditched in the ocean made emergency landings on Iwo Jima. As U.S. Secretary of War Henry Stimson said shortly afterward, "The price has been heavy. But the military value of Iwo Jima is inestimable. Its conquest has brought closer the day of our final victory in the Pacific."

A more accurate, if more ambivalent, epitaph for Iwo Jima was uttered by Marine General Graves B. Erskine at the dedication of the Marine Corps Cemetery on the island in 1945. "Victory was never in doubt," he said. "Its cost was. What was in doubt, in all our minds, was whether there would be any of us left. Or whether the last Marine would die knocking out the last Japanese gunner." ∎

HIT Coast Guardsmen help a wounded Marine into a landing craft for evacuation. More than a third of all the Congressional Medals of Honor awarded for service in the Pacific Theater were given for bravery on Iwo Jima

REST IN PEACE Below, soldiers tidy up the 5th Division Marine Cemetery on the island after the battle

Joe Rosenthal

Associated Press photographer Rosenthal, then age 33, landed on Iwo Jima with the U.S. Marines on Feb. 19, 1945; four days later, the diminutive, bespectacled cameraman took the famous photograph of troops straining to raise a U.S. flag atop the island's Mount Suribachi. Rosenthal, who spent the postwar decades as a daily photographer for the San Francisco *Chronicle,* came to be haunted by the iconic image; although proud of it, he grew weary of answering charges that it was a bogus propaganda shot, carefully staged for his lens. By February 2005, the six men who raised the flag were deceased, but their chronicler, Joe Rosenthal, was still alive.

■ **GOING IN** Marines hit the beach in the first hours of the invasion of "Sulphur Island." Japanese guns were placed to cover every inch of the area, but the defenders often held their fire as the first men came ashore, then opened up with a huge barrage after many troops had landed and were crowding the shore, sitting ducks

■ **LAST FULL MEASURE** At left, two Marines lie dead amid Iwo Jima's sun-baked sands. The Japanese dug deeply into the terrain of the island to create a vast underground network of tunnels and bunkers connected to pillboxes aboveground

■ A TALE OF TWO FLAGS

Joe Rosenthal's picture of six (yes, six) U.S. Marines raising the American flag atop Mount Suribachi on Iwo Jima has been called the most famous image in the history of photography, and it may be.

For years Rosenthal's photo was shadowed by rumors, and after six decades, many people continue to describe it as "staged." It was not. The real story of the picture was well told for modern audiences in the best seller *Flags of Our Fathers* (Bantam; 2000), written by James Bradley, son of one of the flag raisers, Marine medic John "Doc" Bradley.

The story begins on Feb. 23, the fourth day of the invasion. The Japanese had used artillery fire from Mount Suribachi to rain devastation on the invaders, but now the Marines were ready to test Japan's hold on the mountain. Colonel Chandler Johnson ordered a detachment of 40 men to try to ascend to the top of the dormant volcano, and suggested they take a flag—in case they reached it alive.

Surprisingly, the Marines met little resistance as they hiked to the volcano's crest. Once there, they found a metal pipe, attached the 54-by-28-in. flag to it,

and hoisted it in the air. When soldiers and Navy ships below spotted the Stars and Stripes fluttering atop the mountain, they saluted it with cheers and the roar of guns. Marine photographer Louis Lowery had climbed with the group; he took a few pictures of them posing around the flag.

Back on the ground, Johnson ordered another unit of Marines to head up the mountain—and he asked them to take along a larger flag, one that would send a stronger (96-by-56-in.) signal of U.S.

might. This time Rosenthal, Marine cinematographer Bill Genaust and still photographer Bob Campbell tagged along, hoping to get good pictures from atop Suribachi. When they got to the top, the Marines swapped the two flags, as shown in the inset photo at left. As the cameramen sought good positions to snap the raising of the second flag, Rosenthal almost missed the event; he snapped it without even looking through the viewfinder. The next day, an A.P. photo editor on Guam was first to view the shot. He exclaimed, "Here's one for all time!"

Indeed. The photo was printed on the front page of most U.S. newspapers on Sunday, Feb. 25, and was embraced as an emblem of U.S. resolve. Rosenthal may have been one of the last Americans to see the photo; he didn't get a look at it until March 4, after he left Iwo Jima.

Because the shot shows a second flag raising, and because Rosenthal had trekked up the mountain hoping to get a good picture, it is often charged that he choreographed it. But he did not pose the men; the best element of the image—its magnificent composition—was entirely the product of chance.

Facing the Rising Sun

Although the war would seep into every aspect of U.S. life between 1941 and 1945, few Americans felt themselves in harm's way; as in World War I, the conflict was "over there." The exception was the Pacific Coast, where rumors of Japanese strikes swirled following the surprise attack at Pearl Harbor. The war's first weeks were indeed dangerous: nine Japanese subs prowled the offshore sea lanes in December 1941. The subs fired torpedoes at eight U.S. merchant ships, sinking two and killing six seamen

■ **FIRE!** Above, women in Hawaii take target practice at a shooting range in 1945. The island chain, annexed by the U.S. in 1898, became a U.S. territory in 1900. The naval station at Pearl Harbor became the home of the U.S. Navy's Pacific fleet the same year and was gradually expanded into an enormous facility. Hawaii was placed under martial law in the days following the Japanese attack on Pearl Harbor

■ **CRAB ARMADA** At left, with Japanese submarines firing on merchant vessels and causing panic along California's Pacific Coast in late 1941 and early 1942, a small U.S. Coast Guard boat was assigned to shepherd a fleet of San Francisco crab fishermen out to sea

■ **ELDERS** Women were not the only additions to the wartime work force; above, older men help harvest beans in Oregon

■ **FLOTSAM** At left, a Navy team prepares to detonate an errant Japanese torpedo that washed up near the Golden Gate Bridge in San Francisco in the summer of 1946

■ **HOME FIRES** Volunteers in Oregon quench flames. On Sept. 9, 1942, a Japanese seaplane launched from a sub off the U.S. West Coast dropped two incendiary bombs and started a small blaze in the Siskiyou National Forest. In 1945 a Japanese incendiary balloon killed six people at a church picnic in Oregon

■ **FOOLED?** These two young women appear to be strolling through a Seattle suburb. But look closer, at the trees, for instance: they are actually walking upon a fake suburban "set," erected as camouflage atop a giant factory where Boeing was manufacturing B-29 bombers

■ **WAR PLANT** Students at Jane Addams High School in Portland, Ore., break out hoes to till the school's front lawn. Produce from the victory garden was used in the school cafeteria and in home-economics class

■ **PIONEERS** Women assemble airplanes at the Douglas Aircraft plant in Long Beach, Calif. Just as the war helped erase gender divisions in the work force, it also helped eliminate long-standing racial barriers

Japanese Detention

In the hysteria of wartime, President Roosevelt approved the forced removal of some 115,000 Nisei—people of Japanese heritage living in America—to detention camps in the West, even though more than 60% of them were U.S. citizens, and many Nisei men served in U.S. uniform

■ **MOVING IN** Japanese-Americans sort out their belongings as they arrive at the Heart Mountain Relocation Camp in Wyoming in 1942. Some 45,000 civilians would be interned in this camp over the course of the war. No Americans of German descent were detained

■ **LET'S DANCE!** At left, teens don their saddle shoes for a jitterbug at the Heart Mountain Camp. The 4,600-acre complex was the state's third largest community in the war years

■ **"HOME"** Japanese-American soldiers on leave visit their families at Heart Mountain. The older man in plaid is a World War I vet

■ **CATCHING UP** Women congregate at the Wyoming camp; most able-bodied men served in the U.S. Army, usually in Europe

Embracing Death

When U.S. forces invade Okinawa, a long step closer to the empire's home islands, the Japanese turn suicide into strategy

IN THE *SENJIN KUN*, THE JAPANESE CODE OF BATtle ethics that describes and exalts the attributes of the Bushido warrior, it is written that "I will never suffer the disgrace of being taken alive ... I will offer up the courage of my soul and calmly rejoice in living by the eternal principles."

Three and a half years into the war they began, the Japanese had proved their devotion to the *Senjin Kun* and Bushido. At Guadalcanal, on New Guinea, at Tarawa and Iwo Jima, they had fought nearly to the last man, with many soldiers dying while screaming "banzai" in suicide charges, and others committing suicide either in the ancient knife ritual of seppuku or in such ghastly battlefield improvisations as holding a grenade to one's belly and pulling the pin.

By the time American soldiers landed on the island of Okinawa in the Ryukyu chain on April 1, 1945, Japanese commanders were reduced to assuming defensive positions and taking as many of the enemy as possible with them on the journey to an honorable death. The troops that had once rolled around the Pacific Rim in swift thrusts of aggression now hunkered down in sluggish campaigns of attrition. The few offensive actions the Japanese could mount—the banzai charge and the kamikaze pilot—were suicidal in nature. It was a loser's game. As TIME noted then of the kamikazes: "While they could be sure of committing suicide, they still could not be sure of getting away with enough murder in the process."

At Okinawa such measures, formerly last-ditch tactics, assumed the role of strategy. Here, entrenched Japanese troops fought as if their backs were to the wall. They were. Beginning in August 1942 at Guadalcanal in the Solomons, the U.S. had successfully invaded a chain of Japanese-held islands, moving ever closer to the enemy's home archipelago. In this long campaign, Okinawa was the last link: only 350 miles south of Japan's home island of Kyushu and 1,000 miles from Tokyo, its capture would permit U.S. bombers to fly devastating air raids over Japan's cities, a process already well under way, more frequently and in larger numbers. Even worse for the Japanese, if Okinawa could not be held, Japan's next battle would be fought on its own soil.

Outmanned and outgunned, the Japanese commander, Lieut. General Mitsuri Ushijima, did not contest the U.S. landings, nor did he defend the northern half of the 60-mile-long island. Instead, he withdrew most of his troops to Okinawa's southern half, establishing a base near the ancient castle town of Shuri and creating a defensive barrier, the Shuri Line, that straddled the island and featured extensive underground tunnels (one boasted its own railway), as well as fortified caves and pillboxes.

So when Operation Iceberg's vast invasion armada, made up of some 1,300 ships, landed 150,000 U.S. Army infantrymen and Marines under the command of Army General Simon Bolivar Buckner on the island, the foot soldiers met little opposition. One Marine battalion, hunting the elusive enemy, managed to find and kill just four in 24 hours. One Army colonel wrote to another: "Please send us a dead Jap. A lot of my men have never seen one. We'll bury him for you." The glib colonel and his soldiers would see bodies soon enough, in uniforms of both sides, when they reached the Shuri Line.

OFF OKINAWA'S COAST, U.S. AND BRITISH SAILORS were already seeing bodies—those of their fellow crewmen. Utterly outmatched by the vast resources of the Allied navies, Japanese commanders were now counting on the desperate strategy they had first turned to in the Battle of Leyte Gulf in October 1944: the use of kamikaze pilots. Suddenly, stunned Allied seaman realized that they and their ships had become the front lines.

At Okinawa the kamikazes mounted their most ferocious assaults of the war. More than 1,450 Japanese pilots committed aerial suicide—many of them in a series of 10 mass attacks—and they took a mighty toll on the U.S. fleet, sinking 34 ships (counting small landing craft) and damaging more than 300 others,

ORDEAL The 11-week struggle for Okinawa was history's largest land-sea-air battle. Snapshots:

1. The U.S.S. *Ben Franklin* is on fire and severely listing after being bombed while in action off the Ryukyu Islands before the invasion; it did not sink

2. The Japanese did not contest the first U.S. landings on April 1, 1945—Easter Sunday

3. U.S. troops use flamethrowers to roust the Japanese out of their entrenched positions

4. A civilian emerges from a cave to surrender

5. A kamikaze heads directly for the battleship U.S.S. *Missouri*; once a plane was inside the range of antiaircraft guns, sailors were unprotected

6. With Okinawa under U.S. control by late June, supplies began arriving for the fall invasion of Japan

ON THE MOVE Resembling an infantryman from World War I, a U.S. Marine races across open ground. With the Japanese fighting from deeply entrenched positions, the conflict on Okinawa harked back to Ypres and Verdun

the highest total for any naval engagement in the war—belying tough talk from Admiral "Bull" Halsey that the dive bombers amounted to "no real menace but a hell of a nuisance." Some nuisance: the U.S. Navy listed 4,907 men killed or missing at Okinawa and 4,824 wounded. As with the count of disabled ships, this was the Navy's largest total in the war.

It was during the Okinawa campaign that the U.S. military finally publicly revealed the existence of the kamikazes, information kept under wraps since Leyte Gulf. TIME's April 23 issue described the novel tactic, dispelling a few of the myths that U.S. sailors had already created about the suicide pilots: that they wore flowing kimonos and carried samurai swords, and that some of them were chained into their seats.

The Japanese were now beginning to design special planes for the kamikazes. One such killing machine was a small, darting death device somewhat resembling the unmanned German V-1 "robomb," or buzz bomb, with which Adolf Hitler had terrorized London before his scientists perfected the more powerful V-2. This aircraft—which U.S. troops quickly dubbed with a Japanese term they had learned, *baka* ("stupid")—was a manned vehicle equipped with a pilot's cockpit, steering controls and an explosive warhead in the nose. The "baka bomb" was carried near its target by a bomber, then cut loose; three rockets in its tail gave the kamikaze pilot bursts of speed for the suicide dive of his guided missile.

The Japanese would unveil yet another suicide tactic on Okinawa. On the night of May 24-25, U.S. troops at the captured Yontan airstrip on west central Okinawa were startled when a Japanese bomber, hit by antiaircraft fire, glided in and scraped down the runway to a belly landing. Out scrambled 15 Japanese soldiers, who scattered toward the parked U.S. fighter planes and bombers. Rear-area support staff, some of whom had never seen a Japanese soldier up close, fought back. The Japanese burned a few planes, but by dawn the invaders were all dead—some by their own hand grenades.

Enter the *giretsu* ("unsurpassed loyalists"), whom Japanese communiqués described as "special airborne attack units." Near the Yontan airfield, four more troop transports were shot down that night, killing the 70 soldiers inside them. Like the "baka bomb," the *giretsu*, a last dark flower of Japanese desperation, would have little impact on the battle for Okinawa.

A LONG THE SHURI LINE, IT WAS THE AMERICANS WHO were desperate. General Ushijima's fortifications, backed up by large, effective artillery batteries, were holding strong; by April 9, the U.S. invaders pushing south were completely stalled. Heady with their success, a band of young "fire eater" Japanese commanders, disgusted with playing defense, managed to convince General Ushijima to mount an offensive. On the night of April 12, Japanese troops supported by a massive artillery barrage attacked U.S. troops but were hurled back; a second attack in May met the same fate.

The battle along the Shuri Line began to resemble the killing fields of World War I, with U.S. troops—there were more than 300,000 of them on the island by the campaign's end—taking severe casualties as they assaulted strong enemy positions. This was warfare at its ugliest, with the Americans resorting to the use of flamethrowers to root the Japanese out of their bunkers, caves and trenches. General Buckner called it the "blowtorch and corkscrew" method. Liquid flame—napalm—was the blowtorch; explosives, the corkscrew.

Buckner might have taken a page from General Douglas MacArthur: after losing an inordinate number of soldiers in headlong charges at fortified positions at Buna in New Guinea early in the war, MacArthur had learned to mount swift, unexpected amphibious invasions, supported by tactical air power, that often took the Japanese by surprise from the rear. Not Buckner: overruling many opposing voices, he sent the men under his command straight into the enemy lines, pulled back, counted his dead and attacked again.

Even so, the end was preordained. The last elements of Japanese resistance faded in late June, after 82 days of bloodshed that claimed the lives of some 110,000 Japanese troops and as many as 150,000 native Okinawans, conscripted in the battle. U.S. casualties included 12,520 dead and more than 36,000 wounded, more than at Iwo Jima and Guadalcanal combined.

The lessons of Okinawa were clear: the Japanese would fight to the last. For President Harry Truman and his top military advisers, now planning an invasion of Japan's home islands for the fall of 1945, the costs ahead, in both American and Japanese lives, seemed incalculable. To these men, Okinawa underlined the importance of ending the war as quickly as possible, by whatever means possible.

The means was found, and the invasion of Japan never took place. But the protagonists of the duel on Okinawa would not know it.

On June 18, with his campaign essentially won, General Simon Bolivar Buckner was killed by Japanese artillery fire while inspecting front-line positions. Four days later, General Ushijima and his chief of staff, Lieut. General Isamu Cho, donned their dress uniforms, then knelt side by side on a white sheet, in Japan the color of death. Ushijima's aide stepped forward, bowed and handed each general a gleaming knife. As Ushijima pressed the blade against his belly, one of his aides lopped off his head. General Cho leaned forward against his blade; the adjutant swung again. Neither man would suffer the disgrace of being taken alive. ∎

The Healing Touch

Unarmed in battle, unwavering in the face of danger and all too often unsung among the public, Army and Navy medics won the admiration of the troops for their courage. In addition to treating battlefield wounds, medical teams stationed in the Pacific had to treat a host of exotic tropical diseases they had never encountered in their American practices, ailments that proved every bit as harmful as Japanese fire to soldiers raised far from the tropics.

■ **SOLDIER'S FRIEND** Above, fixed in the dirt by a bayonet, a rifle is a transfusion stand in the 1945 battle for Okinawa

■ **FIRST AID** Left, a Marine medic treats a Filipino child on the island of Saipan while his mother bows low in gratitude

■ **DOG DOWN!** Below, G.I.s tend to a friend wounded in the fighting on the Orote Peninsula on Guam in 1944

■ **BUNKER** Above, a combat surgical unit operates in a reinforced jungle dugout on Bougainville Island in 1944

■ **SANCTUARY** Right, during the campaign to liberate Leyte Island, the cathedral in the city of Sens was turned over to the U.S. military for use as a field hospital

■ **FRONT LINES** Below, amid the bloodshed of the U.S. landing on Iwo Jima, Navy doctors and medical corpsmen set up a field hospital in a gully on the beach. Units of blood plasma were flown in from the West Coast of the U.S.

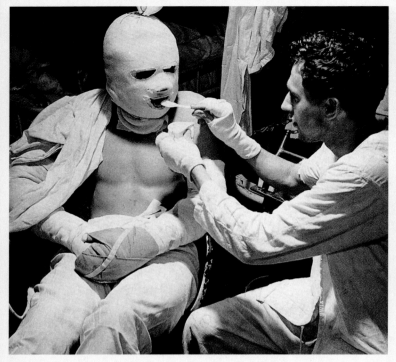

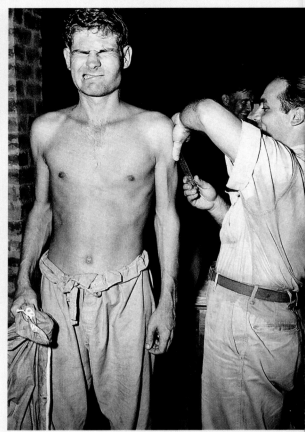

■ **BURN UNIT** Above, aboard the hospital vessel U.S.S. *Solace,* an aide feeds a sailor who was blown off a ship and suffered severe burns in a kamikaze attack

■ **GOING DOWN** Training to acclimate themselves to life in the jungle before taking up their assignment in Burma, Lieut. Laura Hudson of Ohio and a fellow American nurse slide down an incline during an eight-mile hike in 1944

■ **OUCH!** You might think that surviving 18 months as a POW would toughen one up, but Lieut. Allan DuBose of Texas can't help grimacing when he gets a shot after being freed in 1945

■ **STILL LIFE** Right, photographer W. Eugene Smith took this moving image of an American nurse administering glucose and blood plasma to a wounded soldier in 1944

■ **ALLIES** Below, a Filipino nurse tends a wounded American; like the picture at right, it was taken in Sens Cathedral on Leyte

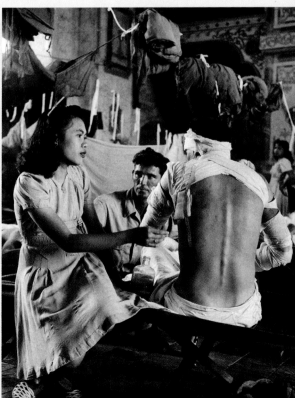

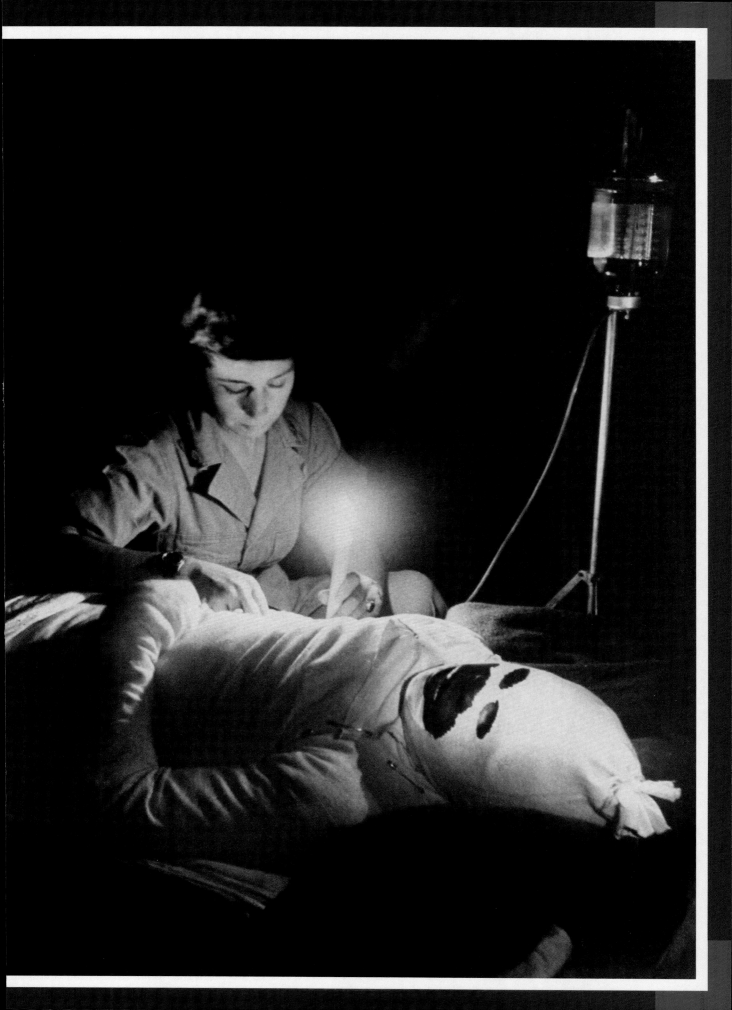

Secrets in the Desert

Working in isolation, U.S. physicists harness the atom's power and create the weapon that will end the war

I N THE SUMMER OF 1945, AS AMERICANS TURNED THEIR FULL ATTEN-
tion to the war in the Pacific after the surrender of Germany, the
future seemed appalling. In the streets of Manila and in the caves
of Iwo Jima and Okinawa, tough Japanese soldiers had shown
they preferred death to surrender. Everyone knew that the next
battle, an invasion of Japan's home islands, would be even
more costly. U.S. soldiers who once chanted, "Win the war
in '44," were now prepared to settle for "The Golden Gate
in '48." In some minds, though, fantasies bloomed—the
same fantasies that had dominated Adolf Hitler's mind
in his last days of life—dreams of a secret weapon, one
of such magnitude that it would shock the enemy into
a realization that he was beaten and would bring the
war to a speedy conclusion, saving millions of lives.

Now, for one last time in this long global conflict that
teemed with surprises, reality outpaced fantasy: in the
desert sands of New Mexico, such a weapon did exist.

Even before the U.S. entered the war, the élite physicists
scattered through American universities—many of them
refugees from fascism in Europe—were buzzing with rumors of a weapon based on the power of atomic fission,
the splitting of the atom. "In the fall of 1941, I was a student at the University of Denver," recalls Dr. Harold
Agnew, then a 20-year-old physics major who had already attracted the notice of his professors.
"And we were all signing up to join the Army
Air Corps. But a professor of mine said, 'Don't
sign up in that program. I think something is
happening where you can be much more useful.' That's all I knew. A couple of weeks later he
said, 'You're going to Chicago.' "

The world of theoretical physics was in quiet
ferment. In 1934, while waiting at a London intersection for a traffic light to change, Hungarian physicist Leo Szilard had stumbled upon a wild surmise: the
insight that if an atom were bombarded with a single neutron and made to release two neutrons, the process would
quickly cascade into a chain reaction that would release enormous quantities of energy. In 1938, Italian physicist Enrico Fermi
had been awarded the Nobel Prize for demonstrating that smashing
neutrons into atoms could kick-start nuclear reactions. And the following
year the world's most famous theoretical physicist, the German Jew Albert Einstein—now a refugee from Hitler, living in America—had quietly written Presi-

dent Franklin Roosevelt that uranium might be used as a powerful new source of energy, adding that "this new phenomenon would also lead to … extremely powerful bombs … A single bomb of this type, carried by boat and exploded in a port, might very well destroy the whole port together with some of the surrounding territory."

It was only after Agnew arrived in Chicago in 1941 that he learned he would be working under Fermi. "In those days there were only a handful of places in the whole country that knew anything about nuclear energy," the scientist, now 84 and living in Solana Beach, Calif., recalls. "The heads of The few physics departments—Ernest O. Lawrence at Berkeley, Arthur Compton at Chicago, John Dunning at Columbia—they contacted all their former graduates and said, 'Come on back.' They were told that if they knew any semiliterate undergraduates, bring 'em too. It's for the war."

The first step in turning an atomic reaction into a weapon was to generate the cascading release of neutrons Szilard had predicted. "We started building the first man-made chain reaction," Agnew recalls, admitting he was still a bit mystified as to the larger purpose of the effort. "I don't think I knew what was going on as far as the bomb was concerned for maybe nine months."

Prompted by Einstein's letter, Roosevelt had ordered the War Department to put together a top-secret "Uranium Committee" to look into the possibility of atomic weapons. Because the initial research was done at Columbia University in New York City, the effort was dubbed the Manhattan Project. But the real action quickly moved to Chicago, where Fermi and his acolytes began assembling a massive "pile" of 60 tons of uranium fuel, enclosed in a protective coating of 400 tons of graphite bricks, on a squash court beneath the University of Chicago's Stagg Field football stadium. For months, they tried different methods of bombarding the pile with neutrons, hoping to provoke a "criticality"—Szilard's predicted chain reaction. They did not succeed.

The work took on new urgency after Pearl Harbor. "People today don't appreciate how frightened we were," Agnew says. "Things were really going down the tube in '41 and '42. We were losing badly in the Pacific. There was Bataan. Hong Kong fell on Christmas Day. The Atlantic was just horrendous." Finally, on Dec. 2, 1942, the Fermi team stumbled on the right configuration,

The Mysteries of Los Alamos

Recalling life on the secret Manhattan Project site in remote Los Alamos, N.M., physicist Harold Agnew says, "I loved the place. Easterners had a hard time getting used to all its primitive discomfort, but I was in hog heaven. It was also a completely democratic society—Oppie saw to that—big shots and flunkies like me all living together. Every week we had a colloquium in one of our two movie theaters, where we would be told what everyone was doing. Once in a while some military guy would come by and give us a pep talk. We worked six days a week, and people enjoyed it. I just thought everything was great. The atmosphere, the intellectual level, it was just fantastic."

Indeed, what Los Alamos lacked in amenities, it made up for in brainpower. The desert community was home, at various times, to such giants of 20th century physics as Niels Bohr, Edward Teller, Ernest O. Lawrence, Glenn Seaborg and a young Richard Feynman, who delighted in picking locks and defying security regulations.

SHHH! Memorable signs greeted visitors to Manhattan Project sites; although this one is at Oak Ridge, Tenn., similar signs were present at the Los Alamos facility

GROUND ZERO After the Trinity test, Oppenheimer, in hat at center, General Groves and others inspect the blast site, where temperatures hit ten million degrees

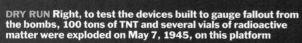

4 RMS, DESERT VU Physicist Agnew: "The first time I saw our bunkhouse, it didn't have any doors. So I borrowed a pickup truck, took the doors off my lab and took them to my house"

DRY RUN Right, to test the devices built to gauge fallout from the bombs, 100 tons of TNT and several vials of radioactive matter were exploded on May 7, 1945, on this platform

LOW TECH In the unsettling picture above, scientists are removing a trolley of radioactive matter from a storage facility

and the mass of uranium achieved criticality, setting off a self-sustaining chain reaction that released large amounts of energy in the form of neutron radiation. "Hearing the counters going faster and faster and seeing the pen recorders continuing to rise was scary," Agnew recalls. But at 3:53 p.m., on Fermi's orders, the fuel was withdrawn, and the reaction stopped without incident. "No flash, no noise, no smoke, no smell," Agnew says. "It was over, and the outside world was unaware of what had happened."

What had happened was that mankind had entered the nuclear age. Once it had been demonstrated that a controlled, man-made chain reaction was indeed possible, efforts to produce an uncontrolled chain reaction, which would release enough energy to vaporize a city, stepped into high gear. For this phase of the project, leadership passed from Fermi to a brilliant young Berkeley professor, J. Robert Oppenheimer, and a hard-charging Army leader, General Leslie Groves.

The two couldn't have more different. Oppenheimer, the brilliant product of a wealthy New York City family, cultivated an interest in Eastern religions. Groves was a no-nonsense military engineer who had established his reputation for getting things done by overseeing the construction of the world's largest office building, the Pentagon, in just over 16 months amid wartime shortages of vital materials like steel.

Seeking secrecy and isolation, Groves and Oppenheimer agreed to move the next phase of the Manhattan Project away from university laboratories to a remote corner of the New Mexico desert. Four months after Fermi's success in Chicago, several hundred scientists and engineers, along with more than 1,000 support personnel, decamped to a large ranch once used as a spa by the wealthy. It was called Los Alamos.

"You want to know how I got to Los Alamos?" Agnew asks. "It was my wife's good looks. She got a job as personal secretary to the administrative head of the project in Chicago. Whenever Oppie came around, he liked to talk to her. Naturally, when Oppie was going to start up the lab in Los Alamos, he decided that he needed someone to work for him who had experience—like Beverly. So he asked her to come to New Mexico. And it was reasonable that I should go too." Agnew's was not an unusual story: like so many others caught up in the global war, the young scientist became a witness to one of history's great events through the power of small coincidences.

The primary problem at Los Alamos, Agnew recalls, was "to figure out how the bomb would be designed. Everyone was working just as fast as possible. We had two designs: a gun assembly that would shoot uranium into the core, and an implosion design that used explosives to crush the core into itself." In the end, both designs would work, but it took more than three years of fine-tuning before workable bombs were created. The gun design, used in a bomb with a uranium core, was deemed so simple that it needed no testing. It became the basis for the "Little Boy" bomb that would be dropped on Hiroshima. But the scientists

were far less certain of the implosion design, used in a bomb that utilized a much more potent fuel, plutonium, a form of enriched uranium created at another secret facility in Oak Ridge, Tenn. This bomb had to be tested.

IN EARLY JULY 1945, EVEN AS THE PLUTONIUM BOMB WAS ready for its test, Agnew and several other members of the team shipped out to an island in the Pacific they had never heard of: Tinian, in the Marianas chain, some 1,200 miles south of Japan's home islands. Their assignment was to measure the radioactivity generated by the bombs after they were dropped. They thus missed by a few days the test of the implosion bomb, which took place at a New Mexico desert crossroads called Alamogordo. On old maps the area was dubbed Jornada del Muerto, "Journey of Death." Oppenheimer christened it Trinity, from a John Donne poem.

On July 16, 1945, at 5:29 a.m., the signal for detonation was given at Trinity—and the sun seemed to rise an hour ahead of schedule. The Bomb's fireball spawned a mushroom-shaped cloud that rose more than six miles into the sky. The single surprise that came from the Trinity test was that the plutonium bomb was four times more potent than the scientists had expected it to be: its power was equivalent to 18.6 kilotons of TNT. In that moment, mankind entered a new and terrible age.

The new device would fulfill the fantasies of those who longed for a secret weapon that would bring the war to an end: five days after it was dropped at Nagasaki, Japan agreed to surrender. Yet the atom bomb would also breed new fantasies, terrible nightmares of its enormous power falling into the wrong hands. Six years of war—six years of death camps and kamikazes and saturation bombing—had exposed man's capacity for evil as never before. The conflict had revealed that some men's urge to annihilate their fellow man was almost unlimited; now it promised to hand them an almost unlimited power to do so. With the atom bomb, science outpaced ethics: as General Omar Bradley would note in 1948, "We live in an age of nuclear giants and ethical midgets." Six decades after the Trinity test, his words have never seemed more relevant. ■

STEADY! A workman stands next to the second atom bomb used in the war, christened "Fat Man," hours before it was deployed at Nagasaki. The notes on its tail, presumably not affectionate, were directed by U.S. soldiers to Japan

"Expect a Rain of Ruin"

The U.S. unleashes its new atom bombs on two Japanese cities, killing hundreds of thousands of civilians and bringing the war to a swift end

THE WAR IS OVER!" AN OFFICER EXCLAIMED BREATH-lessly to General Leslie Groves, the Army's overseer of the Manhattan Project, moments after the first atom bomb was successfully tested in the New Mexico desert on July 16, 1945. "Yes," Groves cynically but prophetically replied. "After we drop two bombs on Japan."

When the Trinity test proved that the bomb worked, plans for the deployment of the deadly creation, in development since the previous September, were set in motion. On July 17, President Harry Truman, attending the Potsdam Conference in Berlin with Winston Churchill and Joseph Stalin, was informed that the test had succeeded. For months Truman had been dreading the necessity of ordering the final invasion of Japan's home islands by U.S. troops. His advisers estimated that U.S. casualties would run to the hundreds of thousands, and perhaps exceed 1 million; Japanese casualties were expected to reach 5 million, if not far more.

Although planning for the invasion, Operation Downfall, was far along, Truman hoped the two bombs America now possessed might make it unnecessary. As he confided to his diary that evening, by sacrificing hundreds of thousands of lives in a demonstration of the atom bomb's power, he might ultimately save many millions more. "It seems to be the most terrible thing ever discovered, but it can be made the most useful," he wrote. Sixty years later, the ethics underlying Truman's grim calculus properly remain the subject of debate, but there is little question that in using the bombs he realized his military goal of bringing the war to a swift and far less deadly end.

U.S. AIR FORCE

LEVELED: Hiroshima after the bomb blast. Very few of the city's buildings remain standing. The area had been left untouched in earlier bombing raids, in order to provide a clear demonstration of the atom bomb's power

So the bombs must be dropped—but where? Although U.S. bombers had been laying waste to Japanese cities for more than a year, leaders in Tokyo were perplexed that four cities had never been targeted: Kokura, Niigata, Nagasaki and Hiroshima. As Kats Kajiyama, then a 7-year-old schoolboy in Hiroshima, now recalls, "We only saw a few American bombers, and they almost never hit our city." Reason: U.S. war planners had set aside, in General Groves' words, "places the bombing of which would most adversely affect the will of the Japanese people to continue the war." For maximum effect, this required cities unscathed by previous bombing, the better to illustrate the might of the new devices.

A special Army Air Force unit, the 509th Composite Group, had been formed in September 1944 to be responsible for de-

livering the bombs. Command was given to Lieut. Colonel Paul Tibbets, a highly respected bomber pilot. He was fully briefed on the unit's mission, but few others among its 225 officers and 1,542 enlisted men were in on the secret.

By the time of the Trinity test the following July, a team of Manhattan Project scientists had already been dispatched to the island of Tinian in the Marianas chain, the 509th Composite Group's headquarters, where the Army had constructed an enormous airfield. For Dr. Harold Agnew, then a young physicist assigned to the bombing mission, reminders of the ferocious battle that had wrested the island from the Japanese—and of other battles taking place beyond the horizon—were everywhere. "All the Japanese buildings were gutted. I

"All around, I found dead and wounded. Some were bloated and scorched ... their legs and bodies stripped of clothes and burned with a huge blister."
—Unnamed Hiroshima survivor, TIME, Aug. 20, 1945

camera. Because a second camera—aboard the *Enola Gay*—malfunctioned, Agnew ended up taking the only film footage of the Hiroshima blast.

Immediately after the dropping of Little Boy, the two planes made steep dives to pick up speed and then swerved into hard right turns, to put as much distance as possible between themselves and the blast. "We must have been seven miles away when the shock waves hit us," Agnew recalls. "And it still felt like enemy fire hitting the plane." So powerful was the bomb's concussion that it hit both planes twice—once directly and a second time when it was reflected up from the ground.

I HAD ARRIVED AT SCHOOL EARLY THAT DAY," RECALLS Kats Kajiyama, now 67 and a professor of Japanese at Brigham Young University's Hawaii campus. "I was playing with my friend when the air-raid siren went off. So we ran inside our school and waited." But this used to watch B-29s, hundreds of them, coming back from missions—some smoking, some with their props feathered."

On July 26 the U.S.S. *Indianapolis*, which was carrying the disassembled pieces of the first bomb, made port in Tinian, and the work of readying the bombs began. The same day, the three Allied leaders meeting in Berlin issued the Potsdam Declaration, which warned that Japan faced "prompt and utter destruction" and demanded the empire's "immediate and unconditional surrender." The Japanese heeded the first of the two adjectives, almost immediately rejecting the declaration. On July 30, Secretary of War Henry Stimson cabled Truman, who was still in Germany, asking for final approval of the order to drop the bomb. Truman wrote out his reply in longhand: "Suggestion approved. Release when ready."

B AD WEATHER—A TYPHOON NEARING JAPAN ON AUG. 1— only delayed what was now inevitable. The skies cleared gradually, and by the afternoon of Sunday, Aug. 5, the 9,700-lb. Little Boy uranium bomb was being winched into the specially modified bomb bay of Tibbets' B-29 on Tinian. The pilot had named the plane for his mother: *Enola Gay*. Agnew and his team made final adjustments to the bomb and took time out for a more personal gesture. "I wrote my name on it," he remembers, "and my wife's daughters' names. I also wrote some nasty words for the Japanese, something like 'To hell with you.'"

After a midnight briefing, the *Enola Gay*, with Tibbets at the controls, took off at 2:45 a.m.; Agnew and the science monitoring team followed in a second B-29, the *Grand Artiste*. Only after his plane was airborne did Tibbets confirm to his 11-man crew that they were carrying an entirely new kind of weapon. At 10 ft. 6 in. long and 29 in. in diameter, the bomb resembled, to one crewman, "an elongated trash can with fins."

"A little before 8:15 a.m.," Agnew recalls, "we caught the tone signal, which meant that the bomb was armed and ready to drop. After we heard the tone, we knew that the bomb was on the way down. Then we saw the flash of light." As the bomb detonated, Agnew was looking through the lens of a movie

TOP: YOSUKE YAMAHATA; BOTTOM: KENICHI KIMURA. BELOW: YOSHITO MATSUSHIGE; FAR RIGHT,

siren was apparently in reaction to a weather plane that preceded the *Enola Gay* by about 20 minutes. "When nothing happened," says Kajiyama, "we went back outside to play some more."

Minutes later, a second siren went off, indicating the approach of more airplanes. "This was a different kind of siren," Kajiyama remembers, "a series of tones sounding at intervals of several seconds. Unlike the continuous siren we had heard earlier, this one meant that the city was about to be bombed."

Once again, Kajiyama and his friend ran inside their schoolhouse. This time, they hid beneath desks and covered their eyes and ears. "A moment later," he recalls, "we saw a light that was like a thousand photographer's flashbulbs going off all at once." That this light was visible through the hands and eyelids that were covering Kajiyama's pupils at that moment is testimony to the force that had been unleashed.

On the ground, seconds after the flash, Kajiyama sensed "a rumbling that felt like an earthquake and sounded like thunder." As the ground shook, he ran outside and saw the city transformed. "Every place," he recalls, "there were buildings burning. All the telephone poles were knocked down. Buildings had their roofs torn off. And people who had been outside when the bomb went off were running around, screaming and blind, with their flesh hanging off their bodies like ribbons." This was the level of devastation in the Ujina district of Hiroshima, more than two miles from the center of the blast zone. At ground zero, nothing recognizable remained. Human beings, buildings, even the landscape's natural geographical features, its knolls and valleys, had been vaporized.

The bomb was triggered at 1,900 ft. above ground, to ensure maximum damage. Temperatures near the hypocenter, the ground point immediately below the explosion, surged to as high as 7200°F. A mile away, the surfaces of objects instantly rose to more than 1000°F. Tens of thousands of people died instantly, perhaps more than 100,000 within a few minutes. In the months to come, many more would die of radiation poi-

DAZED At left, survivors huddle in a Hiroshima street shortly after the bomb blast. This photo was taken about 1.3 miles from the hypocenter

SURVIVORS Right, a mother and child, both wounded in the second bombing, at Nagasaki, clutch balls of rice

BRANDED At bottom right, thermal rays from the bomb burned clothing patterns onto this woman's skin

"If they [the Japanese] do not now accept our terms, they may expect a rain of ruin from the air, the like of which has never been seen on this earth." —Harry Truman, Aug. 6, 1945

soning: the bomb is estimated to have killed a total of some 140,000 Japanese, almost all of them civilians.

IN THE MINUTES AFTER THE BLAST, KAJIYAMA RAN BACK TO his family's home, about three miles away. He found the house deserted and leveled. As the young boy searched frantically for his mother, "a frightening-looking old woman approached me. Her skin was the color of tar, and all the hair was burned off of her head." The woman was limping and nearly blind, and her clothing was burned onto her skin. "But she was calling my name," Kajiyama recalls, "and her voice sounded familiar." The creature standing in front of him was his mother. Working at a factory where she had been sewing uniforms for Japanese soldiers, she had been much closer to the center of the blast than her son. "She held me in her arms and cried," he recalls—and then he remembers one of the triv-

ial details that sometimes linger amid tragic memories. "She apologized over and over again for losing a thermos bottle that I liked very much. I tried to tell her that I didn't care about the bottle, that I was just so happy she was alive, but it was a while before I could make her understand."

In the next few hours, the two would reunite with Kajiyama's father. For several days, the three searched for his brother Masahiro, 12. But the older son's school had been much closer to the center of the blast zone, and when Kajiyama's father finally found the boy, it was at a makeshift site where thousands of dead bodies had been brought for identification by relatives before mass burial.

The family's suffering was not at an end. Weeks later, after they had fled to a relative's home in the countryside, Kajiyama was asleep beside his mother, whose health had begun to deteriorate rapidly from a then unknown disease that would later

Boy. When his primary target, the city of Kokura, was socked in by bad weather, Sweeney had just enough fuel to reach a backup target, Nagasaki, a city of 253,000 on the western side of the island of Kyushu.

With visibility poor, the bomb was dropped off-target, over the Urakami district, about a mile from the city's center. A large part of the city was sheltered from the bomb's force by the hills surrounding the Urakami valley. Even so, the plutonium bomb killed more than 70,000 people—and gave Japan's Emperor Hirohito and his fellow peace advocates in the government the argument they needed to convince the holdouts in their ranks to accept the necessity of surrender.

Harold Agnew, who is now 84 and went on to direct the Los Alamos laboratory after the war, says of the decision to use the bomb, "It brought a very rapid end to a very terrible war. Years afterward, I met a Japanese veteran who told me, 'You saved my life. I would have given my life for the Emperor, but I didn't have to.' So what we did saved a lot of people on both sides, and I don't have any qualms about it."

The boy who was once on the ground agrees with the man who was once in the plane. "What I lived through was tragic and horrifying," says Kats Kajiyama, now a U.S. citizen. "But the tragedy would be even worse if my mother and brother—and so many other people we knew—had died for nothing. But I don't feel that this is so. I believe that their deaths contributed to ending the war and the restoration of world peace. That belief and prayer are what have enabled me to survive."

As TIME pointed out in its initial report of the two bombings, the splitting of the atom ushered in an age when many things were split, including the reaction to the use of the new weapon against innocent civilians. "The knowledge of victory was as charged with sorrow and doubt as with joy and gratitude," the magazine said. "The demonstration of power against living creatures instead of dead matter created a bottomless wound in the living conscience of the race." ■

SHARDS At left, pedestrians walk through a formerly congested area of Nagasaki in the the days after the plutonium bomb was dropped. This location is some 1,000 ft. from the blast center

A TIME FOR MEDITATION Below, Western monks in Nagasaki join civilians in prayer after the bombing. The city was home to some 14,000 Roman Catholics, the largest such group in Japan

be named radiation sickness. "My sister woke me up," he recalls, "and said that our mother had died, lying next to me, while I was asleep. Then my father told me that her last words were to ask him for a promise that he would take care of my sister and me."

THE KAJIYAMAS' NATION WOULD ALSO CONTINue to suffer. After the bombing of Hiroshima, President Truman again called on Japan to surrender, warning that it could "expect a rain of ruin from the air" until it did so. Three days after the Hiroshima blast, as Japan's leaders were debating a surrender, Truman made good on his threat: *Bock's Car*, with Major Charles W. Sweeney at the controls, winged toward Japan carrying the plutonium-powered Fat Man, a far more powerful bomb than Little

Reluctant Surrender

America's potent new weapon and Russia's entry into the war can't persuade Japan's militarists to quit—so the Emperor takes the reins

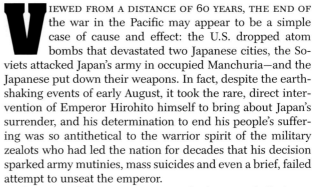

VIEWED FROM A DISTANCE OF 60 YEARS, THE END OF the war in the Pacific may appear to be a simple case of cause and effect: the U.S. dropped atom bombs that devastated two Japanese cities, the Soviets attacked Japan's army in occupied Manchuria—and the Japanese put down their weapons. In fact, despite the earth-shaking events of early August, it took the rare, direct intervention of Emperor Hirohito himself to bring about Japan's surrender, and his determination to end his people's suffering was so antithetical to the warrior spirit of the military zealots who had led the nation for decades that his decision sparked army mutinies, mass suicides and even a brief, failed attempt to unseat the emperor.

The story of the Japanese surrender begins, of all places, in Potsdam, a suburb of Berlin, where the principals of the three great Allied powers who had beaten Germany into surrender convened for the last time in mid-July 1945. It was a contentious, unsettling get-together. Since the conference at Yalta only five months before, Franklin Roosevelt had died, and new U.S. President Harry Truman was an unknown quantity. Britain's Prime Minister Winston Churchill left the conference in midstream, when the Labour Party under Clement Attlee won a stunning victory over Churchill's Conservatives in a general election.

At Potsdam, the Allies agreed on the next steps to be taken in the Pacific, including a major strategic development: as decided at Yalta, now that the European war was over, Russia would enter the conflict against Japan, attacking across the border of occupied Manchuria to establish an entirely new front. On July 26, as the conference concluded, the Allies issued a declaration to Japan, warning of the inevitable "utter devastation of the Japanese homeland" and calling for Japan's "unconditional surrender," as well as for an end to the rule of the militarists, the disarmament of the military and the occupation of Japan by the Allies. In return, the document promised that the Japanese people would be granted freedom of speech, religion and thought and would be allowed to maintain their nonmilitary industries. The Japanese promptly rejected the offer; Foreign Minister Shigenori Togo declared Japan would "ignore" it.

With the dropping of the atom bomb on Hiroshima, the Allies began carrying out their promise to devastate Japan's homeland. Yet even when faced with this immensely power-

THE END General Douglas MacArthur (right, with his back to the camera) presides as Japan's former Foreign Minister Mamoru Shigemitsu signs surrender documents aboard the U.S.S. *Missouri* on Sept. 2. The ceremony followed V-J Day celebrations by 18 days; TIME called it an "anticlimax"

CARL MYDANS-TIME LIFE PICTURES

ful new weapon, most of Japan's military leaders wanted to
keep fighting. Their response was utterly irrational, for by
this time Japan was barely functioning. Its navy and air force
were crippled. Its army had been beaten soundly all across
the Pacific and was now reeling backward in Manchuria. Its
cities had been relentlessly bombed, and its people were
starving. No matter: surrender was at odds with the Bushido
values the Japanese military leaders held most dear, and they
simply refused to accept reality.

A T 1 A.M. ON AUG. 9, THE DAY THE CITY OF NAGASAKI
would be bombed, Joseph Stalin kept his promise:
massive Russian armies, boasting more than 2 million
men, began driving into Manchuria, occupied by Japan's
Kwantung Army. Once a mighty force, this army had been
gradually stripped of men and machines to feed Japan's battles in the Pacific. The veteran, well-equipped Soviet troops,
divided into three main forces and attacking on three fronts,
rolled over the Japanese. Now, for the first time in the war,
Japan's home islands were trapped in a pincer movement.

Close to midnight the same day—hours after news reached
Tokyo of the bombing of Nagasaki—Emperor Hirohito met
with Japan's top civil and military leaders. The Emperor
made clear he had lost faith in the military and urged his
ministers to accept the Potsdam Declaration, saying, "I cannot bear to see my innocent people suffer any longer ... the
time has come when we must bear the unbearable."

On Aug. 10, a cable was sent to the Allies accepting the
terms of the Potsdam Declaration—with the one condition
that the Emperor be allowed to maintain his divine status as
monarch of Japan. U.S. Secretary of State James Byrnes persuaded Truman and the other Allied leaders to respond by
stating that "unconditional surrender" meant just that, while
emphasizing that Japan could retain its monarchy, subject to
the control of Allied occupation leaders. At a second conference with his chief advisers, on Aug. 14, the Emperor repeated the need to accept defeat; his Cabinet agreed, and the surrender cable was sent. When the news reached America and
Europe, it touched off exuberant celebrations.

Throughout these troubled days, Tokyo buzzed with rumors of a coup d'état; they proved reliable when a group of
militant young army officers briefly seized control of the
Imperial Palace on the night of Aug. 14. With the Emperor in
residence, they ransacked the palace, searching for a phono-
graph record already recorded for broadcast, in which
Hirohito announced the surrender to the Japanese people.
But the palace was quickly retaken by troops loyal to the general in command of the Tokyo area, and the leaders of the
rebellion committed seppuku in front of the building.

When the Emperor's recording was played later that day—
it was the first time ordinary Japanese people had ever heard
his voice—spontaneous revolts broke out in military units,
maverick kamikaze attacks were launched, and hundreds of
senior military and government leaders committed suicide.

Japan's formal surrender would not take place for two
more weeks; the official documents were signed on Sept. 2,
aboard the battleship U.S.S. *Missouri* in Tokyo Harbor. TIME
correctly called the moment an anticlimax, but to readers
steeped for years in nerve-shattering climaxes, a glimpse of
tedium may have resembled the promised land. ∎

"Continuing the war can only mean destruction for the nation and [the] prolongation of bloodshed and cruelty in the world. I cannot bear to see my innocent people suffer any longer."
—Emperor Hirohito, imperial conference, Aug. 9, 1945

Victory's Sweet Song

False starts and a lengthy wait for the final curtain can't stop the world from celebrating the end of more than three years of war in the Pacific

LIKE THE PARTIES IN MAY 1945 HERALDING VICTORY IN Europe, the world's celebration of V-J day was preceded by a series of premature announcements of peace—and it's always easier to pop the cork on the champagne bottle than to put it back in. No matter: Americans and their Allies threw themselves a memorable party in mid-August after the Japanese declared they would surrender, then cheered again, if a bit less lustily, on Sept. 2, when the formal surrender documents were finally signed in Tokyo Bay. In effect, the Allies ended up celebrating two V-J days,

and we still do: the first on Aug. 14-15, the second on Sept. 2.

Poor communications were to blame for the stop-and-start nature of the big victory party. The first signal of Japanese surrender was picked up by a San Francisco electrical engineer named D. Reginal Tibbets, sitting up late amid a clutter of radio equipment in his bedroom. At 4:27 on the morning of Aug. 14, be began transcribing a Morse code broadcast from Japan's official radio station, the Domei News Agency: "The Japanese Government are ready to accept ..." At the same time, in a white frame house in Portland, Ore., an FCC moni-

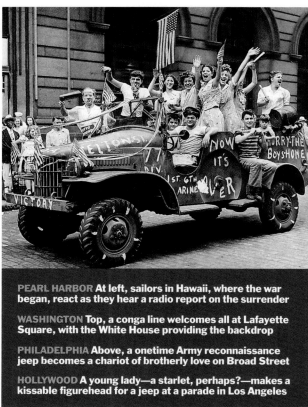

PEARL HARBOR At left, sailors in Hawaii, where the war began, react as they hear a radio report on the surrender

WASHINGTON Top, a conga line welcomes all at Lafayette Square, with the White House providing the backdrop

PHILADELPHIA Above, a onetime Army reconnaissance jeep becomes a chariot of brotherly love on Broad Street

HOLLYWOOD A young lady—a starlet, perhaps?—makes a kissable figurehead for a jeep at a parade in Los Angeles

tor picked up the same exciting news: Japan was officially offering to surrender. But the broadcast went dead, leaving a waiting world breathless, through what TIME called "too many hours and too many false alarms."

The news of the surrender was finally confirmed by President Harry Truman that evening at 7, touching off a victory party that lasted into the night and picked up steam all over again the next day. When the news reached the fighting fronts,

G.I.s yelled wildly, pounded backs, fired guns and drank hoarded whiskey. On Okinawa—won at an enormous cost only seven weeks before, and the staging area for the dreaded autumn invasion of Japan's home islands that now would be unnecessary—the night was lighted by millions of tracer bullets as men fired rifles, machine guns and antiaircraft guns. Ships offshore, fearing kamikazes, laid down a smoke screen and opened up with antiaircraft guns. These actions

were not misplaced: several rogue kamikaze attacks did occur after the surrender. Sadly, though, the party on Okinawa turned ugly, then deadly: six men were killed and 30 wounded.

Wherever servicemen gathered, euphoria was contagious. The big Cunard liner *Queen Elizabeth,* on duty as a troop transport, steamed into New York Harbor with a captured Nazi flag flying at her main mast, a prank by laughing home-bound troops. Soldiers and sailors paraded in triumph through Times Square, staging daring daylight raids on willing nurses, WACs and civilians. The rampant public smooching, LIFE reported, "ran the osculatory gamut from mob assault upon a single man or woman, to indiscriminate chain-kissing."

As at Okinawa, the festivities in San Francisco got out of hand. The harbor city was teeming with sailors on shore leave, many of whom now decided to become drunken sailors on shore leave. For three days, store windows were smashed and shops looted; women were attacked, statues defaced and streetcars overturned. Finally, authorities ordered the sailors back to their ships and bases and urged civilians to stay home.

IF THE MERRIMENT GOT TOO MERRY AT TIMES, IT WAS ALSO dimmed for more profound reasons. On both fronts, the final months of the war had ended with scenes that demanded tears, not cheers. Victory in Germany was accompanied by the liberation of Hitler's death camps, exposing a nation that practiced genocide with assembly-line efficiency. Victory in Japan, although clearly in the service of a righteous cause, was achieved by using wondrous advances in physics for mass annihilation. Nor was the future bright. Russian troops occupied many nations in Eastern Europe, which now faced the prospect of Kremlin hegemony. A showdown between Soviet communism and American capitalism was loom-

ing, a duel that would be shadowed by an eerie new image of peril, the mushroom-shaped cloud.

Yet despite rowdy sailors, Russians who stayed put in Eastern Europe and atomic genies who threatened not to stay put in their bottles, the Allies had earned their party. They had beaten the forces of aggression, had crushed two evil empires into unconditional surrender. Perhaps the most lasting tribute to the Allies' achievement would come in the following decades, when the vanquished nations of Germany and Japan became steadfast friends of their conquerors.

On Dec. 8, 1941, the day after Japan's surprise attack on Pearl Harbor, President Franklin D. Roosevelt had declared to Americans: "Always will we remember the character of the onslaught against us. No matter how long it may take us to overcome this premeditated invasion, the American people in their righteous might will win through to absolute victory."

How Roosevelt would have beamed to know that his countrymen had fulfilled his pledge. They had indeed won absolute victory, and not once but twice: over imperial Japan in the Pacific, and over Nazi Germany in Europe. And how Roosevelt would have rejoiced to learn that his unlimited commitment—"No matter how long"—could now be measured. For the record, Mr. President, "how long" turned out to be three years, eight months and six days. ∎

NEW YORK CITY One of the war's most iconic images was taken at its very conclusion, when TIME-LIFE photographer Alfred Eisenstaedt snapped a sailor and a nurse getting acquainted in Times Square